An Essay on Free Will

An Essay on
FREE WILL

PETER VAN INWAGEN

CLARENDON PRESS · OXFORD

Oxford University Press, Walton Street, Oxford OX2 6DP

Oxford New York Toronto
Delhi Bombay Calcutta Madras Karachi
Kuala Lumpur Singapore Hong Kong Tokyo
Nairobi Dar es Salaam Cape Town
Melbourne Auckland

and associated companies in
Beirut Berlin Ibadan Nicosia

Oxford is a trade mark of Oxford University Press

Published in the United States by
Oxford University Press, New York

British Library Cataloguing in Publication Data

Van Inwagen, Peter
An essay on free will.
1. Free will and determinism
I. Title
123   B945.v/

ISBN 0–19–824624–2
ISBN 0–19–824924–1 (Pbk)

Printed in Great Britain
at the University Press, Oxford

Preface

This book considers several questions about free will, but the bulk of it is addressed to the question whether free will and determinism are compatible. Its answer is that, contrary to received opinion, they are not.

There have appeared, in the last twenty years or so, a fair number of books wholly or mainly about the problem of free will and determinism. One should certainly mention M. R. Ayers's *The Refutation of Determinism*, Austin Farrer's *The Freedom of the Will*, R. L. Franklin's *Freewill and Determinism*, Anthony Kenny's *Will, Freedom and Power*, J. R. Lucas's *The Freedom of the Will*, A. I. Melden's *Free Action*, and D. J. O'Connor's *Free Will*. I have made no mention of these books in the body of the present work. This does not reflect my judgement of the quality of these books, but rather the fact that the concerns of their authors are largely irrelevant to the topics I propose to discuss. I shall treat the problem of the compatibility of free will and determinism seriously and at length. The books I have listed either do not treat this problem at all, or, at best, pass very quickly over certain arguments the correct evaluation of which is essential to its solution. In particular, none of these books contains anything like an adequate discussion of the following argument:

> If determinism is true, then our acts are the consequences of the laws of nature and events in the remote past. But it is not up to us what went on before we were born, and neither is it up to us what the laws of nature are. Therefore, the consequences of these things (including our present acts) are not up to us.

The present book is essentially a defence of this argument and an exploration of the consequences of supposing it to be right, and, therefore, it owes little to any of the books I have mentioned.

There are, I think, only five twentieth-century works that have had any very extensive influence on the present book: C. D. Broad's "Determinism, Indeterminism and Libertarianism",[1] R. E. Hobart's "Free Will as Involving Determination and Inconceivable Without It",[2] R. M. Chisholm's "Responsibility and Avoidability",[3] Carl Ginet's "Might We Have No Choice?"[4] and Richard Taylor's *Action and Purpose*[5]. I discuss Hobart's article in Chapter IV. I do not discuss the other works, but their influence is pervasive. From the articles I have learned what arguments about free will are worth serious and extended consideration. Taylor's book has deeply influenced me; it is, I think, the source of a "picture" of human beings that is partly responsible for my most basic convictions about free will.

Two works that have influenced me as regards special but important points are Harry Frankfurt's "The Principle of Alternate Possibilities"[6] and G. E. M. Anscombe's inaugural lecture, *Causality and Determination.*[7]

W. P. Alston read the book in manuscript. His comments have resulted in the rewriting of many confused and unclear passages.

I have benefited from discussing the problem of free will and determinism with Keith Lehrer, Richard Taylor, Alvin Plantinga, and Carl Ginet. I have benefited from discussing the problem of future contingencies with Margery Naylor.

Parts of this book have appeared elsewhere. I wish to thank the editor of *Noûs* for permission to reprint a few paragraphs of "Laws and Counterfactuals" (1979), the editors of *The Philosophical Review* for permission to reprint parts of "Ability and Responsibility" (1978), D. Reidel Company for permission to reprint parts of "The Incompatibility of Free Will and Determinism" (*Philosophical Studies*, vol. 27, no. 3, 185–9, copyright © 1975 by D. Reidel Publishing Company, Dordrecht, Holland), the editor of *Theoria* for permission to reprint parts of "A Formal Approach to the Problem of Free Will and Determinism" (1974), and the Philosophy Documentation Center for permission to reprint parts of "The Incompatibility of Responsibility and Determinism", which appeared in M. Brand and M. Bradie, eds., *Action and Responsibility* (Bowling Green: 1980).

Contents

Chapter I	The Problems and How We Shall Approach Them	1
Chapter II	Fatalism	23
Chapter III	Three Arguments for Incompatibilism	55
Chapter IV	Three Arguments for Compatibilism	106
Chapter V	What Our Not Having Free Will Would Mean	153
Chapter VI	The Traditional Problem	190
Notes		225
Index		246

Chapter I

The Problems and How We Shall
Approach Them

1.1 There is no single philosophical problem that is "the problem of free will". There are rather a great many philosophical problems *about* free will.[1] In this book I shall solve one of these problems and worry another at great length.

The problem I shall solve is the problem of "fatalism" or "future contingencies". This problem will be dealt with in Chapter II, which is a more or less self-contained essay. That chapter might have been left out of the book with almost no impairment of the argument of the remainder. It is included because it does, after all, bear on the question whether we have free will. And perhaps the fact that what it says is right will go some way toward making up for its irrelevance to the other parts of the book.

The problem of future contingencies is an old and honourable philosophical problem, but it is not one of the great central problems of philosophy. The main topic of this book is one of the great central problems: the problem of free will and determinism.

1.2 It is difficult to formulate "the problem of free will and determinism" in a way that will satisfy everyone. Once one might have said that the problem of free will and determinism —in those days one would have said 'liberty and necessity'— was the problem of discovering whether the human will is free or whether its productions are governed by strict causal necessity. But no one today would be allowed to formulate "the problem of free will and determinism" like that, for this formulation presupposes the truth of a certain thesis about the conceptual relation of free will to determinism that many, perhaps most, present-day philosophers would reject: that free will and determinism are incompatible. Indeed many philosophers hold not only that free will is compatible with determinism but that free will *entails* determinism. I think it would be fair to say that almost all the philosophical writing on the problem of free will and determinism since the time of Hobbes that is any good, that is of any enduring philosophical interest, has been about this presupposition of the earlier debates about liberty and necessity. It is for this reason that nowadays one must accept as a *fait accompli* that the problem of finding out whether free will and determinism are compatible is a large part, perhaps the major part, of "the problem of free will and determinism".

I shall attempt to formulate the problem in a way that takes account of this *fait accompli* by dividing the problem into two problems, which I will call the Compatibility Problem and the Traditional Problem. The Traditional Problem is, of course, the problem of finding out whether we have free will or whether determinism is true. But the very existence of the Traditional Problem depends upon the correct solution to the Compatibility Problem: if free will and determinism are compatible, and, *a fortiori*, if free will *entails* determinism, then there is no Traditional Problem, any more than there is a problem about how my sentences can be composed of both English words and Roman letters.

One of the main theses of this book is that the correct solution of the Compatibility Problem does not imply the non-existence of the Traditional Problem; therefore my division of the problem of free will and determinism into two is no idle exercise. But before I say more about this division of the problem and about the ways in which I shall use it to organize this book, I shall explain what I mean by *free will* and *determinism* in sufficient detail to forestall certain possible misunderstandings.

1.3 In Chapter III, I shall formulate the thesis of determinism with as much precision as I am able to give it. Our present purposes will be served by a short, preliminary account of what is meant by determinism. Determinism is quite simply the thesis that the past *determines* a unique future. But let us see what that might mean.

Presumably, at any given moment there are many "possible futures", many ways in which the world might go on. Or at least this is true if we understand 'possible' in a sufficiently liberal way: there are certainly many "picturable" or "conceivable" or "consistently describable" futures. But many of the futures that are possible in this sense are impossible in another: they are *physically* impossible. For example, though I can picture to myself what it would be like for there to be a total eclipse of the sun this afternoon, though I can say without contradicting myself that a total eclipse of the sun will be visible this afternoon, there is an obvious sense in which this future I might imagine or describe is physically impossible. To say this is not to say that it is contrary to the laws of nature— if we may allow ourselves this piece of terminology—that there should be an eclipse this afternoon, for the laws of nature do not by themselves dictate when particular events like eclipses shall occur.[2] To say that a "possible future" containing an imminent eclipse is physically impossible is rather to say that given the past, the *actual* past, *and* the laws of nature, no eclipse will occur; that the past and the laws of nature together rule out any possibility of an eclipse this afternoon. Those who, like me, do not object to talk of "possible worlds" may think of the matter this way: while there are presumably possible worlds in which the laws of nature are the actual laws and in which there is an eclipse this afternoon, there is no possible world in which (i) the laws of nature are the actual laws, (ii) the past is the actual past, and (iii) there will be an eclipse this afternoon.

This example shows that there is a clear sense in which certain "imaginable", "conceivable", or "consistently describable" futures are physically impossible. *Determinism* may now be defined: it is the thesis that there is at any instant exactly one physically possible future.[3] There must, of course, be *at least* one physically possible future; if there is more than one, if at some instant there are two or more ways in which the world could go on, then *indeterminism* is true.

Determinism in this sense must be carefully distinguished from what we might call the Principle of Universal Causation, that is, from the thesis that every event (or fact, change, or state of affairs) has a cause. It is far from obvious what the logical relations that hold between these two theses are. I doubt, for example, whether the Principle of Universal Causation *entails* determinism. In order to deduce the latter from the former, we should need at least three premisses:

(1)   if an event (or fact, change, state of affairs, or what have you) has a cause, then its cause is always itself an event (or what have you) and never a substance or continuant, such as a man;

(2)   if an event (or what have you) *A* was the cause of an event *B*, then it follows, given that *A* happened and given the laws of nature, that *A* "causally *necessitated*" *B*, that *B* could not have failed to happen;

(3)   every chain of causes that has no earliest member is such that, for every time *t*, some event in that chain happens earlier than *t*.

It is easy to see why each of these premisses is necessary for the deduction of determinism from the Principle of Universal Causation.

Suppose that the Principle of Universal Causation is true and suppose that premiss (1) is false. Suppose, that is, that the doctrine of *immanent* or *agent* causation is true.[4] Suppose, to be more specific, that a certain change occurs in an agent, Tom, and Tom himself is the cause of this change, and no earlier state of affairs necessitated this change. Then the thesis of determinism is false. But our description of this case is internally consistent, for it does not entail that any event is without a cause. In particular, the change in Tom has a cause: Tom himself. The cause of this change, it is true, has no cause, but this does not entail the falsity of the Principle of Universal Causation, since its cause is not an event or change but a man, that is, a continuant.[5]

Suppose that the Principle of Universal Causation is true and suppose that premiss (1) is true and suppose that premiss (2) is false. That is, suppose that every event is caused by some earlier event or events but that these earlier causes do not *necessitate*, but merely *produce*, their effects. (That this supposition is consistent with our concept of causation—that is to say, with *the* concept of causation, for every concept is the concept it is and is not some other concept—has been argued by Professor Anscombe in her inaugural lecture.[6] I shall present and defend similar arguments in Chapter IV.) I think it is easy to see that, if these suppositions are correct, then, while every event has a prior cause, the past nevertheless does not determine a unique future.

Suppose that the Principle of Universal Causation is true and suppose that both premiss (1) and premiss (2) are true and suppose that premiss (3) is false. Then every event is caused by an earlier event that necessitates it; nevertheless, determinism might be false, for as Łukasiewicz pointed out, there might be a pair of times, t_1 and t_2, such that (i) a certain event A happens at t_2, (ii) A is the final member of an infinite chain of causes, and (iii) every member of this chain occurs later than t_1.[7] In that case, we could consistently suppose that the past (up to and including t_1) and the laws of nature do not together determine whether A shall or shall not happen at t_2, and do not, therefore, determine a unique future.

It follows that to deduce determinism from the Principle of Universal Causation we must assume (1), (2), and (3) as premisses. I doubt whether all three of these propositions are true. I am particularly doubtful about (2).[8] Therefore, I doubt whether universal causation entails determinism.

I am uncertain what to say about the question whether determinism entails universal causation. Could there be, e.g., an explosion that was not caused by any earlier events but which was none the less inevitable, given the past and the laws of nature? I think that anyone who answers immediately "Of course not!" reveals that a certain picture, or definition, or theory of causation has a very firm grip on him (which is not to say that he is wrong). But any real discussion of this question would lead us needlessly, for we need not answer it, into a discussion of causation, something I shall avoid whenever it is possible.

Having distinguished determinism from the Principle of Universal Causation, let us return to our examination of determinism. Our definition of determinism presupposes some understanding of the notion of a law of nature. I should like to define 'law of nature' in its turn, but I do not know how. I will mention, however, some constraints on an adequate definition of this concept and some necessary conditions for its application. These remarks, though they will not constitute a definition of 'law of nature', will at least show how my use of this term differs from that of some other writers. I should require any definition of 'law of nature' to have the following three consequences:

(i)   the phrase 'is a law of nature' is a real predicate: it is typically and properly used in ascribing a certain property to certain objects (unlike, say, 'exists', according to Kant, or 'is good', according to R. M. Hare);

(ii) the objects that have this property are sentences or propositions (non-linguistic entities expressed by sentences) or whatever it is that are the bearers of truth-value: anything that is a law is *also* either true or false;

(iii) whether a proposition or sentence is a law is independent of what scientists or others happen to believe or happen to have discovered: a proposition, if it is a law, is unchangeably and objectively so, just as, according to the prevailing view of mathematics, a proposition, if it is a theorem, is unchangeably and objectively so, whatever mathematicians or others happen to believe or happen to have proved.

Philosophers have on occasion proposed necessary conditions for a proposition's being a law of nature. A law, for example, is supposed to be true, to be contingent, to entail the existence of no particular (contingent) individual and to "support its counter-factuals" or "warrant inference to subjunctive conditionals". But even if these conditions are individually necessary for lawhood, they are certainly not jointly sufficient.[9] Consider, for example, the proposition that all men who are deprived of vitamin C develop scurvy. This proposition is presumably both true and contingent. Moreover, we may suppose that it "supports its counter-factuals": every man, past, present, or future, is such that if he were deprived of vitamin C, he would develop scurvy.[10] But it hardly follows that this general proposition is a *law of nature*, for the fact that it supports its counter-factuals might depend on quite accidental circumstances. Suppose, for example, that there is such a thing as "vitamin X", which could be used as an effective replacement for vitamin C; but suppose that all the vitamin X there is is

locked in a vault on Mars. If that is true, then while our proposition does in fact support its counter-factual instances, its
supporting them depends upon the accidental circumstance
that the sole supply of vitamin X is inaccessible to human
beings. Or, again, we may imagine that all men are such that
they would develop scurvy if they were deprived of vitamin
C, but that if an accident involving certain radioactive materials
had happened at a certain time and place, some of the wit-
nesses *would have had* descendants whose bodies were capable
of synthesizing vitamin C and who would therefore *not* develop
scurvy under any conditions of diet. It seems to me to be
obvious that our concept of a law of nature entails that the
possession of lawhood by a proposition cannot depend on such
accidental occurrences as these. Therefore, these examples
show that the conditions we have been examining are not
jointly sufficient for lawhood. I know of none that are—except,
of course, sets of conditions that are trivially sufficient, such
as sets involving the requirement that a law be a physically
necessary proposition—and neither, I think, does anyone else.
Nevertheless, 'law of nature' seems to be an intelligible concept and one we can't get along without if we wish to give a
complete description of the world. Let me give a simple example of this that is quite independent of any problems about
determinism.

I have recently read an article on the possibility of intersidereal travel in which the authors divide the unpleasant
necessities of this sort of travel into two categories: those
imposed upon the travellers by the ignorance of the designer
of their vehicle, and those imposed upon the travellers by
the laws of nature. This is an important distinction. Space-
ships and other artefacts are doubtless never perfect. But
certain disadvantages of intersidereal travel are not going
to be removed by technological advance as the corresponding disadvantages of inter-continental travel were removed.
Inter-continental travel, now a matter of hours, was once a
matter of months or years. But intersidereal travel, if it should
ever come to pass, will always be a matter of years or centuries. No technological advance could ever change this
unfortunate fact, for it is a consequence of the laws of
nature.[11]

Now I have just said something about the way things are; what I have said is as much a part of a complete description of the world as are the most ordinary factual statements of the geographer or the historian. And I think it is plain that what I have said I could not have said without employing the concept of a law of nature, or, at least, without employing some essentially equivalent concept like the concept of physical necessity. Therefore the notion of a law of nature makes sense, even if no one knows how to explain it to one who has not yet acquired it. (How you and I *did* acquire it is a question for the epistemologist or the historian of science; I am content to point out that we have it.) And, therefore, my definition of determinism, though it may rest on an undefined concept, at least rests on an undefined concept we *have*.

Let us now see what can be done about defining *free will*.

1.4   I use the term 'free will' out of respect for tradition. My use of the term is not meant to imply that I think there is such a "faculty" as "the will". When I say of a man that he "has free will" I mean that very often, if not always, when he has to choose between two or more mutually incompatible courses of action—that is, courses of action that it is impossible for him to carry out more than one of—each of these courses of action is such that he can, or is able to, or has it within his power to carry it out. A man has free will if he is often in positions like these: he must now speak or now be silent, and he *can* now speak and *can* now remain silent; he must attempt to rescue a drowning child or else go for help, and he is *able* to attempt to rescue the child and *able* to go for help; he must now resign his chairmanship or else lie to the members, and he has it within his power to resign and he has it within his power to lie.

'Free will', then, is to be defined in terms of 'can'. But how is 'can' to be defined? I am afraid I do not know how to define 'can', any more than I know how to define 'law of nature'. Nevertheless, I think that the concept expressed by 'can' in the examples given in the preceding paragraph—the concept of the power or ability of an agent to act—is as clear as any philosophically interesting concept is likely to be. In fact,

I doubt very much whether there are any simpler or better understood concepts in terms of which this concept might be explained. There are, however, concepts with which the concept of human power or ability might be confused, either because they really are similar to the concept of power, or because they are sometimes expressed by similar words. Perhaps what I say in the sequel will be clearer if I explicitly distinguish the concept of power or ability from those concepts with which it might be improperly conflated.[12]

(i) The concept of the power or ability of an agent to act is not the concept of *moral* or *legal permissibility*. I might say to a hard-hearted landlord, "You can't simply turn them out into the street", knowing full well that, in the sense of 'can' that is our present concern, he very well *can*. The popular retort, "Oh, can't I? Just you watch!" is, I should think, usually a play on these two senses of 'can', though sometimes it may be an expression of a genuine confusion between them. And in some few cases, cases typified by the use of words like 'I can't go through with it', it may be that no one, either agent or spectator, can say with any confidence whether *can* is being used to express the idea of power or the idea of permissibility.

(ii) The concept of the power or ability of an agent to act is not the concept of *physical possibility*, nor is power or ability entailed by physical possibility. This can be shown by a simple example. Suppose I have been locked in a certain room and suppose that the lock on the door of that room is a device whose behaviour is physically undetermined; it may come unlocked and it may not: there is a future consistent with both the actual past and the laws of nature in which an internal mechanism unlocks the lock and another such future in which it doesn't. Then it is physically possible that I shall leave the room. But it does not follow that in any relevant sense I *can* leave the room.

(iii) The concept of the power or ability of an agent to act is not the concept of *epistemic possibility*. Consider the sentence, 'Castro could have arranged for Kennedy's assassination'. Clearly there are at least two things that someone who spoke these words might mean by them. He might mean, 'For all we know, Castro *did* arrange for Kennedy's assassination', or he might mean, 'Castro had it within his power to arrange for Kennedy's assassination'. These senses are obviously quite different and the first is of no particular interest to us.

(iv) The concept of the power or ability of an agent to act is not the concept of *causal power* or *capacity*. We say that penicillin *has the power to* kill certain bacteria, that a hydrogen bomb *is capable of* destroying a large city, and that a certain computer *can* perform a thousand calculations per second. (These are statements about capacities that may be unrealized. The vocabulary of our talk about the realization of causal capacities and the vocabulary of agency similarly overlap: we talk about the *action* of hydrochloric acid on zinc and the *action* of an automatic pistol.) But this sort of talk is really very different from talk of the power of an agent to act, despite their common origin in the technical terminology of medieval Aristotelianism. Perhaps the best way to appreciate this difference is to examine some ascriptions of causal capacity to human agents and to contrast them with ascriptions of ability to human agents.

We ascribe a capacity, rather than an ability, to an agent when we say he:

can digest meat (being an omnivore);

has absolute pitch;

has normal colour vision;

can understand French.

We ascribe an ability, rather than a capacity, to an agent when we say he:

can cook meat;

can sing correctly;

can name the colours;

can speak French.

Despite their superficial similarity, there is all the difference in the world between the sort of property that the predicates in the first list ascribe to an agent and the sort of property that those in the second list ascribe to an agent. Consider, for example, the last item in each list. For a man to have the capacity to understand French is for him to be such that if he were placed in certain circumstances, which wouldn't be very hard to delimit, and if he were to hear French spoken, then, willy-nilly, he would understand what was being said. But if a man can *speak* French, it certainly does not follow that there are any circumstances in which he would, willy-nilly, speak French. The concept of a causal power or capacity would seem to be the concept of an invariable disposition to react to certain determinate changes in the environment in certain determinate ways, whereas the concept of an agent's power to act would seem not to be the concept of a power that is dispositional or reactive, but rather the concept of a power to *originate* changes in the environment.[13]

Three points need to be made about what I have said about capacities and abilities.

First, it does not pretend to be an *analysis* of the distinction between capacities and abilities. It is, rather, an argument by example for the existence of this distinction. I do not know how to give a general account of it. (The reader may have noticed that I rarely attempt to give any general account or analysis of a concept, being content, in problematical cases, to try to show that we *have* a concept answering to a certain description and to try to distinguish it from other, similar concepts. In general, I am suspicious of philosophers' "analyses" of concepts, which seem to me to be only rarely correct and almost always tendentious. In the course of this book, I shall frequently appeal to our understanding of various unanalysed concepts—such as the concept of an agent's power to act—in order to convince the reader that one of my premises is true. But note that if I were to offer a philosophical analysis of these concepts, I should have to appeal to our pre-analytical understanding of them as part of my argument for the correctness of my analysis. The appeal to intuition must turn up at some level of discourse. I prefer making "nonce" appeals to intuition at specific points in the argument to making the very abstract and general appeals to intuition that are inevitable when one is defending a philosophical analysis. This rationale for my procedure is, of course, self-serving, since I almost never *know* of any plausible analysis of the concepts I employ. I should add that my *definitions* of terms—such as 'determinism' —are not supposed to be analyses of concepts but explanations of my own technical terminology.)

Secondly, I do not mean to imply that this distinction is, at least in any very straightforward way, supported by ordinary usage. There is certainly nothing wrong with saying that someone is able to understand French, and probably nothing wrong with saying that a certain king lacks the capacity to rule.

Thirdly, I have been making a *conceptual* distinction. No ontological conclusions should be drawn from the existence of this distinction. Nothing I have said entails that the abilities of agents are not in some sense "reducible to" or do not "supervene upon" the causal capacities of the agents—or of some parts of agents, such as organs, cells, or atoms—and their environment. Here are two analogous cases that may make this point clearer: the concept of a number is not the concept of a set, but that does not mean that statements about numbers cannot be reduced to statements about sets or that there are numbers *in addition to* sets; the concept of a mental event is not the concept of a physical event, but that does not mean that statements about mental events cannot be reduced to statements about physical events or that there are mental events *in addition to* physical events.

I repeat: the purpose of this discussion of abilities and capacities, unlike the purposes of the discussions of most other philosophers who have made this distinction, has been conceptual and not ontological. My only purpose has been to state as clearly as I can *what* concept it is I shall be using 'can' and 'able' and 'power' to express. It is this sense, of course, that these words bear in the above definition of free will. And it is free will as defined in the present section that I shall argue is incompatible with determinism as defined in the previous section.

(v) The concept of the power or ability of an agent to act is not the same as the concept of a *skill* or an accomplishment. In the preceding discussion of abilities and causal capacities, I used the predicate 'can speak French' as an example of a predicate that expresses the power of an agent to act. I did this because 'can speak French' stands in instructive opposition to the capacity-predicate 'can understand French'. But there is more to be said about 'can speak French'. Suppose that Jean-Paul, a valiant member of the Resistance, has been captured by the Germans and bound and gagged. Can he speak French?

Well, to be able to speak French is to be able to speak, and he can't speak because he is gagged: so he can't speak French. On the other hand, if the German commander ordered all the prisoners who could speak French brought before him, he would be unlikely to look approvingly on the action of the subordinate who produced only the ungagged French-speaking prisoners ("For the others, *Herr Oberst*, cannot speak *simpliciter*, and, *a fortiori*, cannot speak French").

Clearly there is a distinction to be made between a skill, accomplishment, or general ability, on the one hand, and, on the other, the power to exercise it on a given occasion. This is true despite the fact that the same words might be used in both kinds of situation ('can speak French'; 'can move her left arm'; 'can play the flute'). That is not to say that there may not be a close conceptual connection between the two. I should think, in fact, that a statement ascribing a skill or other general ability to an agent is probably equivalent to some statement asserting that, under certain conditions, that agent has the power to perform acts that fall under certain descriptions. But I shall not pursue this question, since it is not relevant to our present concerns. It is plain that the 'can' that figures in discussions of free will and determinism is not the 'can' of skill: the thesis of determinism may or may not be relevant to the question whether someone on a particular occasion can or cannot speak French; it is certainly irrelevant to the question whether that person is a French-speaker.

1.5   It is in these senses that I shall understand 'free will' and 'determinism'. In Chapters III and IV, I shall argue that free will is incompatible with determinism. It will be convenient to call this thesis *incompatibilism* and to call the thesis that free will and determinism are compatible *compatibilism*. I have no use for the terms 'soft determinism', 'hard determinism', and 'libertarianism'. I do not object to these terms on the ground that they are vague or ill-defined. They can be easily defined by means of the terms we *shall* use and are thus no worse in that respect than our terms. Soft determinism is the conjunction of determinism and compatibilism; hard determinism is the conjunction of determinism and incompatibilism; libertarianism is the conjunction of incompatibilism and the thesis that we have free will.[14] (I should like to appropriate 'libertarianism' as a name for the thesis that we have free will, but the incompatibilistic associations of this term are too firmly ingrained in too many readers for this to be wise. I have toyed with the idea of using 'elutherianism' for this purpose, but reason has prevailed. I have finally and reluctantly settled on 'the free-will thesis'.) I object to these terms because they lump together theses that should be discussed and analysed separately. Even having them on hand is a permanent temptation to conflate the Traditional Problem and the Compatibility Problem. They are therefore worse than useless and ought to be dropped from the working vocabulary of philosophers.

There is one other term that commonly figures in discussions of free will and determinism that I shall avoid: 'contra-causal freedom'. This term is highly ambiguous and, moreover, in accepting incompatibilism the believer in free will commits himself to accepting none of the things it *might* mean.

'Contra-causal freedom' might mean the sort of freedom, if freedom it would be, that someone would enjoy if his acts were uncaused. But, as we shall see in Chapter IV, that someone's acts are undetermined does not entail that they are uncaused. (This point was briefly touched on in Section 1.3.)

'Contra-causal freedom' might mean the sort of freedom, if freedom it would be, that someone would enjoy if in acting he *violated the laws of nature*, that is, if he worked miracles—even if only small miracles, local to the motor centres of his brain. Now I am not one of those philosophers who think that miracles are conceptually impossible. It seems to me that if God created *ex nihilo* a spinning object, then the proposition we call 'the law of the conservation of angular momentum' would be false. Yet, it seems to me, it might be a law of nature for all that. I think I understand the notion of a supernatural being, that is, the notion of an agent who is superior to and not a part of Nature (this enormous object that the natural sciences investigate), and I think that the falsity of a proposition counts against its being a law of nature if and only if that falsity is due entirely to the mutual operations of natural things, and not if it is due to the action of such an "external" agent upon Nature. But it does not follow from this perhaps rather quaint thesis about the concept of *miracle* that *we* can perform miracles, for there is no reason to suppose we are supernatural beings. And even if we are supernatural beings, *that* we are is not a consequence of the joint truth of the free-will thesis and incompatibilism. If these two theses are true, then determinism is false, and, moreover, one's free choices are undetermined: if I have a free choice between A and B, then my doing A is consistent with the past and the laws of nature and so is my doing B. Incompatibilism, therefore, *entails* that neither my freely doing A nor my freely doing B would "violate" a law of nature. It follows that it is sheer confusion to attribute a belief in contra-causal freedom, in the present sense, to the incompatibilist who believes in free will.

Finally, "contra-causal freedom" might be attributed to an agent if that agent has it within his power to act contrary to the laws of nature; that is, if the agent is *able* to perform certain acts whose performance *would be* sufficient for the falsity of certain propositions that are *in fact* laws of nature. But the incompatibilist, whether or not he accepts the free-will thesis, does not believe in contra-causal freedom in this sense. Quite the contrary: it is *because* the incompatibilist believes that we do not possess this power with respect to the laws of nature that he believes free will requires indeterminism. The precise sense in which this is true will be evident from an inspection of the arguments for incompatibilism that will be presented in Chapter III.

Incompatibilism, therefore, may perhaps be described as the thesis that free action is "extra-causal"; to say it is the doctrine that free action is "contra-causal" can only lead to confusion.

1.6 Incompatibilism can hardly be said to be a popular thesis among present-day philosophers (the "analytic" ones, at any rate). Yet it has its adherents and has had more of them in the past. It is, however, surprisingly hard to find any *arguments* for it. That many philosophers have believed something controversial without giving any arguments for it is perhaps not surprising; what is surprising is that no arguments have been given when arguments are so easy to give. Perhaps the explanation is simply that the arguments are so obvious that no one has thought them worth stating. If that is so, let *us* not be afraid of being obvious. Here is an argument that I think is obvious (I don't mean it's obviously right; I mean it's one that should occur pretty quickly to any philosopher who asked himself what arguments could be found to support incompatibilism):

> If determinism is true, then our acts are the consequences of the laws of nature and events in the remote past. But it is not up to us what went on before we were born, and neither is it up to us what the laws of nature are. Therefore, the consequences of these things (including our present acts) are not up to us.

I shall call this argument the *Consequence Argument*. In Chapter III, I shall argue for incompatibilism by presenting three very detailed versions of the Consequence Argument. Or, if you like—how does one count arguments, anyway?—I shall present three detailed arguments each of which is suggested by the Consequence Argument.

In Chapter IV, I shall examine three arguments for compatibilism: the "Paradigm Case Argument", the "Conditional Analysis Argument", and an argument I shall call the *Mind* Argument because it has appeared so often in the pages of that journal.[15]

The Paradigm Case Argument attempts to establish the compatibility of free will and determinism by an examination of cases of human action that, it is alleged, serve as paradigms for the teaching of the meanings of words like 'free'.

The Conditional Analysis Argument maintains that statements ascribing to human agents the power or ability to act otherwise are to be analysed as disguised conditionals, which, when their disguise is removed, can be seen to be compatible with determinism.

The *Mind* Argument proceeds by identifying indeterminism with chance and by arguing that an act that occurs by chance, if an event that occurs by chance can be called an act, cannot be under the control of its alleged agent and hence cannot have been performed freely. (In this brief statement of the *Mind* Argument I have left entwined three strands of reasoning that I shall disentangle in Chapter IV.) Proponents of the *Mind* Argument conclude, therefore, that free will is not only compatible with determinism but entails determinism.

I shall argue in Chapter IV that these arguments fail. There are, I think, no other arguments for compatibilism that need be taken seriously. Let me give just one example of an argument that need *not* be taken seriously. Some philosophers have urged that to suppose that free will and determinism are in conflict is to confuse compulsion with determination by causal laws. For, these philosophers argue, to do something of one's own free will is to do that thing without being compelled to do it, and to behave in accordance with a deterministic set of causal laws is not to be compelled. I reply that this argument confuses doing things of one's own free will with having free will about what one does. These are not the same thing. The following case shows this. Suppose a certain man is in a certain room and is quite content to be there; suppose, in fact, that he wants very much to remain in that room and that it would be difficult indeed to induce him even to consider leaving it. Then, I should think, he remains in the room of his own free will. But we can with perfect consistency go on to suppose that he has no free will about whether he leaves the room: suppose that, unknown to him, the only door is locked and that it is not within his power to open it.

Now someone might want to say that our imaginary agent did *not* remain in the room "of his own free will". I don't think this is right, but I will not argue the point. For if it is true that our agent did not remain in the room "of his own free will", then we cannot establish that a person does something "of his own free will" by establishing that his doing it is *uncompelled*. But the "compulsion" argument we have been considering certainly does depend on the premiss that one *can* so establish that a person has acted "of his own free will". Let us grant this premiss. The example of the man locked in the room shows that it does not follow from a person's doing something "of his own free will" that he *can* do otherwise. And thus it does not follow from the undoubted fact that we often do things of our own free will that what I have called the free-will thesis is true. And, therefore, the Compatibility Problem is not going to be solved by jejune reflections on compulsion.

1.7 If the arguments of Chapter III are correct, then incompatibilism is true. These arguments have premisses. Some of the premisses are more controversial than others. That is, some of the premisses of Chapter III will be accepted without question by the compatibilist and others he will want to argue about. Let us call the conjunction of these "controversial" premisses P. Suppose I am willing to grant that *if* any of my premisses are false, the false ones are conjuncts of P. The compatibilist and I will thus agree that if compatibilism is true, then P is false. One compatibilist has actually argued (in effect) that this proposition on which he and I agree entails that I am begging the question against compatibilism by assuming the truth of P.[16]

It should suffice to point out that the situation in which this argument places the compatibilist and me is a perfectly symmetrical one: I am in a position to employ the same argument, *mutatis mutandis*, to prove the conclusion that his choice of premisses begs the question, and I should be as well justified in employing the argument against him as he is in employing it against me. Now why, I have asked myself uneasily, would anyone say something that can be so easily refuted? I think there are two possible answers. (i) The compatibilist thinks that compatibilism is prima facie true and that the burden of proof lies on the incompatibilist. (When a philosopher says, "The burden of the proof lies on you", he means, "You must deduce your conclusion from the truths of immediate sensory experience by means of an argument that is formally valid according to the rules of elementary logic; I on the other hand may employ any dialectical tactic I find expedient".) (ii) He thinks that the premisses from which he derives compatibilism are more plausible than those from which I derive incompatibilism.

As to the first of these possibilities, I deny that compatibilism is prima facie right and incompatibilism prima facie wrong. Quite the other way round, if you ask me. But I shall not assume that either of these propositions is prima facie right. I shall treat them as philosophical theses of equal initial plausibility, and this, it seems to me, is the only reasonable way to approach the Compatibility Problem.

In Section 4.3, I shall attempt to undermine the thesis that the premisses of the compatibilist are prima facie more plausible than my own by comparing the premisses of one argument for compatibilism, the Conditional Analysis Argument, with the premisses of one of the incompatibilist arguments presented in Chapter III. I think that the unprejudiced reader— if such can be found: very likely anyone willing to read as far as Chapter IV will have brought strong feelings about the Compatibility Problem to his reading of this book—will agree that if the premisses of my argument and the premisses of the Conditional Analysis Argument are considered independently of their implications for the Compatibility Problem, then the former will be seen to be considerably more plausible than the latter.[17]

1.8 If the arguments of Chapters III and IV are cogent, then I shall have provided good reasons for thinking that free will and determinism are incompatible. Suppose I am right. Suppose these theses are incompatible. Which, if either, ought we to accept? As a first step towards answering this question, I shall, in Chapter V, address the question, "What would it mean to reject free will?" I shall argue that such a rejection would have at least two interesting consequences.

First, anyone who rejected free will could not consistently deliberate about future courses of action. This is so, I shall argue, owing simply to the fact that one cannot deliberate without believing that the things about which one is deliberating are things it is possible for one to do. How important one takes this consequence to be will, of course, depend on how important one thinks consistency is.

Secondly, and, I think, much more importantly, to deny the existence of free will commits one to denying the existence of moral responsibility. Until a short while ago, most philosophers would have taken this to be obvious. But if any of these philosophers had been asked to defend this obvious thesis, he would almost certainly have appealed to the following principle: a person can be held morally responsible for what he has done only if he could have done otherwise. In a recent remarkable article, however, Harry Frankfurt has presented convincing counter-examples to this principle. I shall devote the bulk of Chapter V to showing that even if Frankfurt is right, it is none the less true that moral responsibility is possible only if we have free will.

Now some philosophers will perhaps want to protest at this point in the argument that while I may indeed have shown that in *some* sense free will is incompatible with determinism, and while I may have shown that free will in *some* sense is logically necessary for moral responsibility, I have not shown that there is any single notion of free will that has both these features. Therefore, these philosophers may allege, I am not in a position to say that considerations having to do with moral responsibility can be used to show that we ought to accept the doctrine *called* 'free will' in Chapters III and IV and there shown to be incompatible with determinism.

I shall meet this possible objection in two ways. First, I shall ask the reader to examine the premises of the arguments of Chapter III after they have been rewritten according to the following rule: at each place at which the words 'free will' occur in the premises of these arguments, replace them with the words 'free will in just that sense of *free will* that is relevant to questions of moral responsibility'. I contend that the reader will find that the rewritten premises are no less plausible than the original ones. Secondly, I shall present an argument for the incompatibility of moral responsibility and determinism that makes no mention whatever of free will, though it will be structurally identical with one of the arguments for the incompatibility of free will and determinism that occurs in Chapter III. I think this "direct" argument for the incompatibility of responsibility and determinism will have the following feature: it will clearly be sound if and only if the corresponding argument of Chapter III is sound. But if this is true, then it seems very unlikely that it is only some sort of "free will" that has nothing to do with moral responsibility that is shown in Chapter III to be incompatible with determinism.

The principal conclusion of Chapter V will therefore be that to reject free will—in just that sense of 'free will' in which we have earlier argued that free will is incompatible with determinism—is to reject moral responsibility.

In Chapter VI, I shall discuss the Traditional Problem, that is, the problem of finding out whether determinism is true, or whether the free-will thesis is true, or whether neither is true.

I shall proceed by asking what reasons we have for thinking that determinism is true and what reasons we have for thinking that the free-will thesis is true.

There are two sorts of reason for believing in determinism. First, one might believe in determinism because one believes that science has shown determinism to be true. I shall argue at length that science has, if anything, shown determinism to be false. Secondly, one might believe that determinism is a truth of reason, on the ground that it is a logical consequence of the Principle of Sufficient Reason. I shall show that, whether or not determinism is a consequence of the Principle of Sufficient Reason, the Principle of Sufficient Reason must be rejected, since it entails the collapse of all modal distinctions.

In addition to asking what reasons might be brought in support of determinism, we shall also ask what reasons might be brought in support of a certain closely related but weaker thesis: the thesis that human beings, like typical digital computers, behave in ways that are entirely determined by their past states and their current "input". It is important to consider this thesis because: (i) it would seem to be incompatible with free will if and only if determinism proper is; (ii) unlike determinism proper it is not in even prima-facie conflict with current physical theory; and (iii) it is commonly contended that the empirical study of human beings has uncovered facts that strongly support it. I shall argue that this common contention is sheer bluff.

The conclusion of the argument whose course is summarized in the last few paragraphs is that neither physics nor pure reason supports determinism, and, moreover, that the scientific study of human beings does not support the thesis that the behaviour of human beings is "for all practical purposes" determined.

What reasons can be brought in support of the free-will thesis? It cannot, I think, be seriously maintained that we can know by some sort of introspection that we have or that we do not have free will. And neither can it be maintained that the empirical study of human beings is likely to show us that we have or that we do not have free will. The only relevant argument would seem to be this: if we do not have free will, then there is no such thing as moral responsibility; therefore, since there is such a thing as moral responsibility, there is such a thing as free will. (Moreover, since free will is incompatible with determinism, determinism is false.) The first premiss of this argument is defended in Chapter V in the way outlined above. In Chapter VI, we shall examine its second premiss, and I shall defend my use of this argument against the charge that for an incompatibilist so to argue amounts to his claiming to be able to prove that determinism—a thesis about the motion of matter in the void—can be shown to be false by *a priori* reflection on moral responsibility. I shall also examine a condition of certain philosophers (their having fallen under the spell of "scientism") that makes it psychologically very difficult for them to believe that such "tender-minded" arguments as this could possibly provide one with good reason to reject determinism.

I shall finally address the question, "What would you say if, after all, the progress of science did show that indeterminism was untenable?"

Chapter II

Fatalism

2.1 Fatalism, as I shall use the term, is the thesis that it is a logical or conceptual truth that no one is able to act otherwise than he in fact does; that the very idea of an agent to whom alternative courses of action are open is self-contradictory.[1] The word 'fatalism' is used in philosophy in at least two other senses: it is used (i) for the thesis that what is going to happen is *inevitable*, and (ii) for the thesis that no one is able to act otherwise than he in fact does. (This latter thesis is entailed by but does not entail what I am calling fatalism.) So long as it is understood that neither of these theses is what *I* mean by 'fatalism', no confusion will result from this plurality of senses. But the idea of the inevitability of what is going to happen is so commonly associated with the word 'fatalism' that I feel I should say something about it.

2.2 Suppose a witch predicts that I shall drown within the next twenty-four hours. She also predicts that I shall attempt to evade this fate, and that my efforts will be in vain. Here are two stories about how her prediction might come true.

(a) I determine to spend the next twenty-four hours at the top of a high hill. But as I leave the witch's hovel, I am overpowered by three assailants in the employ of an enemy of mine, who, despite my struggles, carry me to a nearby pond and hold me under water till I am dead.

(b) I determine to spend the next twenty-four hours at the top of a high hill. While climbing the hill, I fall into a hidden well and drown. Moreover, if I had simply gone about my business and done nothing in particular to avoid drowning, I should not have drowned.

In each of these stories, the witch's prediction, that my efforts to avoid drowning would be in vain, came true. But

there is an important difference between them. In story (a), I
should have drowned no matter what I had done, and this is
not a feature of story (b). And yet story (b) produces—in me
at any rate—the sort of feeling one might express by saying,
"Yes, that's what inescapable fate means". How is this feeling
produced? Let us examine a more artful story of the same
kind.

SHEPPY: I wish now I'd gone down to the Isle of Sheppey when the
doctor advised it. You wouldn't 'ave thought of looking for me there.

DEATH: There was a merchant in Bagdad who sent his servant to market
to buy provisions and in a little while the servant came back, white
and trembling, and said, Master, just now when I was in the market-
place I was jostled by a woman in the crowd and when I turned I saw
it was death that jostled me. She looked at me and made a threatening gesture; now, lend me your horse, and I will ride away from this
city and avoid my fate. I will go to Samarra and there death will not
find me. The merchant lent him his horse, and the servant mounted
it, and he dug his spurs in its flanks and as fast as the horse could gallop
he went. Then the merchant went down to the market-place and he
saw me standing in the crowd and he came to me and said, Why did
you make a threatening gesture to my servant when you saw him this
morning? That was not a threatening gesture, I said, it was only a
start of surprise. I was astonished to see him in Bagdad, for I had an
appointment with him to-night in Samarra.

SHEPPY: [With a shudder.] D'you mean there's no escaping you?

DEATH: No.[2]

Death seems to imply that she and the merchant's servant
would have met that very night, no matter what he had done.
But this is false. They would not have met that night if he
had remained in Bagdad. (Otherwise, the point of the story is
lost.) But then why does Death's story have the effect on us
of making her seem inescapable? Well, because her story leads
us to believe that whatever one attempts to do to avoid her
will be just the wrong thing. In this sense, she is inescapable.
But notice that the fact that there's no escaping her depends
on our inevitable ignorance of what she has got written down
in her little (presumably black) book. Such stories as story (b)
above and Death's story and the story of Oedipus depend for
their effect on the ignorance of their protagonist about the
way in which a prediction will come true. Story (a) does not
depend on the ignorance of its protagonist. Even if the witch

in story (a) had told me exactly how I should be drowned, this would not have enabled me to escape drowning.

Let us introduce some philosophical jargon. Let us say of a certain future event (an event that is in fact going to happen) that it is *strongly inevitable for me* if it would happen no matter what I did.[3] Similarly, a future *state of affairs* is strongly inevitable for me if it would *obtain* no matter what I did. Let us say that a future event, or state of affairs, is *weakly inevitable for me* if both of the following conditions hold: (i) it is not strongly inevitable, and (ii) if I tried to take measures to prevent it, then I should choose the wrong measures out of ignorance, and it is strongly inevitable for me that I should be ignorant of the right measures.

In story (a), my death by drowning at a certain moment was strongly inevitable for me at the time of the witch's prediction. In story (b), my death by drowning at a certain moment was weakly inevitable for me at the time of the witch's prediction, at least assuming that nothing I might have done thereafter would have been sufficient for getting a more detailed prediction from the witch. In Death's story, it was weakly inevitable for the servant that he should meet her in Samarra that night, at least assuming that nothing he might have done before arriving in Samarra would have been sufficient for discovering that it was 'Samarra' and not 'Bagdad' that was written beside his name in her appointment book. (The "effect" of these stories, their "atmosphere" of inescapable fate, is not due solely to the fact that they are stories about men whose death at a certain moment is weakly inevitable. These literary qualities also owe a great deal to the fact that their protagonists' incomplete foreknowledge has magical or supernatural sources, to the fact that their protagonists *in fact* attempt to escape death, and to the fact that the very measures their protagonists take to escape death contribute to their deaths.)

It is obviously possible, magical or supernatural prediction aside, that *some* events be strongly inevitable, and possible that *some* events be weakly inevitable. It is, for example, strongly inevitable for me and for anyone else that the sun rise tomorrow. As to weak inevitability, suppose I am in a burning building—I do not yet realize it is burning, but shall in a moment—from which there are exactly two possible exits. And suppose that all the following propositions are true:

(i)　if I do not try to leave the building, I shall be burned to death;

(ii)　if I try to leave by the nearer exit, I shall be burned to death;

(iii)　if I try to leave by the more remote exit, I shall succeed and save my life;

(iv)　I have no reason to think that either exit is more likely to lead to safety than the other, and have no way of finding out if either exit is preferable;

(v)　if I believed I were in danger and saw two routes of possible escape, I should always choose the nearer unless I had some good reason to regard the more distant as preferable.

If (i)–(v) are true, then my death by burning is now weakly inevitable for me.

But if it is possible that some events be inevitable, in either sense, for someone, could it be that all events are inevitable, in either sense, for anyone or everyone? Let us first consider weak inevitability. Taken literally, this question must be answered "No": it is certainly not weakly inevitable for me that I shall continue writing for at least the next five minutes, though, unless I am very much mistaken, I *shall* in fact do this. A more interesting question is whether some important subclass of the class of future events is weakly inevitable for everyone. For example, everyone will die at some particular moment; could it be that, for every living person, there is some future moment such that it is weakly inevitable for him that he shall die at that moment?

Let us look carefully at this question. Consider the class of people who will die at noon tomorrow. Many of these people, unfortunately, are in excellent health, and no one could now predict any of the fires, bathing accidents, acts of political terrorism, and so on, that will cause their deaths. But this is not sufficient for the weak inevitability of any of their deaths. It seems enormously likely that at least one of these people is such that *if* now, contrary to fact, he were to come to think that there was good reason to believe he should die tomorrow at noon, then he would *not* die tomorrow at noon. Consider, for example, Mergendus, who will die in a boating accident at noon tomorrow. Suppose, contrary to fact, that you or I were to predict in Mergendus's hearing that he should die at noon tomorrow, and that Mergendus—he is a superstitious man—took our prediction seriously enough to believe that his life was in danger, and that he had better take care. What would happen? What I should *expect* would happen is that Mergendus would refuse to leave his house tomorrow (much less, go boating) and that, owing to this precaution, he would *not* die at noon tomorrow. But, of course, there is no intrinsic absurdity in supposing that what would happen is that Mergendus would refuse to leave his house tomorrow and would be killed in his own bed by a meteorite at just the moment at which he would have drowned if he had gone boating. In fact, *someone* or other has probably been in just this doubly unfortunate position: even if he had taken steps sufficient to avoid whatever it was that in fact caused his death at a certain moment, he would, none the less, have died at just that same moment because, to speak theromorphically, another death was lying in wait for him.

There seems to be no conceptual absurdity in supposing that this is *always* the case: it is conceptually possible that, for every person, there is a moment such that he will die at that moment and such that his death at that moment is weakly inevitable for him if it is not strongly inevitable. But we cannot take seriously any suggestion that this conceptual possibility is in fact realized. If it were realized, this would either be simply an enormous, meaningless multiple accident, an accident of more than astronomical improbability, or else the result of the manipulations of some cosmic "puppet-master" like Death or Death's employers in Maugham's play. And surely a belief in a personified Death or Fate, or whatever one might want to call a cosmic puppet-master, is a belief for which 'superstition' is, if anything, too flattering a word.[4]

Let us turn now to strong inevitability. Is there any reason to think that all future events, or some important and interesting class of future events, are strongly inevitable for us? To believe this is to believe that the future would be the way it is in fact going to be, even if we should choose to behave differently and no matter *how* we should choose to behave. To affirm this thesis is simply to deny the reality of cause and effect. Thus baldly stated, the thesis that all future events (or all those of some important kind) are strongly inevitable has nothing whatever to recommend it. It is therefore not surprising that there exist philosophical arguments for it. I offer the reader two. One is a chestnut, and one is, as the White Knight would say, my own invention. It may be regarded as a generalization of the first.

> It's no good summoning a physician if you are ill, for a physician can't help you. For either you're going to recover or you aren't. If you aren't going to recover, the physician can't help you. If you are going to recover, the physician can't help you, since you don't need help.[5]

> Let E be any event that might happen. Consider the theorem of logic '$(q \supset p) \lor (r \supset \sim p)$'. In virtue of this theorem, one or the other of the following two propositions must be true:

> If I try, by any means whatever, to prevent E, E will happen;

> If I try, by any means whatever, to bring about E, E will not happen.

> Therefore, either E or the non-occurrence of E is strongly inevitable for me.

Each of these arguments is sheerest sophistry. (I leave them to the reader to expose.) And, so far as I know, there is no reason for thinking that all events, or all events of some important kind, are strongly inevitable always and for everyone, other than the reasons, such as they are, that are supplied by sophistical arguments like these.

We may summarize our conclusions about the "inevitability of what is going to happen" as follows. If one's belief that what is going to happen is inevitable is a belief in the *weak* inevitability of all, or all of some important class of, future events, then one's belief is a belief in an accidental, meaningless, and staggeringly improbable aggregation of circumstances, or else mere superstition. If one's belief is a belief in the *strong* inevitability of all, or all of some important class of, future events, then one's belief, if it is founded upon anything at all, is founded upon sophistry.

2.3 Let us now turn to fatalism proper. The fatalist is not an "inevitabilist", strong or weak. The strong inevitabilist affirms the counter-factual conditional

> If Caesar had taken ship for Spain on 14 March, Caesar would have been murdered on 15 March

but neither the fatalist nor the weak inevitabilist affirms this proposition. (Perhaps they don't *deny* it either; after all, for all anyone knows, if Caesar had suddenly decided to leave for Spain on 14 March, a storm would have forced his ship back to port, and the assassination would have gone through as planned. But the fatalist and the weak inevitabilist see no particular *reason* to affirm this proposition.) The weak inevitabilist affirms the counter-factual conditional

> If Caesar had taken seriously the soothsayer's warning, Caesar would have been murdered on 15 March

and the fatalist does not affirm this proposition, though perhaps he doesn't *deny* it; he simply sees no particular reason to think it's true. What the fatalist does believe is that, since Caesar *didn't* take ship for Spain on 14 March, he *couldn't* have done this. And since Caesar didn't in fact take the soothsayer's warning seriously, he *couldn't* have. And, of course, he believes this not because he thinks he knows some special facts about Caesar, but as an instance of a general thesis: it is a logical or conceptual truth that if an agent in fact does some particular thing, then that thing is the *only* thing the agent is able to do. And, as regards the future, the fatalist believes that if an agent is in fact going to do some particular thing, then that thing is the only thing he can do, the only thing it is open to him to do.

Now if there is any good reason to think that fatalism is true, it is a very important thesis. It seems to be a feature of our concept of moral responsibility that we hold a person morally responsible for the way he has acted only if we believe he could have acted otherwise. And it seems to be a feature of our concept of deliberation that we can deliberate about which of various mutually exclusive courses of action to pursue only if we believe that each of these courses of action is open to us. Therefore, anyone who accepts fatalism must regard all ascriptions of moral responsibility as incorrect, and must, on pain of self-contradiction, refrain from deliberating about future courses of action.[6] But deliberation and the ascription of moral responsibility are extremely important; in fact it is hard to imagine what human life would be like without them. But these very facts that show that fatalism is extremely important if there is any reason to think it true, also seem to show that there could not be any reason to think it true. If fatalism is true, then the ideas expressed by sentences like 'he alone is to blame for the accident' and 'I am trying to decide whether to have my father declared mentally incompetent' are conceptually defective. The former is, if fatalism is true, a straightforward conceptual falsehood, like 'he alone has trisected the angle'. The second, while it could be used to express a truth even if fatalism were true, would be like 'I am trying to devise a method for trisecting the angle': these sentences could be used to express a truth only by one who *believed* a conceptual falsehood.

I think it is incoherent to suppose that any thesis could be true that has the consequence of rendering conceptually defective sentences so utterly *basic* to human life as the sentences about blame and deliberation mentioned above. But I shall not argue for this thesis. It could not, I think, be adequately argued for in print: philosophers who disagree about such deep matters as these can hope to resolve their disagreement, if at all, only in conversation. In any case, this is not a book of metaphilosophy but of metaphysics. In such a book as this, the wisest course is to look at various arguments for fatalism and see what can be made of them. It will probably not surprise the reader to discover that I think that the arguments we shall examine are houses built upon sand. But I shall not claim to show that fatalism is false, since, for all I shall show, there may be arguments for fatalism that are not open to the objections I shall raise. Unless I am mistaken, however, most arguments for fatalism depend upon premisses that are among or are variants on the premisses of the two arguments I shall discuss.[7] Therefore, what I shall say will be directly relevant to, if it does not actually refute, just about any argument for fatalism.

I shall not examine directly the classical sources of fatalism. The meaning of Aristotle's famous passage (*De Interpretatione*, IX) is in dispute; the very structure of the Master Argument of Diodorus is a matter of scholarly conjecture. I, who am no historian, do not propose to undertake an investigation of what these philosophers may have meant. If any of the blunders I shall doubtless make in the sequel could have been avoided by more careful attention to Aristotle, Cicero, Epictetus, or their modern commentators, I expect someone will be good enough to point this out.

2.4 Fatalistic arguments typically depend on the notions of truth and falsity. But what are truth and falsity? Truth and falsity are properties. But properties of what? They are properties of propositions. I do not mean anything mysterious by 'proposition'. I use this word as a general term for the things people *assent to, reject, find doubtful, accept for the sake of argument, attempt to verify, deduce things from*, and so on.[8] (Some of the phrases in this list take more than one sort of object. One may, for example, reject not only propositions but bribes. I hope no one is going to be difficult about this.) We have plenty of "specialized" words for propositions in the language of everyday life, just as we have plenty of specialized words for human beings. On various occasions we call propositions 'doctrines', 'theses', 'theories', 'premisses', 'conclusions', 'theorems', 'views', 'positions', 'conjectures', 'statements', 'hypotheses', 'dogmas', 'beliefs', and 'heresies', just as, on various occasions we call human beings 'women', 'babies', 'thieves', 'Trotskyites', 'Australians', and 'Catholics'.

It is thus uncontroversial that there are propositions. The only question that could arise is: "What *are* propositions?" Many philosophers apparently think propositions are sentences, since they think sentences are what are true or false. But I can make no sense of the suggestion that propositions are sentences, and I shall not discuss it further. It is true that

I am willing on occasion to speak of sentences being true or false, but this is only shorthand. When I say that a given sentence is *true*, I mean that the proposition—a non-sentence—that that sentence expresses is true. (To say that an English sentence *expresses* a given proposition is to say, roughly, that the result of concatenating 'the proposition that' and that sentence *denotes* that proposition.) Similarly, when I say that a name is *honourable*, I mean that the individual or family that bears that name is honourable. I can no more understand the suggestion that a sentence might be true otherwise than in virtue of its expressing a true proposition than I can understand the suggestion that a name might be honourable otherwise than in virtue of its being borne by an honourable individual or family.

There are philosophers who will demand at this point that I state a "principle of identity" for propositions. I will not do this. When one attempts to give a general way of determining whether two predicates applying to propositions are coextensive, a number of vexed questions arise. What I want to say about fatalism can be said without answering most of them. But there is one sort of question about propositional identity that we must be able to answer. We might call questions of this sort, 'questions about propositions expressed by sentences containing indexical expressions'. Suppose a madman says, "I am Napoleon", and that a second madman, perhaps at another time and in another place, speaks these same words. Do these madmen assert or express the same thing?—what we might call 'the proposition that one is Napoleon'. Or, again, suppose that at a certain moment I believe I am about to die and that at another moment, years later, I believe I am about to die. Do I believe the same thing to be true on these two occasions ("the proposition that one is about to die"), or two different things?

It seems to me that only one answer is possible: the madmen say, and I believe, different things.[9] Take the former case. Suppose, to simplify the argument, that one of the madmen *was* Napoleon. Then what one said was true and what the other said was false, and, therefore, by the non-identity of discernibles, what one said was not what the other said. (If we had supposed neither of the madmen to be Napoleon, then what each said would have been false; but this would not have changed matters essentially, since they would none the less have been in *disagreement* about the identity of Napoleon, and therefore saying distinct things.) More or less the same argument can be given in respect of the two occasions on which I believe I am about to die: there are possible circumstances in which what I believe on the earlier occasion is false and what I believe on the later occasion is true. But there are no possible circumstances in which some one thing is both true and false. Of course someone might say that what I believed on the earlier occasion was *then* false but later *became* true. But if that were right, I could say on the later occasion, "When I thought I was about to die twenty years ago I was *then* wrong. But what I then believed has now become true. When I look at my diary of twenty years ago and see the words 'I am about to die', I am comforted in my present affliction by the thought that what I wrote has become true and that, in consequence, nothing said in my diary is *now* false." And this would be an absurd thing to say.

So the two madmen said, and I believed, two different things. That is, in each of our two cases, two numerically distinct propositions are involved. To take a more extreme example, if someone asks me how I feel and I say, "I am tired", and, five seconds later I am again asked how I feel and again say, "I am tired", then I assert or express two distinct propositions: at a certain moment, I express the proposition that I am then tired; five seconds later, I express a distinct proposition, the proposition that I am *then* tired.[10]

This is a very sketchy account of "propositions", but perhaps it will do for our purposes. Truth and falsity are, as we said earlier, properties of propositions. There are, of course, many other properties whose extensions comprise propositions. Propositions, in addition to being true or false, may be empirically verifiable, hard to understand, inexpressible in the tongue of a certain tribe, and so on. But I take it that each of us knows *what* properties truth and falsity are. Anyone sufficiently pervicacious to claim *not* to know, may perhaps be helped by two famous passages from Aristotle's *Metaphysics* (Ross's translation):[11]

To say of what is that it is not, or of what is not that it is, is false, while to say of what is that it is, and of what is not that it is not, is true ... (Γ, 1011ᵇ.)

It is not because we think truly that you are white that you *are* white, but because you are white that we who say this have the truth. (Θ, 1051^{b}.)

Let us now turn to an argument for fatalism.

2.5 The argument we shall now consider turns on the notion of an agent's "ability to render a proposition false". This notion will be defined in Section 3.4. For the present, however, let us suppose that we have a sufficient intuitive grasp of the schema 's can render *p* false' to go on with.

Let us consider some proposition about the future—say the proposition that I shall shave tomorrow morning. This proposition—call it 'S', for short—is true if and only if I shall shave during the morning of 4 June 1976. Since I shall shave during this period (I *might* be wrong about this; but then I *might* be wrong about almost anything), S is true. That is, S is true *now*. But it would seem that if a proposition is true at some particular moment then it must be true at every moment. If this were not the case, then the following would be part of a conceivable "history" of S: S was false all through April 1902, but early in May it became true and remained true till Good Friday 1936, after which it was false until V-E day. . . . But this sort of history is not conceivable, and, hence, if S is true, S is unchangeably true. We might put the matter this way: there are possible worlds in which S is always true and possible worlds in which S is always false; but there are no possible worlds in which S is at one time true and at another false. But if S is unchangeably true, then I cannot render S false, for the same reason that, if a certain king is unchangeably powerful, then I cannot render him helpless. But if I cannot render S false, then I cannot refrain from shaving tomorrow morning; for if I could refrain from shaving tomorrow morning, then I could render S false.

Now this argument is sound only if a certain factual claim I have made—that I shall shave tomorrow morning—is true.[12] But even if I am mistaken in thinking I shall shave tomorrow morning, then, though the argument we have been considering is not sound, an essentially identical argument for the conclusion that I cannot shave tomorrow morning *is* sound. Thus, either I cannot refrain from shaving tomorrow morning or else I cannot shave tomorrow morning: my belief that, of two incompatible courses of action, shaving and not shaving, both are open to me, is shown to be false.

This reasoning can, of course, be generalized. If it is correct, then for every true proposition about the future there is a similar argument, also sound, for the conclusion that I cannot (nor can anyone else) render that proposition false. That is to say, if anyone is in fact going to act in a certain way then just *that* way is the only way he *can* act. Or, to put our conclusion another way, fatalism is true.

Various philosophers have found this way of arguing compelling. Such philosophers do not usually, at least in modern times, become fatalists. But they do think that this way of arguing forces us to choose between fatalism and some almost equally unattractive alternative, such as the recognition of some third truth-value in addition to truth and falsity. I cannot myself say whether this is the case, for the above paragraphs contain phrases I do not understand.[13] Among them are: 'true at some particular moment', 'true at every moment', 'became true', 'remained true', 'is unchangeably true', and so on. That is—and we must be very careful about this—I do not see what these phrases mean if they are used as they are used in the above argument for fatalism. If I were to say, "Municipal bonds are a good investment", and someone replied, "That used to be true but it isn't true any more", his words would be a model of lucidity. But if someone were to speak to me as follows:

> Consider the proposition that municipal bonds are a good investment. *This very proposition* used to be true but is no longer true

then I should have grave problems in understanding what he meant. Let us pretend that 'T' denotes in our dialect, yours and mine, the moment at which my imagined respondent spoke. When he spoke the words 'the proposition that municipal bonds are a good investment' he referred to a proposition that is true if and only if municipal bonds were a good investment at T. (I do not say the proposition he referred to *is* the proposition that municipal bonds were a good investment at T; whether this is the case is one of the questions about identifying propositions that I don't have to answer.) If he had spoken these same words one day earlier, he would have referred to a proposition that is true if and only if municipal bonds were a good investment one day earlier than T. What could he mean by saying of such a proposition that it "was once" true but "is no longer" true? My understanding of the ordinary use of 'was once true' and 'is no longer true' is of no help to me. Normally, if I utter a certain sentence and am told, "That was once true",[14] my respondent means *something* like: 'If you had used those same words on a certain *earlier* occasion, then you *would have* said something true' or 'The words you have spoken *used* to express a true proposition'.

If anyone thinks this an *ad hoc* description of what 'was once true' means, let him consider the following case, which raises exactly analogous difficulties. Suppose I say, "The number of committee members is odd, so the vote won't be a tie", and you, who know of a change in the structure of the committee reply, "It used to be odd, but it isn't any more". You are *not* saying that there is a certain number—twelve, say—that used to be odd but isn't nowadays; rather, you are saying *something* like this: the phrase 'the number of committee members' *used* to denote an odd number, but now it denotes a different number, one that isn't odd. I think that most philosophers will agree that we are on the right track in the "used to be odd" case; I think we are also on the right track in the "used to be true" case.

In any event, the analogy between the two cases is instructive. Suppose someone were to say, "There is a number that used to be odd", and I replied, as indeed I should, that I didn't understand what he meant. My failure to understand him might or might not be justified, but, however this might be, clearly I should not be helped towards understanding him by an explanation like this one: 'Look, you understand what I mean if I say that the number of committee members used to be odd. But the number of committee members is a number; therefore you understand what it means to say there is a number that used to be odd'. Similarly, my difficulties about sentences like 'There is a proposition that used to be true' are not going to be cleared up by explanations like: 'The proposition that municipal bonds are a good investment used to be true. So it is clear what it means to say that there is a proposition that used to be true'.

I have argued that, when, in ordinary speech, we appear to say of a certain proposition that it used to be true, we are in fact saying of a certain propositional name that it used to denote, or of a certain sentence that it used to express, a proposition that is true, just as when we appear to say of a certain number that it used to be odd, we are in fact saying of a certain descriptive phrase that it used to denote a number that is odd. If I am right, then our ordinary use of 'used to be true' and similar phrases (of which a parallel account could be given) will not enable us to understand the use made of such phrases in the argument for fatalism that we are considering.

What I have done so far is to argue that temporal qualification of a copula connecting 'true' or 'false' and a name of a proposition cannot be explained in a certain way, namely, by reference to *apparent* instances of it in ordinary speech. But it may very well be that there is some other way to make sense of such qualification. To make sense of this idea, it would be sufficient to make sense of the open sentence:

(The proposition) x is true at (the moment) t,

since all the other locutions involving temporal qualification of the possession of truth by a proposition that are required by the fatalistic argument we are examining can be defined in terms of this sentence.

I know of only one explanatory paraphrase of this open sentence that is worthy of serious consideration.[15] It is this:

If someone were to assert x and nothing else at t, then what he asserted at t would be true.

Thus, for example, according to the proponents of this explanation, the sentence

The proposition that Queen Victoria died in 1901 was true in 1878

expresses a truth, since, if anyone had said in 1878, "Queen Victoria will die in 1901"—which are words that were suitable in 1878 for asserting the proposition we *now* call 'the proposition that Queen Victoria died in 1901'—he would have been right. (This sort of device can be applied in all manner of cases. For example, someone could say, "The number twelve

is even in Tibet", and explain these strange words as just
another way of saying, "If someone were to refer to the number twelve in Tibet, he would be referring to something even".)
Now I do not think that what we have been offered is a good
explanation of the meaning of 'x is true at t' since I don't
think this sentence means anything—just as I don't think 'The
number twelve is even in Tibet' means anything—and thus I
don't think that *anything* is or could be an explanation, good
or bad, of its meaning. But perhaps this is not terribly important, since we can always regard what we have been offered as
a stipulative definition: it is, after all, a sentence containing
the proper variables free, and that is the only formal requirement on the *definiens* of a stipulative definition. That is to
say, we may regard 'x is true at t' as simply a convenient abbreviation, without antecedent meaning, for what has mis-
takenly been offered as an analysis or explanation of 'x is true
at t'.[16] We now have a way of interpreting (apparent) temporal
qualifications of the ascription of truth-values to propositions.
Let us return to our argument for fatalism and see whether its
premisses appear plausible when the temporal qualifications
they contain are interpreted in this way.

The crucial premiss in this argument seems to be the proposition that S is unchangeably true. The sentence 'S is unchangeably true' can, I think, be paraphrased in terms of our "basic"
locution 'x is true at t' in this way (by analogy to, e.g., 'God
is unchangeably powerful'):

$$(\exists x) \text{ (S is true at } x) \ \& \ \sim \Diamond (\exists x)(\exists y) \text{ (S is true at } x \ \& \ \sim S \text{ is true at } y)$$

where '$\Diamond$' abbreviates 'it is possible that'. Expanding the second conjunct of this sentence in terms of our stipulative
definition of 'x is true at t', we obtain:

(a) $\sim \Diamond (\exists x)(\exists y)$ (If someone were to assert S at x, then
what he asserted at x would be true $\&$ $\sim$If someone were
to assert S at y, then what he asserted at y would be true).

Now this sentence seems to express a truth: consider the con-
junctive open sentence got by dropping '$\sim \Diamond (\exists x)(\exists y)$' from
it; there is no possible world in which there exists a pair of
moments of time that satisfies this open sentence. Have we

then proved fatalism? Not unless we can deduce 'I cannot
render S false' from 'S is unchangeably true'. Why should anyone accept this consequence? Earlier I wrote:

> But if S is unchangeably true, then I cannot render S false,
> for the same reason that, if a certain king is unchange-
> ably powerful, then I cannot render him helpless (p. 34),

and this appears to be a conclusive argument. But does the
analogy really hold? When we say, "Edward III was powerful
in 1346", our use of the adverbial phrase 'in 1346' is transparent; it does not need to be *given* a meaning. But when we
say, "S was true in 1346", the phrase 'in 1346' is not transparent; it needs to be given a meaning. Well, we gave it a meaning in the only way in which anything can be given a meaning:
by stipulation. Having done this, we proceeded to define 'S is
unchangeably true' in such a way that this phrase would have
the same logical properties as 'Edward is unchangeably powerful', *provided* 'S is true at *t*' had the same logical properties as
'Edward is powerful at *t*'. Do they have the same logical properties? The answer to this question is not obvious. After all,
the logical properties of, for example, 'Edward III was powerful in 1346' are determined by the rules, embedded in our
linguistic practice, for the use of the words it contains, and
this is not the case with 'S was true in 1346': *its* logical properties are determined by the rules for the use of the words
contained in its stipulated *definiens*. Perhaps the wisest course
we could take would be to refrain from framing our questions
in terms of the stipulatively defined sentence 'S is unchangeably true' and, instead, frame them in terms of the *definiens*
we have provided for this sentence. That is, instead of asking
whether 'I cannot render S false' follows from 'S is unchangeably true', let us ask whether it follows from the conjunction of

($\exists x$) (if someone were to assert S at x, then what he
asserted at x would be true)

with proposition (a). Informally, suppose S has these two
features: (i) there is a time such that if anyone were to assert
S at that time, his assertion would be true, and (ii) there *could
not be* a pair of times such that, if someone were to assert S
at one of these times, he would say something true, *and* if

someone were to assert S at the other of these times, he would
say something false. Does it follow from this supposition that
I cannot render S false? Well, perhaps it does; but I don't
see any reason to think so. Suppose someone said yesterday
(Thursday) that I should shave on Saturday morning, and that
what he said on Thursday is true. It is, of course, quite impossible for this to be the case *and* for it to be the case that
he should say tonight, "You are going to shave tomorrow
morning", and be wrong. Moreover, it is simply not possible
that he should have said on Thursday "You are going to shave
on Saturday" *and* have been right *and* it be the case that I
shall not shave on Saturday. But, I think, nothing of interest
about my free will with respect to shaving on Saturday follows;
the argument-form

$$p$$
$$\sim\!\Diamond(p \;\&\; q)$$
$$hence, \sim\!\Diamond q$$

is notoriously fallacious. But perhaps clever fatalists do not
rely on this fallacious form of reasoning. The clever fatalist
may claim to reason as follows:

> Look, you admit that S was true yesterday. But it's not
> *now* up to you what was the case yesterday: it is not
> within your power to change the fact that S was true
> yesterday. And it is a logical consequence of S's having
> been true yesterday that you will shave tomorrow. There-
> fore, it is not within your power to change the fact that
> you will shave tomorrow. If I am making use of any
> "modal" argument-form, it is this:
>
> $$\sim\!P\,p$$
>
> the fact that q is a logical consequence of the fact that p
> $$hence, \sim\!P\,q,$$
>
> where 'P' abbreviates 'it is within one's power to change
> the fact that'.[17]

I am not convinced by this argument. Its proponent says,
"But it's not now up to you what was the case yesterday", and
this has the ring of an extremely plausible assertion. If the adverb 'yesterday' that occurs in 'It's not now up to you what
was the case yesterday' has its usual sense, then it can hardly

be denied that this sentence expresses a truth. But if the argument we are considering is to avoid the fallacy of equivocation, then 'yesterday' must be used in the same sense in the argument's first and second sentences. And if its first sentence is to make sense, then 'yesterday' must have in that sentence a sense of the sort we have stipulated for temporal adverbs that qualify copulae flanked by 'true' or 'false' and propositional names, or some other purely stipulative sense. I shall ignore this second possibility, since I do not know what other sense might be given to these adverbs. Therefore, in evaluating this argument we must interpret

It's not *now* up to you what was the case yesterday

in accordance with our stipulation. And I see no reason to think that this sentence, so interpreted, expresses a truth. In particular, I see no reason to assent to

If S was true yesterday, then it's not now up to me whether S was true yesterday,

though I see every reason to assent to, for example,

If S was believed yesterday, then it's not now up to me whether S was believed yesterday.

In the second of these sentences, 'yesterday' has the sense it has in everyday usage; in the first it has a peculiar sense stipulated by the fatalist, just as 'in Tibet' has a special sense in 'The number twelve is even in Tibet' if this peculiar sentence is interpreted as was suggested earlier.

If we expand the first of these sentences in accordance with our stipulation, we obtain:

If (if someone had asserted S yesterday, then he would have asserted something true), then it's not now up to me whether it is the case that (if someone had asserted S yesterday, then he would have asserted something true).

Now I think the antecedent of this conditional is true. But I see no reason to think that its consequent isn't false. That is, I see no reason to think that the truth-value of

If someone had asserted S yesterday, then he would have asserted something true

isn't now up to me, for it is up to me just in the case that I can
shave tomorrow and can refrain from shaving tomorrow. And
I see no reason to doubt that both these things are within my
power. Moreover, even if I am wrong about this and I am either
unable to shave or unable to refrain from shaving, I do not see
that the fatalist has ever suggested any *logical* or *conceptual*
reason why this might be so. Someone might, I suppose, offer
the following argument: 'If S was true yesterday and if you
have it within your power to render S false, then you have the
power to make it the case that S was at one time true and at
another time false, which is impossible'. But such a consequence doesn't follow. What follows is that it is within my
power to make it the case that S was always false. When I say
this, I am talking the fatalist's language. If it sounds strange
to say that I now have it within my power to make it the case
that a certain true proposition was always false, that is the
fatalist's fault. It is he, after all, who has invented a strange
sense for the word 'always', a sense such that, using the word
in that sense, I can truly describe my ability to refrain from
shaving tomorrow morning as an ability to make it the case
that the true proposition S "was always" false.

I realize that neither the fatalist nor the philosopher who
feels drawn to fatalism is likely to be convinced by these arguments. Richard Taylor has responded to them in conversation
along these lines: 'You say you have the ability to render false
the proposition that you will shave tomorrow—that is, to
make it the case that this proposition has always been false—
even though this proposition is in fact true. And you say there
are ever so many true propositions about the future that you
have this sort of power over. Very well then, let us see you
exercise this power that you claim: pick any true proposition
about the future, and then so act that this proposition has
always been false'. But this is an illegitimate demand. I claim to
have a certain power and the description I give of this power
depends for its application on this power's not being exercised.
(The description is 'the power to render certain always true
propositions always false'.) What Taylor demands is that I
show that I have such a power by exercising it. If this sort of
demand were legitimate, fatalism could be established very
easily. Fatalism may be looked upon as the doctrine that the

only powers one has are—of logical necessity—powers that one in fact exercises. Suppose I say that fatalism is false since I have powers I never in fact exercise, and the fatalist replies, "Very well then, if you have such powers, *let's see you exercise one*". This is not perhaps a very convincing argument. In fact, it depends on the same fallacy as an infamous sophistical demand sometimes made by not very able Berkeleians: 'You say that objects continue to exist while they're not being observed; very well then, *let's see one*'.

To recapitulate: Either the use that the fatalist makes of "temporal" qualifications of the possession of truth and falsity by a proposition is meaningless, or else this use must be explained by a stipulation like the one I have suggested. If it is explained by such a stipulation, then sentences like 'Every proposition is, if true, unchangeably true' express, in *his* usage, truths. (And there is no other usage in which they express anything.) But the proposition expressed by this sentence is quite consistent with its being the case that there are many true propositions about, for example, what will happen tomorrow that I have it within my power to render false. Or, at least, I have never seen any compelling argument for the conclusion that this is not the case.

2.6 Richard Taylor has offered a puzzling and ingenious argument for fatalism.[18] His argument may be put as follows:

Suppose I am a naval commander who is deliberating about whether to issue order O or to refrain from issuing order O. Suppose that, under the conditions that in fact prevail, my issuing O would result in there being a naval battle tomorrow, while my refraining from issuing O would result in there being *no* naval battle tomorrow.

We shall show that either it is not within my power to issue O, or else it is not within my power to refrain from issuing O.

(i) Suppose no naval battle will occur tomorrow. Then a condition necessary for my issuing O is absent: namely, a naval battle tomorrow. For, since my issuing O is a condition *sufficient* for there being a naval battle tomorrow, then a naval battle tomorrow is a condition *necessary* for my issuing O. If someone feels it is odd to talk of my *now* doing something "in the absence of", for example, a naval battle *tomorrow*, we may agree with him. Let us say that our use of 'in the absence of' is an *extension* of normal English usage. We may in our present usage say I am now writing *in the absence of* an earthquake in London tomorrow, provided there will be no earthquake in London tomorrow. As regards the past, we may say I am now writing *in the absence of* a German invasion of the British Isles in 1940. While there is an element of artificiality in this way of speaking, the truth-conditions for assertions that involve it are none the less intelligible enough. The first of our illustrative sentences expresses just the same proposition as, or a proposition necessarily equivalent to, that expressed by

> I am now writing and there will be no earthquake in London tomorrow.

The second illustrative sentence expresses the same proposition as, or a proposition necessarily equivalent to, that expressed by

> I am now writing and the Germans did not invade the British Isles in 1940.

Now consider the following principle:

(A) No agent is able to perform an act in the absence of a condition necessary for its accomplishment.

Taylor says of this principle, "This is no law of logic, and in fact cannot be expressed even in the contemporary modal logics, but it is nonetheless manifestly true" (p. 58). It follows from (A) and from what we have already established—that a condition necessary for my issuing O is absent—that I cannot issue O.

(ii) Suppose a naval battle will occur tomorrow. Then a condition necessary for my refraining from issuing O is absent: namely, the non-occurrence of a naval battle tomorrow. But then, by principle (A), I cannot refrain from issuing O.

Therefore, either I cannot issue O or else I cannot refrain from issuing O. That is to say, it is not up to me whether I issue O. This argument, of course, can be generalized. If it is sound, then, for any case of an agent who is deliberating about which of various courses of action to pursue, we can show by a similar argument that at most *one* of these courses of action is open to him; that at most one is such that he can pursue it; that it is not up to him which if any of these courses he shall pursue.

The crucial premiss in Taylor's argument is Principle (A). If we accept this principle, then we can derive fatalism by a much simpler argument than Taylor's. For it is obvious that whenever I am *not* performing a certain act, then there is absent a condition necessary for my performing it: namely, my performing it.[19] And, of course, whenever I am performing a certain act, there is absent a certain condition necessary for my *not* performing it: my not performing it.[20] Thus, Principle (A) leads *directly* to the collapse of the distinction between what one does and what one can do: one who accepts Principle (A) has already got fatalism in his pocket and need not shop for it in Taylor's elaborate naval bazaar, diverting though the wares offered there may be.

Is Principle (A) true? The question is complex, for Principle (A) is ambiguous. We shall see that there are two ways it might be interpreted. Interpreted in one of these ways, it is obviously true but does not yield Taylor's conclusion; interpreted in the other way, it indeed yields Taylor's conclusion, though there is no reason to think it is true.

Let us call an *ability-sentence* a complete, grammatical, declarative sentence that consists of a subject term that denotes or purports to denote a person ('I'; 'Richard Taylor'), followed by an "ability-copula" such as 'can', 'am able to', or 'has it within his power to', followed by any string of words.

Ability-sentences containing adverbs or adverbial phrases are often ambiguous. Consider:

I can refrain from talking at any time.

Does the adverbial phrase 'at any time' modify the verb-phrase 'refrain from talking' or does it modify 'can'? In the former case, the sentence means something like 'It is within my power to keep a vow of perpetual silence'; in the latter case, something like 'At any given moment, I can at that moment refrain from talking'.

In normal English usage, this ambiguity is usually not very important. It is resolved by such factors as intonation or one of the syntactically possible interpretations being wildly inappropriate. If there were some real possibility of confusion, the speaker might reposition the adverbial phrase:

> I can, at any time, refrain from talking.

It will be convenient for us to introduce a more explicit device than these for the disambiguation of ability-sentences. Let us use round brackets in this fashion:

> I can (refrain from talking) at any time;
>
> I can (refrain from talking at any time).

The import of the round brackets is this: in the first of these sentences, 'at any time' must modify 'can', since both 'can' and 'at any time' are outside the brackets; in the second sentence, 'at any time' must modify 'refrain from talking', since both these phrases are inside the brackets. Roughly speaking, the presence of a pair of disambiguating brackets in an ability-sentence "forces" an adverb or adverbial phrase to modify a verb or verb-phrase that is on the "same side" of the pair of brackets.

Or, if the reader is willing to include in his ontology abstract entities called "acts" and is willing to recognize 'refraining from talking' and 'refraining from talking at any time' as phrases naming acts, then he may regard the round brackets as marking the boundaries of names of acts. Thus, on this way of looking at matters, the above pair of sentences may be read:

> I can perform the act *refraining from talking* at any time;
>
> I can perform the act *refraining from talking at any time*.

Perhaps even the reader whose ontology is not so copious as to include such acts will regard this explanation as intuitively useful if ontologically dubious, like an explanation of the derivative as a quotient of infinitesimal quantities.

A third way of looking at this pair of sentences is to regard them as marking the same distinction as:

> I can obey the command 'Refrain from talking' at any time;
>
> I can obey the command 'Refrain from talking at any time'.

But this is not quite satisfactory, since the propositions expressed by these sentences seem to have unwanted entailments, as, for example, that I can understand English. Let us, therefore, regard our first explanation of our use of brackets as official, and the second and third explanations as being offered for the sake of such intuitive value as they may have.

Let us now return to principle (A). Let us look at some instances of this principle. First a "trivial" instance:

(a) I cannot move my finger when my finger is not moving.

This sentence may be disambiguated as follows:

(b) I cannot (move my finger) when my finger is not moving;

(c) I cannot (move my finger when my finger is not moving).

If an English speaker were to utter sentence (a), he would most naturally be taken to mean (c). But (b) is a *possible* reading of (a), though what is expressed by (b) would normally be expressed by 'Whenever my finger is not moving, I lack the ability to move my finger'. Obviously, if someone uttered sentence (c), or uttered (a) *meaning* (c), he would be right. But what about (b)? Could a person utter this sentence and say something true? Well, consider the following case. My finger is paralysed, but it is important to me that it move, so I am continuously straining to move it. During intermittent and unpredictable intervals I become able to move my finger and then, of course, it begins to move; then it again becomes paralysed and ceases to move. In that case, if I were to utter (b), I should say something true. There is therefore a semantic difference between (b) and (c); sentence (a) is not merely syntactically ambiguous. But if (a) is an instance of (A), then it would seem to follow that (A) is ambiguous. Is it (b) or (c) that is an instance of (A)?

A similar point can be made about

(d) I cannot issue O in the absence of a naval battle tomorrow.

Does Taylor intend this sentence to mean (e) or (f)?

(e) I cannot (issue O) in the absence of a naval battle tomorrow.

(f)   I cannot (issue O in the absence of a naval battle tomorrow).

Which of these sentences is an instance of (A)? Obviously this question has no answer. For (A) itself is ambiguous. We must distinguish between:

(A)1   No agent is able to (perform an act) in the absence of a condition necessary for its accomplishment,

and

(A)2   No agent is able to (perform an act in the absence of a condition necessary for its accomplishment).

In which of these ways shall we read (A)? Let us try it both ways. Suppose (A) means A(2). From A(2) we may deduce (f), though there seems to be no reason to think we can deduce (e). Does it follow from (f) together with the proposition that there will be no naval battle tomorrow that I cannot issue O? I see no reason to think it follows. Certainly not just any inference of this *form* can convincingly claim to be valid. For example, the inference

> I cannot (move my finger in the absence of my finger's moving);
>
> My finger is not moving;
>
> *hence*, I cannot move my finger

does not *seem* to be valid. In fact, it seems to be invalid. For its premisses are true, but its conclusion certainly seems to be false. As one philosopher (an unlooked-for ally) has put the matter:

The statement "I can move my finger," as well as the statement "I can hold my finger still," are both true (though their joint truth obviously does not entail that I can do both at once). This I take to be quite certain . . . if there is any philosophical theory implying that one or the other of these statements must be false, then that theory is doubtful.[21]

Is there then some special reason, some reason having to do with naval battles and orders, to suppose that the proposition that I cannot issue O follows from (f)? This would be hard to maintain. Proposition (f) is the same proposition as, or, at least, is entailed by, the proposition that I cannot issue O without a naval battle tomorrow resulting. And the following inference hardly seems valid:

> I cannot issue O without a naval battle tomorrow resulting;
>
> There will be no naval battle tomorrow;
>
> *hence*, I cannot issue O.

Of course, if fatalism is true, then this inference *is* valid, as is the inference about the movement of my finger we looked at earlier. But I am not arguing that fatalism is false; rather that a certain argument does not show that it is true.

It seems, therefore, that, while A(2) is true, there is no reason to think that it can be used to prove fatalism. What about A(1)? A(1) does indeed entail (e), and hence fatalism. But is there any reason to think that A(1) is true? I see none. The only argument Taylor offers in support of (A) does not produce—in me, at any rate—any tendency to accept A(1). His argument consists simply in exhibiting instances of situations in which he is unable to perform some act and in which a condition necessary for his performing that act is absent and in which his inability to perform that act is a result of the absence of that condition:

> I cannot, for example, live without oxygen, or swim five miles without ever having been in water, or read a given page of print without having learned Russian, or win a certain election without having been nominated, and so on. (p. 58.)

But this argument is invalid. Since my being able to perform a certain act is a necessary condition for my performing it, any condition necessary for my being able to perform that act is a condition necessary for my performing it. Therefore, since there are indeed conditions necessary for my being able to perform various acts, there are conditions that are necessary for my performing various acts that are also necessary for my being *able* to perform those acts. What Taylor has done is simply to list certain conditions necessary for his being able to perform certain acts, conditions that are *a fortiori* necessary

for his performing those acts. But such a list lends no support
to A(1). One might as well try to show that one cannot live
in America if some condition necessary for one's living in
California is absent by arguing:

> I cannot, for example, live in America, if I do not live
> in the Western Hemisphere, live upon dry land, live north
> of the Equator . . .

I conclude that Taylor's attempt to establish fatalism is a failure. Principle A is ambiguous. On one interpretation, A(2), it
is true but there is no reason to think it entails fatalism; on
the other, A(1), it entails fatalism but there is no reason to
think it true.

2.7 Discussions of the "Law of the Excluded Middle" bulk
large in most treatments of fatalism. But I have not discussed
this "law" at all, and it does not appear as a premiss in either
of the fatalistic arguments we have examined. It would be
possible to maintain, however, that these two arguments do
make covert use of the Law of the Excluded Middle. My formulation of Taylor's argument, for example, depends for its
validity on the validity of the inference-form

$$p \supset q$$
$$\sim p . \supset q$$
$$hence, q$$

which certainly seems to depend, in some sense, on the Law
of the Excluded Middle. And perhaps it is arguable that the
argument discussed in 2.5 depends, again "in some sense", on
the Law of the Excluded Middle.

But what is the Law of the Excluded Middle (hereinafter
'LEM')? Here are three candidates:

(i)   If p is any English sentence, then the sentence that re-
      sults from writing p and then writing 'or it is not the
      case that' and then once more writing p, expresses (as an
      English sentence) a true proposition;[22]

(ii) Every proposition is either true or false;

(iii) For every proposition, either that proposition is true or
      its denial is true.

Candidate (i) must be provided with some informal qualification if it is even to be plausible. Obviously 'sentence' must
be understood to mean 'declarative sentence', where, one
hopes, the class of "declarative" sentences of English is one
that can be specified by purely syntactical means. But even if
this can be done, a more serious problem remains: (i) seems to
be a report of a fact about English that is at best contingently
true. And this would be the case even if 'true' in (i) were replaced with 'necessarily true'. After all, 'or' and 'not' might
have meant something other than what they in fact mean. Of
course, (i) might be elaborated to meet this difficulty, but the
objection might be elaborated, too. On the whole, I think it
would be more profitable for us to turn our attention to (ii)
and (iii), than to play modification-and-counter-example
with (i).

There are two main differences between (ii) and (iii): (ii)
contains 'false' and (iii) does not, and (iii) contains 'denial'
and (ii) does not. But what does 'false' mean if not 'not true';
what is falsehood but the complement of truth in the domain
of propositions? And what is the "denial" of a proposition if
not the proposition that it is not true? Some philosophers, I
know, think that 'true' and 'false' are like 'transparent' and
'opaque': just as there are visible objects that are neither transparent nor opaque, so there are propositions that are neither
true nor false. It has been argued, for example, that the proposition that the present king of France is bald is neither true
nor false. These well-known arguments, however, establish
at best that it is not clear whether 'the proposition that the
present king of France is bald' denotes anything, given the
political conditions that actually prevail in France. But if this
description does denote something—presumably it denotes the
proposition that someone is now the only king of France and
is bald, if it denotes anything—what it denotes is, I should
think, either true or false; if it denotes nothing, then no
counter-example to the thesis that falsehood is, in the domain
of propositions, the complement of truth, has been produced.
(The thesis that propositions "about the future" are neither
true nor false we shall consider presently.)

If, as I have argued, 'false' means 'not true', and the denial
of a proposition is the proposition that it is not true, then (ii)

and (iii) come to much the same thing. I shall treat them as equivalent and equally good expressions of LEM.

Is LEM true? Various reasons for saying it is not have been offered. One class of interesting reasons for rejecting LEM arises in physical science, from considerations involving the physical interpretation of the formal mathematical theory of quantum mechanics; another class of reasons arises in pure mathematics from considerations involving non-constructive descriptions of infinite sets. I have nothing interesting to say about these reasons, which are, in any case, of no direct relevance to those questions about LEM that arise in discussions of fatalism. (They may, of course, be of indirect relevance; if they are persuasive, they may lead the erstwhile champion of LEM to mistrust his intuitions concerning the application of this principle even in cases involving only macroscopic objects and constructive predicates.)

What *is* of direct relevance to the problem of fatalism is the question whether LEM "applies" to propositions "about the future". Does this principle give us licence to say that, for example, the proposition that I shall one day kill myself (K) is either true or false? Let us say that it does, and then ask whether the principle, so interpreted, is true. It will, I think, be sufficient to ask whether K is either true or false. If K is neither true nor false, then LEM is false; if K is either true or false then—I should think—just any proposition "about the future" is either true or false, at least assuming it involves only assertions about macroscopic objects and properties expressible by means of constructive predicates.

The question whether K is either true or false is just the question whether it is the case that either I shall kill myself or I shall not. For consider the argument:

(1) The proposition that I shall kill myself is true if and only if I shall kill myself

(2) The proposition that I shall kill myself is false if and only if I shall not kill myself

(3) Either I shall kill myself or I shall not

hence, (4) Either the proposition that I shall kill myself is true or it is false.

By way of commentary on this argument: (a) it is formally valid, being an instance of the form '$p \equiv q; r \equiv s; q \vee s; hence\ p \vee r$';[23] (b) the sentence displayed to the right of '(1)' is formed by filling the blank in 'The proposition that . . . is true if and only if . . .'. Such a sentence expresses—as a sentence of English and relative to a given context of utterance (I shall from now on leave it to the reader to supply such qualification as this)— a *true* proposition provided the sentence that fills the blank expresses *any* proposition. (I shall presently discuss the contention that 'I shall kill myself' does not express *any* proposition.) If anyone denies this, I do not understand what he means by 'true'. The same remarks apply *mutatis mutandis* to the sentence to the right of '(2)'. (c) Therefore—leaving aside the question whether 'I shall kill myself' and its negation express propositions—(4) is true if (3) is true.

Is (3) true? It is certainly the case that if I were to utter the sentence displayed to the right of '(3)' above, I should say something true. (Or at least this is the case if we suppose I utter this sentence in a context in which my uttering it constitutes my asserting that I either shall or shall not kill myself, and not a mere phonetic exercise. But such a context is easily imagined: suppose you and I are discussing the advisability of my buying a certain type of life insurance, and I utter this sentence as a preface to an argument by cases.) But if that is the case, then how could (3) be anything but true? Could it be the case that there is a certain sentence s such that (i) if I were to utter s I should in uttering s say something true, and (ii) the proposition expressed by s is *not* true? To answer "Yes" to this question is surely to contradict oneself.

Therefore, (4) is true unless 'I shall kill myself' fails to express a proposition, unless there *is* no such proposition as the proposition that I shall kill myself, just as there is no such proposition as the proposition about kangaroos I just now asserted. How could there be no such proposition? Surely someone may believe or assert or even know that I shall one day kill myself. But if a sentence can be meaningfully concatenated with 'he believes that . . .' or 'he knows that . . .' or can be used as the vehicle of an assertion, then that sentence expresses a proposition. That is what it *is* for a sentence to express a proposition.

Perhaps the opponent of LEM will want to protest: "I grant you that it is possible for someone to utter, say, 'he will some-day kill himself' and make an assertion. What I am saying is that the assertion he makes, or the proposition he expresses, is neither true nor false". But to say this is simply to grant the premiss of my argument—that it is possible to make assertions about the future—and to deny the conclusion: that any such assertion is either true or false. And that would be to deny that my argument is valid without attempting to find a flaw in it.

There is a good deal more that could be said about LEM, but I shall not say it. I have attempted in 2.7 to show that LEM is true because I think it *is* true and because certain writers on fatalism have denied it, thinking that such a denial constitutes the only escape from fatalism. But since there are no known compelling arguments for fatalism, this is not the case. Such writers are like atheists who become Parmenideans in order to deny the premiss of St. Thomas's First Way. To enter into an extended debate about LEM would be as profit-less an undertaking as writing a treatise proving that some things are in motion.

Chapter III

Three Arguments for Incompatibilism

3.1 The main contested question in current discussions of free will is not, as one might expect, whether we *have* free will. It is whether free will is compatible with determinism. It seems to me that free will and determinism are incompatible, and in this chapter I shall try to demonstrate this incompatibility.

Discussions of this question are usually not on a very high level. In the great majority of cases, they are the work of compatibilists and consist to a large degree in the ascription of some childish fallacy or other to incompatibilists (conflation of "descriptive" and "prescriptive" laws; failure to distinguish between causal necessity and compulsion; equation of freedom and mere randomness). Donald Davidson places himself in this tradition when he writes:

I shall not be directly concerned with [arguments for the incompatibility of freedom and causal determination], since I know of none that is more than superficially plausible. Hobbes, Locke, Hume, Moore, Schlick, Ayer, Stevenson, and a host of others have done what can be done, or ought ever to have been needed, to remove the confusions that can make determinism seem to oppose freedom.[1]

It is not my purpose in this book to defend any previous writer against a charge of fallacious argument. My own arguments will be explicit, and any fallacies they commit should be correspondingly visible. (It is doubtful whether anyone has ever been seduced by the fallacies with which incompatibilists are customarily charged; if anyone indeed has achieved such a level of philosophical incompetence, I, at least, fall short of it.) Now the line between arguing for a certain view and ascribing fallacious reasoning to the opponents of that view, while clear enough in theory, is often blurred in practice. Entangled with the charges of fallacy and confusion made in the writings of the philosophers Davidson mentions, there are positive arguments for the compatibility of free will and determinism. In so far as these arguments can be disentangled from diagnoses of ills I am not heir to—if, indeed, these ills exist at all—I shall examine them in Chapter IV.[2]

3.2 In Chapter I, I mentioned the following simple argument for incompatibilism, the Consequence Argument:

> If determinism is true, then our acts are the consequences of the laws of nature and events in the remote past. But it is not up to us what went on before we were born, and neither is it up to us what the laws of nature are. Therefore, the consequences of these things (including our present acts) are not up to us.

This, I think, is a *good* argument. But I must admit it's rather sketchy. The present chapter is an attempt to fill in the details of this sketch in three different ways. (I have called this chapter "Three Arguments for Incompatibilism", but the principle of individuation for arguments is far from clear; I might have called it "One Argument for Incompatibilism Done Three Ways".) These three arguments, or versions of one argument, or whatever they are, are intended to support one another. Though they have essentially the same point, they are very different in structure and vocabulary. I intend to exploit these differences as follows. If anyone has a vague feeling of unease about one of the arguments—because it's not stated in anything like ordinary language, say, or because its logical structure is rather complicated and may serve to conceal some muddle— he may find, I *hope* he will find, that this feeling of unease does not arise when he contemplates one or both of the other two arguments. This, I think, will tend to show that the cause of his feeling of unease is an *accident of a particular mode of presentation* of the features common to the three arguments and does not reside in these common features themselves. Of course, it does not follow logically that this is the case: the cause of the feeling of unease that someone feels when he considers one of these arguments may be present but inoperative when he considers another, owing to the fact that this cause, which may or may not be a real defect in the arguments, is masked by features peculiar to the other.

I intend these remarks to apply only to cases of "a vague feeling of unease". If a philosopher has a specific and detailed objection to one of the arguments, then I do not propose to hide behind the others. In fact, I think this would be impossible: I am quite sure that any specific and detailed objection to one of the arguments can be fairly easily translated into specific and detailed objections to the others; and I think that any objection to one of the arguments will be a good objection to *that* argument if and only if the corresponding objections to the others are good objections to *them*. I may be wrong about this. Perhaps one of the arguments fails in some way to which no defect in either of the others corresponds; indeed, perhaps all the arguments are defective, but for, loosely speaking, different reasons. I hardly think this is the case, however. We shall see.

There is a second dialectical advantage in my presenting three arguments, provided I am right in thinking that they stand or fall together. If I relied on only one of these arguments, a compatibilist might reason as follows: "Since the conclusion of this argument is fundamentally wrong, the argument contains a fundamental mistake. I admit I can't put my finger on this mistake, though I'm sure I could uncover it if I were willing to take the time and trouble. But life is short..." Now I am not at all unsympathetic to such an attitude, at least provided that the philosopher who expresses it does not claim to be an expert on the problem of free will and determinism. Life *is* short. But I do think that this attitude is a *less* reasonable one to express in the face of three arguments that seem intuitively to have the same point and which are yet very different in the vocabulary they employ and in their logical structure. Surely if there were some fundamental mistake *common* to all three arguments, it would be at least *likely* to reveal itself in one of them, however well hidden it was in the others?

Each of the three arguments has its peculiar virtues and vices. The virtue of the first argument is its vocabulary, which is close to that of traditional discussions of the free-will problem. Its vice is its extremely complex structure. The virtue of the second argument is its extremely simple structure. Its vice is its vocabulary, which is radically different from the traditional vocabulary of arguments about free will. The third argument is an intermediate case as regards complexity of logical structure and departure from traditional terminology. Its peculiar logical vice is a dialectical virtue: while the first two arguments are valid in first-order extensional logic, the third employs special modal principles. This is a logical vice because I endorse no extensional semantics for the modal operator involved in the argument, and, therefore, my contention that the modal principles I employ in the argument are valid rests only on intuition. But the use of a modal operator is a dialectical virtue, since many people seem to think that a modal fallacy in some way underlies incompatibilism, and this charge is best evaluated in its application to an explicitly modal argument.

3.3 In this section, and in the following section, I shall explain what I mean by certain terms that will be used in the first argument for incompatibilism.

I shall begin by attempting to say what I mean by *determinism*. In order to define determinism I shall need three subordinate notions: the notion of a *proposition* (and allied notions such as *truth*, *denial*, *conjunction*, and *entailment*) and the notion of *the state of the entire physical world at an instant*, and the notion of a *law of nature*.

Propositions (that is, non-linguistic bearers of truth-value) were introduced in Section 2.4. I have little to add to what I said there and in 2.7 about propositions, truth, and falsity. I shall assume only that propositions have the following four properties. (i) To every possible way the world could be, there corresponds at least one proposition, a proposition that is necessarily such that it is true if and only if the world *is* that way. Since there are doubtless ways things could be that are too complex to be described in any natural language, this means that there are propositions that cannot be expressed in any natural language. (ii) Every proposition is either true or false. (iii) The conjunction of a true and a false proposition is a false proposition. (iv) Propositions obey the Law of Contraposition with respect to entailment. That is, for every x and every y, if x and y are propositions, and if it is impossible for x to be true and y false, then it is impossible for the denial of y to be true and the denial of x false.

One "model" for propositions that gives them these features is this: propositions are identified with sets of possible worlds.[3]

A proposition in this sense is *true* if it contains the actual world; the *denial* of a proposition is its complement on the set of all possible worlds; the *conjunction* of two propositions is their intersection; one proposition *entails* a second if the former is a subset of the latter. I am not wedded to this model. It has features that unfit the "propositions" it models for certain tasks traditionally assigned to things called 'propositions'. For example, in Section 2.4, "propositions" were introduced as things that could be accepted, asserted, proved, denied, and so on. But the objects of such activities can hardly be modelled on sets of possible worlds, for on that model, for example, the proposition that some Albanian barber shaves all those and only those Albanians who do not shave themselves is identical with the proposition that there are Greek geometers who know how to trisect the angle: each is the empty set. Yet if these propositions are objects of assertion or denial, surely they must be distinct propositions. Still, this model yields all the features of propositions that I need for my present purposes, and shows, assuming the consistency of the notions of *set* and *possible world*, that these features are consistent.

Let us now turn to *the state of the entire physical world* (hereinafter, *the state of the world*) *at an instant*. I shall leave this notion largely unexplained, since my argument is very nearly independent of its content. Provided the following two conditions are met, one may flesh out 'the state of the world' in any way one likes.

(i) Our concept of *state* must be such that, given that the world is in a certain state at a certain instant, nothing *follows* about its state at any other instant: if x and y are any "states", and some possible world is in x at t_1 and y at t_2, there is a world that is in x at t_1 and *not* in y at t_2. For example, we must not choose a concept of *state* that would allow as a part of a description of the momentary state of the world, the clause, '. . . and, at T, the world is such that someone's left hand will be raised 10 seconds later than T'.

The theory of relativity has the consequence that this notion —the state of the world at an instant—has no application to things as they are, and is perhaps even incoherent. But there is a relativistically acceptable concept—the state of things on the surface of a light-cone—that could be used in its place. This refinement, however, could be implemented only by tedious and philosophically irrelevant (in the present context) elaboration of definitions and arguments that are already rather more elaborate than I like. I shall therefore ignore relativistic considerations in the sequel. The second and third arguments will be similarly unsophisticated.

(ii) If there is some observable change in the way things are —if a white cloth becomes blue, a warm liquid cold, or if a man raises his hand—this change must entail some change in the state of the world. That is, our concept of *state* must not be so theoretical, so divorced from what is observably true, that, for example, it be possible for the world to be in the *same* state at t_1 and t_2, despite the fact that someone's hand is raised at t_1 and not at t_2. It is arguable that this requirement is incompatible with our interpreting *state* as *quantum-mechanical state*, for it is arguable that there exists a moment t and possible worlds w_1 and w_2 such that w_1 and w_2 are in the same quantum-mechanical state at t, although a certain cat is, in w_1, alive at t and, in w_2, dead at t.[4] But I shall say nothing about the deep and difficult problems this contention raises.

Having defined—or, at any rate, discussed—the notions of *proposition* and *state of the world at an instant*, we shall now combine them. Let us say that a proposition *expresses the state of the world at t* provided it is a true proposition that asserts of some state that, at t, the world is in that state. (We may put the matter this way in terms of our "sets of possible worlds" model of propositions: a proposition *p purports to express the state of the world at t* if there is some state such that p contains all those and only those worlds that are in that state at t; *p expresses the state of the world at t* if it purports to express the state of the world at t and is, moreover, true.)

Finally, I need the notion of a *law of nature*. I have no idea how to explain this term, much less define it. But I can say what I do *not* mean by it: as I said in Section 1.3, it is not an *epistemological* term. Ontologically speaking, a law of nature is a proposition: some propositions have the feature *being a law of nature* and some don't, and which do and which don't is a matter utterly independent of the present state of scientific knowledge and the history of scientific knowledge. The laws of nature would be just as they are even if there had never been any human beings or other rational animals. *Law of nature*, at least in my usage, is no more an epistemological term than is *star*. (Ontologically speaking, a star is a material body: some material bodies have the feature *being a star* and some don't, and which do and which don't is a matter utterly independent of the present state of astronomical knowledge and of the history of astronomy. The stars would be just as they are even if there had never been any human beings or other rational animals.)

Despite the parallels I want to draw between the stars and the laws of nature, I want also to insist on an important difference between our *powers* with respect to these two classes of objects. It is quite conceivable that human power will grow to the extent that we shall one day be able to alter the stars in their courses. But we shall never be able to do anything about the laws of nature. There are presumably many propositions that are in fact true, but which it is within our power to falsify. Probably the proposition that no one ever has read or ever will read all of the *Oxford English Dictionary* aloud is true. I should think, however, that someone *could* falsify this proposition if he were willing to devote a large part of his life to this pointless task. But suppose someone has set out to falsify the Principle of the Conservation of Angular Momentum. That is, suppose someone is attempting to construct a piece of laboratory apparatus the behaviour of which would violate this principle. If the principle is a law of nature, he cannot succeed. If he *can* succeed (even if he doesn't), that is, if he has it within his power to succeed, then it is not a law. We might even imagine that the principle is in fact *true* but is not a law simply because someone can falsify it. Suppose that a certain physicist designs a certain piece of apparatus and that all competent physicists agree that if this piece of apparatus were built and put into operation it would violate the Principle of the Conservation of Angular Momentum. Suppose a respected firm of engineering contractors, having examined the physicist's specifications, state that it would be possible, given "the state of the art", to build the device. Suppose the physicists and engineers are right. But suppose that actually to construct the device would require an *enormous* expenditure of resources, a fact that results in its never being constructed. We may consistently add to these suppositions the supposition that angular momentum is conserved, that is, that the Principle of the Conservation of Angular Momentum is *true*. But this principle would simply not be a law of nature if such a device *could* be constructed: if human beings *can* (have it within their power to) conduct an experiment or construct a device that would falsify a certain proposition, then that proposition is not a law of nature. A law of nature must be immune to such possible disconfirmation. This of course is consistent with our saying that for any given law we could *conceive* of an experiment that would disconfirm it.

The conclusion of the above argument may be restated this way: the laws of nature impose limits on our abilities: they are partly determinative of what it is possible for us to do. And indeed this conclusion is hardly more than a tautology. The oddness of denying it can be brought out if we think of someone ordering a subordinate to violate a law of nature. Suppose a bureaucrat of the future orders an engineer to build a spaceship capable of travelling faster than light. The engineer tells the bureaucrat that it's a law of nature that nothing travels faster than light. The bureaucrat concedes this difficulty, but counsels perseverance: "I'm sure", he says, "that if you work hard and are very clever, you'll find some way to go faster than light, even though it's a law of nature that nothing does." Clearly his demand is simply incoherent.

I should point out that the above conclusion does not rest on the premiss that the laws of nature are *true* propositions. I am not saying that it is impossible for us to alter the laws of nature owing simply to the fact that it is logically impossible to cause any proposition simultaneously to satisfy the conditions 'x is a law of nature' and 'x is false' (laws of nature being by definition true).[5] If this argument were valid, one could derive fatalism from the premiss that it is logically impossible to cause any proposition simultaneously to satisfy the conditions 'x is a true proposition' and 'x is false'. But, as I said in Chapter II, many true propositions are such that one can render them false: the schema 'If P is a true proposition, then no one can render P false' has many counter-instances, at least in my opinion. The instance got by replacing 'P' with 'the proposition that no one ever reads all of the *OED* aloud' is one. No law of nature, however, is such that anyone can render it false: the schema, 'If P is a law of nature, then no one can render P false' has *no* counter-instances. Or put the matter this way: it is true and trivial, and not what I am arguing for, to say, "It is impossible for there to be a person x and a proposition y such that x can bring it about that y is a law of nature and y is false". Call this 'the *de dicto* principle'. It is also true to say, "It is necessary that, for every person x and every proposition y, if y is a law of nature, then x cannot render y false". This is at least *less* trivial and it is what I have been arguing for. Call this 'the *de re* principle'. From the *de re* principle and 'the proposition that momentum is conserved is a law of nature', we may validly deduce, 'Feynman cannot render the proposition that momentum is conserved false'. But from this premiss and the *de dicto* principle, no such conclusion follows. Note that such applications of *modus ponens* to instances of the *de re* principle may yield contingent truths, since the proposition that a given proposition is a law of nature may very well be a contingent truth. Feynman, for example, may be unable to render the proposition that momentum is conserved false because this proposition is a law of nature. But, for all I know, there are possible worlds in which he exists and in which this proposition (though perhaps true) is not a law of nature and in which he is able to render it false.

If we interpret 'law of nature' very broadly, there seem to be exceptions to the *de re* principle, and these must be dealt with. Consider *psychological* laws, including laws, if such there be, about the voluntary behaviour of rational agents. If there are such laws, it is at least arguable that they should be included among the "laws of nature"; rational agents are, after all, in some sense part of "nature". But it is hard to see how to avoid the conclusion that, if we have free will, we have it within our power to act differently from the way such laws say we shall act. Let us look at a particular case.

Suppose psychologists discover that no one who has received moral training of type A in early childhood ever spreads lying rumours about his professional colleagues. Suppose you and I in fact received such training. Does it follow that we *can't* engage in this odious activity? I don't see why it should be supposed to follow. (Mark Twain: "I am morally superior to

George Washington. He couldn't tell a lie. I can and I don't.")
Suppose further that you and I are in fact *able* to spread lying
rumours about our colleagues. Does it follow that a statement
of the regularity we have imagined psychologists to have discovered is, though true, not a law? Well, suppose the existence of this regularity is a logical consequence of some well-
confirmed theory of human moral development that has great
explanatory and predictive power. In that case, it would certainly be very *tempting* to call this statement a 'law'; I should
hardly want to counsel resistance to this temptation. "But
why", someone may ask, "does this regular pattern of behaviour occur if people don't *have* to conform to it?" Note
that the only people in a position to depart from it are those
who have in fact had training of type A. Perhaps it is just these
people who *see the point* in not spreading lying rumours. To
come to see the point in not exercising an ability one has is
not to *lose* that ability.

So it seems at least plausible to suppose that the *de re* principle might be false if 'law of nature' were interpreted broadly
enough. I shall simply narrow the interpretation of 'law of
nature' by fiat: "laws of nature" in the sequel shall be by
definition propositions that apply non-vacuously to things
that are *not* rational agents. (Things such as teacups, electrons,
and galaxies.) For such laws, I maintain, the *de re* principle
holds good. This stipulation has an important consequence. It
may well be that, for all that is said in this book, human behaviour is wholly predictable on the basis of laws that are
about the voluntary behaviour of rational agents. Moreover, I
see no reason to think that such predictability would be incompatible with free will.

Let us make one further stipulation about the laws of nature:
the logical consequences of any set of laws of nature are also
laws. This stipulation produces what is in some ways a rather
artificial notion of a law of nature. It has, for example, the
consequence that the conjunction of Snell's Law with the
Principle of the Conservation of Angular Momentum (assuming these propositions to be laws) is a law. If anyone is troubled
by this stipulation, which I adopt only because it will simplify
the statement of my argument, he may read 'the laws of nature'
in the sequel as 'the logical consequences of the laws of nature'.

Thus, on our "sets of possible worlds" model for propositions, a law of nature is any set of worlds that has as a subset the set of all worlds in which the laws of nature are the same as those of the actual world, or, as we might say, are *nomologically congruent with* the actual world.

We may now define 'determinism'. We shall apply this term to the conjunction of these two theses:

> For every instant of time, there is a proposition that expresses the state of the world at that instant;[6]

> If p and q are any propositions that express the state of the world at some instants, then the conjunction of p with the laws of nature entails q.

This definition seems to me to capture at least one thesis that could properly be called 'determinism'. Determinism is, intuitively, the thesis that, given the past and the laws of nature, there is only one possible future. And this definition certainly has that consequence. It *also* has the consequence that the future determines a unique past. This consequence, however, does not trouble me. The only *physical* theories that are known to be deterministic "from-past-to-future" (two-particle classical mechanics and certain mathematically similar theories) are also known to be deterministic "from-future-to-past". There are "theories" in a certain broad sense of the word that are only "one-way" deterministic—"theories" describing the behaviour of certain Turing machines, for example—but I should be at least mildly surprised to see any plausible *physical* theory that had that feature. But if anyone is really troubled about this, he may add a suitable "later than" clause to the definition. Such an addition will not affect the use I shall make of this definition in what follows.

The reader will note that the horrible little word 'cause' does not appear in this definition. Causation is a morass in which I for one refuse to set foot. Or not unless I am pushed. Certain arguments for the compatibility of free will and determinism will force me to say something about the relation between determinism and "universal causation". (See Section 4.4.)

3.4 Determinism is a thesis about propositions, but the free-will thesis is a thesis about agents. If we are going to investigate the conceptual relations between these two theses, we shall do well to state the free-will thesis as a thesis about agents and propositions. I propose to do this by devising a way to describe our powers to act—and, by acting, to modify the world—as powers over the truth-values of propositions. This can be done as follows. Consider the propositions I should express if I were to utter any of the following sentences at the present moment:

(a) $27 \times 15 = 405$;

(b)   Magnets attract iron;

(c)   Mary Queen of Scots was put to death in 1587;

(d)   I have never read *The Teachings of Don Juan*;

(e)   No one has ever read all of Hume's *Enquiry* aloud;

(f)   The cup on my desk has never been broken.

(All these propositions are, I think, true.) There is at least one important and interesting difference between the relations I bear to (a)-(c) and those I bear to (d)-(f). The difference I have in mind might be described in various ways: there is nothing I can do, or ever could have done, about the fact that (a)-(c) are true, and this is not the case with (d)-(f); the truth of (a)-(c) is something it is not and never has been within my power to change, though the truth of (d)-(f) is something that it is within my power, or once was within my power, to change; (a)-(c) are true and I do not have, and never have had, any choice about this, but, though (d)-(f) are true, this is something I have a choice about, or is something I once had a choice about. (In making these assertions about the difference between (a)-(c), on the one hand, and (d)-(f), on the other, I assume I have free will. If I don't, then this apparent difference between the two sets of statements is illusory.)

I shall mark this distinction by using an idiom I introduced in Section 2.5: I *can render*, or once *could have rendered*, all of (d)-(f) *false*; I *cannot render*, and never *could have rendered*, any of (a)-(c) *false*. I rather like the name *being able to render false* for this relation that I bear to (d)-(f) and do not bear to (a)-(c). But I admit that this name could be misleading. In fact it has been misleading. My use of this phrase has on occasion created the impression that I believe that human beings can somehow enter into *causal* relations with propositions.[7] But being able to render a proposition false is nothing so metaphysically exotic as that; to be able to render a proposition false is to be able to arrange or modify the concrete objects that constitute one's environment—shoes, ships, bits of sealing wax—in a way sufficient for the falsity of that proposition.

But how shall we understand this sufficiency? We might understand 'sufficient' to mean 'logically sufficient'. That is, we might understand '*s* can render *p* false' to mean 'It is within *s*'s power to arrange or modify the concrete objects that constitute his environment in some way such that it is not possible "in the broadly logical sense" that he arrange or modify these objects in that way and *p* be true'.[8] For example, I can, according to this proposal, render false the proposition that this cup is never broken, since I can break this cup—at least if I have free will—and it is not possible that I break this cup and this cup never be broken. If I *could* move my hand faster than light, then I *could*, in the sense proposed, render false the proposition that nothing ever travels faster than light, since it is not possible that I should move my hand faster than light and nothing ever travel faster than light.

I do not believe that this proposal exactly captures the intuitive notion of being able to render a proposition false, that is, the notion of "having control over" the truth-value of a proposition. Let us suppose that in 1550 Nostradamus predicted that the Sphinx would endure till the end of the world. And let us suppose that this prediction was correct and, in fact, that *all* Nostradamus's predictions were correct. Let us also suppose that it was within Gamal Abdel Nasser's power to have the Sphinx destroyed. Then, I should think, it was within Nasser's power to render false the proposition that all Nostradamus's predictions were correct. But this would not be the case according to the definition proposed in the preceding paragraph, since it is possible in the broadly logical sense that Nasser have had the Sphinx destroyed and yet all Nostradamus's predictions have been correct. That is, there are possible worlds in which the proposition that all Nostradamus's predictions were correct is true and in which Nasser had the Sphinx destroyed: worlds in which Nostradamus did *not* predict that the Sphinx would endure till the end of the world and made no other predictions that would have been falsified by Nasser's destruction of the Sphinx.

The best way to rule out such counter-examples would seem to be to "build the past into" our definition. More precisely, we may define '*s* can render *p* false' as follows:

> It is within *s*'s power to arrange or modify the concrete objects that constitute his environment in some way such that it is not possible in the broadly logical sense that he arrange or modify those objects in that way and the past have been exactly as it in fact was and *p* be true.

I believe that this definition captures the notion that is suggested by the words 'being able to render a proposition false', except, perhaps, for the case of false propositions about the past.[9] For example, it has the consequence that I can render the proposition that Socrates died of old age false, since it is not possible that the past should have been exactly as it in fact was and Socrates have died of old age. There are three reasons why this feature of our definition need not trouble us, however. First, it would be easy enough to remove it by some *ad hoc* fiat. Moreover, the first argument for the incompatibility of free will and determinism will involve only *true* propositions. Finally, the 'can render false' idiom will not appear in the *conclusion* of the argument. Thus the odd consequences of the definition can affect the conclusion of the argument only if they result in some defect (such as falsity) in at least one of its premisses.

3.5 Now the first argument. I shall imagine a case in which a certain man, after due deliberation, refrained from performing a certain contemplated act. I shall then argue that, if determinism is true, that man *could not have* performed that act. Because this argument will not depend on any features peculiar to our imagined case, the incompatibility of free will and determinism in general will be established, since, as will be evident, a parallel argument could easily be devised for the case of any agent and any unperformed act.

Let us suppose that there was once a judge who had only to raise his right hand at a certain time, T, to prevent the execution of a sentence of death upon a certain criminal, such a hand-raising being the sign, according to the conventions of the judge's country, of a granting of special clemency. Let us further suppose that the judge—call him 'J'—refrained from raising his hand at T, and that this inaction resulted in the criminal's being put to death. We may also suppose that J was unbound, uninjured, and free from any paralysis of the limbs; that he decided not to raise his hand at T only after a suitable period of calm, rational, and relevant deliberation; that he had not been subjected to any "pressure" to decide one way or the other about the criminal's death; that he was not under the influence of drugs, hypnosis, or anything of that sort; and, finally, that there was no element in his deliberations that would have been of any special interest to a student of abnormal psychology. I shall argue that, despite all these advantages, J could not have raised his hand at T if determinism is true.

My argument for this conclusion will take the form of comments on the premises of an "argument" in the logic-text sense: a numbered sequence of propositions, all but the last of which are the argument's *premises* and the last of which is its *conclusion*. One critic has supposed that my use of an argument in the logic-text sense constituted my attempting to provide a "formal proof" for a philosophical thesis, and has derided the very possibility of such an enterprise.[10] I applaud his values while deploring his exegesis. Formal proofs of philosophical theses are not to be had and I should be a fool to attempt any. My critic has mistaken what is really no more than a bookkeeping device for an argument, and, in fact, for a proof. The numbered sequence of propositions below is not my first argument for incompatibilism. My first argument for incompatibilism, rather, takes the form of a commentary on the premises of the "argument in the logic-text sense". My argument, in fact, is conterminous with Section 3.5 of this book. I shall distinguish my argument from the numbered sequence of propositions it discusses by calling the former the First Argument and the latter the First Formal Argument. These are mere convenient labels and should be understood in the light of the present paragraph.

In the First Formal Argument and in my subsequent commentary upon it, I shall use 'T_o' to denote some arbitrarily chosen instant of time earlier than J's birth, 'P_0' to denote a proposition that expresses the state of the world at T_0, 'P' to denote a proposition that expresses the state of the world at T, and 'L' to denote the conjunction into a single proposition of all the laws of nature. All these symbols are to be regarded as "rigid designators". Thus, if I discuss certain counter-factual situations or unrealized possibilities or such, and if I use, for example, 'P' in the course of this discussion, I mean 'P' to designate a proposition that *in fact* expresses the state of the world at T, whether or not it would express the state of the world at T if those situations obtained or those possibilities were realized.

The First Formal Argument consists of seven propositions, the seventh of which follows from the first six:

(1) If determinism is true, then the conjunction of P_0 and L entails P

(2) It is not possible that J have raised his hand at T and P be true

(3) If (2) is true, then if J could have raised his hand at T, J could have rendered P false

(4) If J could have rendered P false, and if the conjunction of P_0 and L entails P, then J could have rendered the conjunction of P_0 and L false

(5) If J could have rendered the conjunction of P_0 and L false, then J could have rendered L false

(6) J could not have rendered L false

(7) If determinism is true, J could not have raised his hand at T.

That (7) follows from (1)–(6) can easily be established by truth-functional logic. Note that all the conditionals that occur in (1)–(7) are material conditionals: the 'could have' that occurs in them is merely the past indicative of 'can'. ("John hasn't read this letter, has he?" "I don't know, but I hope you've kept it under lock and key. You know what a dedicated snoop he is. If he could have read it, he did read it.")

One critic has supposed that the premises of this argument are supposed to be necessary truths.[11] But this is not the case.

If the premises of the argument were necessary truths, then its conclusion would be a necessary truth. But its conclusion is false in any possible world in which determinism is true and J raised his hand at T. Of course, in such worlds at least one of the premises will be false. This is a simple consequence of the formal validity of the argument. Take, for example, a world in which L is the conjunction of all laws of nature, determinism is true, and J raised his hand at T. In such a world, (5) is false, since its consequent is false and its antecedent true. The antecedent of (5) is true in such a world because J could in that world have done something incompatible with the truth of the (false) conjunction of P_0 and L: raising his hand. He could have done this in that world simply in virtue of the fact that he did.

So I don't say that all the premises of the First Formal Argument are necessary truths. But I do say that they are true in all possible worlds in which the story we have told about J is true. That is, the premises of the First Formal Argument, and hence its conclusion, *follow from* our story about J. The story of J is, or we are pretending it is, true. But it's obviously only contingently true: there are possible worlds in which J raised his hand at T; there are possible worlds in which J never existed at all. And in many such worlds, (7) will be false and at least one among (1)–(6) will therefore be false. And this is just the way things should be, for the conclusion of the First Formal Argument *oughtn't* to be a logical consequence of incompatibilism alone.

Let us now examine the premises of the First Formal Argument. The preceding paragraph should make it clear that in this examination we are entitled to draw upon any facts about J and his situation that were presented in the story we told about J.

Premiss (1). This premiss follows from our definition of determinism and our specifications of the designations of 'P_0', 'L', and 'P'.

Premiss (2). The symbol 'P' is our name for the proposition that expresses the state the world was in fact in at T, a time at which J's hand was not raised. It is therefore impossible for P to be true if J's hand was raised at T, or, indeed, if things were in any way different at T from the way they actually were.

Premiss (3). The clause 'J could have raised his hand at T' is ambiguous. Using the system of disambiguating brackets introduced in Section 2.6, we may represent this ambiguity as follows: this clause could mean either 'J could have (raised his hand at T)' or 'J could have (raised his hand) at T'. I mean this clause to be understood in the former sense.[12]

As to the *truth* of (3): it is obvious that if (2) is true and if J could have raised his hand at T, then there is a certain "arrangement or modification of the concrete objects constituting J's environment"—J's hand rising at T—such that (i) it is not possible that J should arrange things this way and P be true, and (ii) J could have arranged things this way.

Premiss (4). This premiss is an instance, allowing for a shift of tense, of the following general principle:

> If s can render r false, and if q entails r, then s can render q false.

(Substitute 'J' for 's', 'P' for 'r', and 'the conjunction of P_o and L' for 'q'.) This principle is a trivial truth. For if q entails r, the denial of r entails the denial of q. Thus anything sufficient in the broadly logical sense for the falsity of r is also sufficient for the falsity of q. Therefore, if there is some arrangement of objects that s can produce, which is such that s's producing it would be sufficient for the falsity of r, there is some arrangement of objects—the very same one—that s can produce, which is such that his producing it would be sufficient for the falsity of q.

Premiss (5). This premiss is an instance of the following general principle:

> If q is a true proposition that concerns only states of affairs that obtained before s's birth, and if s can render the conjunction of q and r false, then s can render r false.

Consider, for example, the propositions

> The Spanish Armada was defeated in 1588

and

> Peter van Inwagen never visits Alaska.

For all I know, the conjunction of these two propositions is true. At any rate, let us assume it is true. Given that it is true, it seems quite clear that I can render it false if and only if I can visit Alaska. If, for some reason, it is not within my power ever to visit Alaska, then I *cannot* render it false. This is a quite trivial assertion, and the general principle of which it is an instance is hardly less trivial. And it seems incontestable that premiss (5) is also an instance of this principle.

The general principle of which (5) is an instance need not be defended only by an appeal to intuition. Let us assume that the antecedent of this principle is true. That is, let us assume the truth of both:

(a) q is a true proposition that concerns only states of affairs that obtained before s's birth,

and

(b) s can render the conjunction of q and r false.

We shall proceed to derive the consequent of the principle.

Let W (for 'was') be the conjunction into a single proposition of all true propositions about the past. Then we have, from (b) and from the definition of 's can render p false' that was given in Section 3.4:

(c) There is a possible arrangement of objects a such that s can bring it about that a is realized and such that the conjunction of W with the proposition that a is realized (call this conjunction 'W & a') entails the denial of the conjunction of q and r ("d (q & r)").

It follows from (a) that W entails q and thus that W & a entails q. From this and (c) it follows that W & a entails the conjunction of q and d (q & r). And from this it follows that W & a entails the denial of r. And, therefore, since s can bring it about that a is realized, s can render r false.

Premiss (6). This premiss would seem to be an obvious consequence of what we said about our powers with respect to the laws of nature in Section 3.3. But a compatibilist might reject this contention. I can imagine a compatibilist arguing as follows:

> Suppose determinism is true and suppose I am not in fact going to raise my hand one minute from now. It follows that there is a certain possible arrangement of objects—any arrangement that includes my hand's being raised would do—such that it is not possible in the broadly logical sense that I should arrange objects in that way and the past have been exactly as it was and L be true. But since I *can* raise my hand one minute from now, I therefore *can* render L false, though, of course, I am not going to do so. If this result *sounds* queer, that's not my fault; the queerness derives entirely from your definition of '*s* can render *p* false'.

Well, there is obviously *some* sense in which I can't render the laws of nature false: I have no choice about what the laws of nature are; there's nothing I can *do* about them. There are many propositions whose truth-values are within my power, but surely the laws of nature are not among them. Let us therefore simply set aside the definition of '*s* can render *p* false' that was given in Section 3.4 and ask: aren't the premisses of the First Formal Argument evidently true, however '*s* can render *p* false' may be defined? Isn't our pre-analytic understanding of the notion of one's power over a proposition sufficiently clear that we can simply *see* that the premisses of the First Formal Argument are true? The unregenerate compatibilist is likely to respond to these questions this way:

> I'm not willing to grant that. The premisses of the First Formal Argument may be plausible at first glance, but that can be said of many false propositions. I can't say for sure which of your premisses is false since, now that you have set aside the definition given in Section 3.4, I'm not clear about what you mean by *can render false*. But I am confident that for any reasonably precise specification of this notion—one, that is, that is as clear as that given in Section 3.4—I shall be able to show that at least one of your premisses is false when it is interpreted according to that definition. If you should devise a definition

that does justice to our pre-analytic conviction that no one can render false a law of nature, then, I predict, I shall be able to show, according to the strict terms of that definition, that one of the other premisses of the argument—I expect it would be either (4) or (5)—is false if compatibilism is true.[13]

But now, I think the compatibilist is doing no more than calling our attention to the fact that, if compatibilism is true, then some premiss of our argument is false. That is, he is calling our attention to the fact that the argument is valid.

The reader who accepts the characterization of *can render false* that was presented in Section 3.4 will perceive a certain ironic consequence of the compatibilist's argument (which is perfectly correct) for the conclusion that compatibilism entails the falsity of premiss (6): it is the compatibilist, and not the incompatibilist, who believes in "contra-causal freedom".

This completes my presentation of the First Argument. While this argument contains a great deal of detail, the general idea behind it is a simple one. Consider any act that (logically) someone might have performed. If it should turn out that this act was incompatible with the state of the world before that person's birth taken together with the laws of nature, then it follows that that person could not have performed that act. Moreover, if determinism is true, then just *any* deviation from the actual course of events would be incompatible with any past state of the world taken together with the laws of nature. Therefore, if determinism is true, it never has been within my power to deviate from the actual course of events that has constituted my history.

Some philosophers seem to think the statement, 'if an act was incompatible with the state of the world before a person's birth taken together with the laws of nature, then it follows that that person could not have performed that act' *must* be based on some sort of muddle. But if one examines an actual case in which a certain act is "ruled out" by the state of the world before someone's birth and the laws of nature, then this conclusion does *seem* to follow, and it is very hard indeed to see what muddle one's conviction that this is so is based on. Let us ask, for example, whether I could have visited the star

Arcturus half an hour ago. My having visited Arcturus at that moment seems to be ruled out by the state of the world before I was born and the laws of nature. Let us consider the state of the world one minute before I was born. At that moment, I was approximately 3.6×10^{17} metres from Arcturus. The temporal interval separating the moment one minute before I was born from the moment that occurred one half hour before now is about 1.16×10^9 seconds. It is a law of nature—or so we believe at present; let's suppose we're right—that no two objects have a relative velocity greater than 3×10^8 metres per second.[14] It follows, by simple arithmetic, that I did not visit Arcturus one half hour ago.

Here we have a case in which the proposition that I *did not* do a certain thing is deducible from the state of the world before I was born taken together with a law of nature. And it certainly *seems* to follow from the fact that this deduction is possible that I *could not* have done this thing. It is at any rate *true* that I could not have done this thing (could not have visited Arcturus one half hour ago). Is there some further fact, beyond the fact of the deducibility of my non-visit to Arcturus from the state of the world before I was born and the laws of nature, to which we should need to refer to justify our belief that I couldn't have visited Arcturus one half hour ago? I don't see what this further fact could be. Is there some feature of this "deduction of non-performance" that is not a universal feature of deductions of non-performance, which we have capitalized upon? What is it, then? In order to drive this point home, I shall construct an argument parallel to the First Formal Argument for the conclusion that I *could not* have visited Arcturus one half hour ago. Let us use 'T' to designate the moment of time that occurred one half hour ago. Let 'P' designate the proposition that I did not visit Arcturus at T. Let 'P_0' designate the proposition that expresses the state of the world one minute before my birth. (Note that P_0 entails the proposition that at that moment Arcturus and I were separated by a distance of about 3.6×10^{17} metres.) Let 'L' designate the proposition that nothing travels faster than 3×10^8 metres per second. We may now argue:

(1)   The conjunction of P_0 and L entails P

(2)   It is not possible that I have visited Arcturus at T and P be true

(3)   If (2) is true, then if I could have visited Arcturus at T, I could have rendered P false

(4)   If I could have rendered P false, and if the conjunction of P_0 and L entails P, then I could have rendered the conjunction of P_0 and L false

(5)   If I could have rendered the conjunction of P_0 and L false, then I could have rendered L false

(6)   I could not have rendered L false

(7)   I could not have visited Arcturus at T.

This seems to be a perfectly cogent and unexceptionable argument for the conclusion that I could not have visited Arcturus at T. Anyone who thinks he can demonstrate that one of the premisses of the First Formal Argument is false, must either show that his argument does not also "demonstrate" the falsity of the corresponding premiss of the "Arcturus" argument, or else he must accept this conclusion and explain why the apparent truth of the premisses of the "Arcturus" argument is only apparent. Perhaps someone will be able to do one of these things, but this project does not look very promising to me.

On page 74, I said that "the unregenerate compatibilist" was likely to maintain that if premiss (6) of the First Formal Argument is true, then either premiss (4) or premiss (5) is false, or, at least, is inconsistent with compatibilism. (*Which* of (4) and (5) is false, according to this compatibilist, would depend on exactly how one defines 'can render false'.) This thesis about (4) and (5) is quite implausible when it is applied, *mutatis mutandis*, to the corresponding premisses of the "Arcturus" argument. Perhaps the reader will find it instructive to reflect on this implausibility and to ask himself whether some of it doesn't rub off on the compatibilist's thesis concerning the First Formal Argument.

Let us look at premiss (4). Suppose I could have rendered P false, that is, could so have arranged things that I have visited Arcturus at T. If P_0 and L entail that I did *not* visit Arcturus at T, then I could so have arranged things that the conjunction of these two propositions is false: my so arranging things as to visit Arcturus at T is logically sufficient for the falsity of this conjunction.

Let us look at premiss (5). P_0 is a proposition about the arrangement of the furniture of the world before I was born—and therefore before I was capable of arranging things. L is a proposition whose truth imposes an upper limit on the relative velocities of physical objects at any time. Surely if I could ever have done something sufficient for the falsity of the conjunction of these two propositions, it would be just this: getting two objects to exhibit a relative velocity incompatible with the truth of L.

These arguments for the truth of (4) and (5) may be combined in the following intuitive way. I believe that one minute before my birth the star Arcturus and I were separated by a distance of about 3.6×10^{17} metres. I believe that between the moment one minute before my birth and the moment that occurred one half hour ago, there elapsed approximately 1.16×10^9 seconds. I believe that no two physical objects ever move toward each other with a velocity greater than 3×10^8 metres per second. Now suppose someone trustworthy—God, say—tells me that, while these beliefs of mine are *true*, I should be wrong to infer from them that it was not within my power to have visited Arcturus one half hour ago. For, God says, this *was* within my power. What could I conclude from this revelation? Only one conclusion seems possible: it was within my power to do something that has in fact never been done, namely to travel (relative to a certain object) at a speed greater than 3×10^8 metres per second. If God should also tell me that it is a *law of nature* that nothing exceeds this velocity, then I could only conclude that it was within my power to violate a law of nature, that is, to work a miracle. This might be an unpalatable conclusion, but not so unpalatable as the conclusion that it was within my power to have been born over a year earlier than I in fact was.

3.6 The structure of the First Argument was complex indeed. The structure of the Second Argument will be simplicity itself. The First Argument made extensive use of the notion of a *proposition*. Our preliminary discussion of propositions touched upon the idea that propositions could be modelled

on sets of possible worlds. We saw that various notions intimately related to the notion of a proposition could be defined
—rather than simply grasped intuitively—and defined in a very
pleasing and elegant way if propositions were taken to be, or
to differ only in irrelevant ways from, sets of possible worlds.
The Second Argument differs from the First Argument by
exploiting the intimate connection between propositions and
sets of possible worlds. This exploitation takes the form of
the elimination of all references to propositions: in the Second Argument we shall discuss the problem of the compatibility of free will and determinism in terms of possible worlds
"directly".

A good deal of the discussion that preceded the First Argument will apply to the Second Argument. The reader may find
a second reading of Section 3.3 helpful.

The concept of a possible world is an extremely useful one.
Yet a considerable number of philosophers who seem to be
otherwise intellectually responsible have taken to amusing
themselves and their graduate students by engaging in what
can only be described as Philistine sneering at this harmless
and fruitful notion. Well, as poor Paley said, who can refute a
sneer? Nevertheless, while some of our discussion up to this
point has involved loose talk about, or loose talk couched in
terms of, possible worlds, the Second Argument will involve
quantification over them that is meant to be taken in full ontological seriousness. Therefore, I had better say a few words
in defence of these inoffensive objects. Since it is better to be
right than original, what I say will be largely cribbed from
Alvin Plantinga's brilliant book, *The Nature of Necessity*.[15]

There is one canard that must be disposed of before I say
anything else. Some philosophers have supposed that talk of
possible worlds is supposed to provide us with a device for
defining modal concepts in terms of non-modal concepts.
Having supposed this, these philosophers proceed to point out
that *possible world* is itself a modal concept. But this is simply
silly. No one, so far as I know, has ever supposed that one
could grasp the notion of a possible world if one had no prior
grasp of the notion of possibility. (One might as well say that
Frege believed he could explain truth and falsity by reference
to the objects the True and the False.)

What are possible worlds? Possible worlds are members of the class of *ways things might be* or *possible ways things might be arranged* or, simply, possibilities.[16] We quantify over such objects when we say, "There are three ways in which the Earth could be destroyed", or "There are still a few possibilities that we haven't investigated". Let us call such objects *possibilities*.[17] Possibilities are designated by phrases consisting of 'the possibility that' followed by a sentence, with main verb in the subjunctive mood, that expresses a possibly true proposition. (Phrases like 'the possibility that $7 + 5$ equal 13' thus fail to designate anything, there being no such possibility.) Possibilities are either realized or unrealized. For example, the possibility that Socrates teach Plato is realized, but, if things had gone differently, it would have been unrealized. To say that a possibility is unrealized is obviously not to say that it doesn't exist. For there obviously exist unrealized possibilities, such as the possibility that Socrates never have met Plato. (To say that there exist no unrealized possibilities is to adopt *Spinozism*, a doctrine equivalent to the doctrine that a proposition is true if and only if it is necessarily true.)

But not just any possibility is a possible *world*, for not just any possibility is sufficiently "filled out" to deserve to be called a *world*. In order to say which possibilities are possible worlds, we shall need two definitions. Let us say that a possibility *includes* a second possibility if it is impossible for the former to be realized and the latter unrealized. (Moreover, every possibility includes itself.) Let us say that a possibility *precludes* a second possibility if it is impossible for them both to be realized. (Moreover, no possibility precludes itself.) Thus, the possibility that Socrates teach Plato includes the possibility that $2 + 2$ equal 4, the possibility that Socrates exist, the possibility that Plato exist, and the possibility that Socrates teach someone. It precludes the possibility that Socrates fail to exist and the possibility that Socrates teach no one. It neither includes nor precludes the possibility that Socrates teach Aristotle or the possibility that the most famous snub-nosed Greek philosopher teach Plato.[18] For every possibility, there is exactly one possibility it both includes and is included by: itself. (The preceding sentence is a statement of the principle of individuation for possibilities.) Most possi-

THREE ARGUMENTS FOR INCOMPATIBILISM   81

bilities are like the possibility that Socrates teach Plato: there are possibilities they neither include nor preclude. If a possibility fails to have this feature it is *comprehensive*. That is, a comprehensive possibility is a possibility that, for every other possibility, either includes it or precludes it. A comprehensive possibility is a possible world: 'comprehensive possibility' and 'possible world' are, in my usage, stylistic variants.

I shall assume without argument that there are comprehensive possibilities. If there are any, there is more than one. (To say there is exactly one comprehensive possibility is Spinozism.[19]) I shall assume without argument that it is false that all comprehensive possibilities are unrealized. But if any comprehensive possibility is realized, exactly one is, since it is an obvious consequence of our definitions that any two comprehensive possibilities preclude each other. The realized comprehensive possibility is the actual world: 'the realized comprehensive possibility' and 'the actual world' are, in my usage, stylistic variants.[20]

Since possible worlds are possibilities and possibilities are abstract objects, possible worlds, including the actual world, are abstract objects. Therefore, what philosophers sometimes call "the world", what, indeed, I have called "the world" in this book, is not the same object as the actual world. *The world* is the universe, or the cosmos, or what Professor Geach has called "the upper limit of the series: the solar system, the galaxy, the system of galaxies . . ." If things were different in some minor way, if, say, I had not shaved this morning, then of course *the world* would still have existed, albeit it or a few of its components would have had different features. But if I had not shaved this morning, the abstract object that is in fact the actual world would not have been actual, though it would still have existed. If I had not shaved this morning, the actual world would have been an unrealized possibility, and some other possible world (some other comprehensive possibility) would have been actual (realized).

Now it may be a bad idea for me to use the word 'world' in this double sense. Perhaps I should call the world 'the cosmos' or 'the universe'. Or perhaps I should refrain from calling comprehensive possibilities 'worlds'. But I like the word 'world' as a name for the cosmos better than its pompous Greek and Latin alternatives. And to call possible worlds 'comprehensive possibilities' outside contexts in which I am specifically discussing what I take to be their nature—that is, *in* contexts in which I am using them as devices for presenting propositions about free will and determinism—would be an inadvisable departure from customary philosophical terminology.[21] At any rate, the construction of my sentences will remove all possibility of ambiguity. If I say *"the* world", I must mean the cosmos, for there are many comprehensive possibilities. If I talk of "worlds", I must mean comprehensive possibilities, for there is only one cosmos. If I say "the actual world", I cannot mean the cosmos, for 'actual' in my usage means 'realized' and it is possibilities not cosmoi that can be said to be realized or unrealized.

We need one more definition and then we shall be ready to present the Second Argument. We say that a proposition is true at, or in, a given world if that proposition *would be* true if that world *were* actual.[22] An important special case of the notion of the truth of a proposition at a world is the notion of the truth of a singular existential proposition at a world. Applied to this special case, the above definition tells us that a given object—the Eiffel Tower, say, or the number four—exists at, or in, a given world provided that object *would* exist if that world *were* actual.[23] It is an obvious consequence of this definition that there are objects that exist in more than one world. For the proposition that Socrates had a long, straight nose, while false, is false only contingently. Therefore there are possible worlds, none of them actual, at which Socrates had a long, straight nose. I am aware that there is supposed to be something called "the problem of trans-world identity", but, though I have assiduously attempted to find out what this problem is, I have never succeeded. To those who think there is such a problem, I make a gift of a rather more pressing problem, the problem of *trans-propositional identity*: how can the proposition that Nixon is a villain and the proposition that Nixon is an honest man both be about the same man, when one is about a villain and the other is about an honest man?

3.7 The Second Argument, like the First Argument, is a commentary on the premises of an argument in the logic-text sense. I shall call the "logic-text" argument 'the Second Formal Argument'. The vocabulary of the Second Formal Argument is that of the first-order predicate calculus with identity, supplemented by four non-logical constants. These constants, with suggested English readings, are:

A: the actual world;

Sxy: x shares a slice with y;

Nxy: x is nomologically congruent with y;

Hxy: x has access to y.

We shall also employ a one-place defined predicate, 'D':

$$Dx =_{df} (\exists y)(Sxy) \& (y)(Syx \& Nyx . \supset y = x).^{24}$$

'Dx' is read, 'x is deterministic'.

The intended sense of 'A' is evident from its suggested English reading. This term is to be understood as short for the definite description 'the actual world': 'A' is not to be taken as a proper name for, or a "rigid designator" of, the world that happens to be actual.

The predicate 'S' represents the symmetrical, reflexive, and non-transitive relation that has the class of all possible worlds as both its domain and its range and which two worlds bear to each other if they are indistinguishable at some instant. One might want to respond to this explanation by asking, "Indistinguishable with respect to what?", for it is not clear whether there is any such thing as absolute-indistinguishability-at-an-instant. Perhaps w_1 and w_2 are indistinguishable at t if, for every property x and object y, y exists and has x in w_1 at t if and only if y exists and has x in w_2 at t? But suppose there are not only well-behaved properties like *being blue* or *being radioactive*; suppose there are also such unruly properties as *being grue* and *having resigned the Presidency five years since*. A moment's reflection should show that if these properties and their relatives indeed exist, then two worlds are indistinguishable, by the above definition, at some instant only if they are indistinguishable at all instants, a result that obviously renders "being indistinguishable at an instant" a worthless notion.

If this problem has no solution, then, I think, determinism is an incoherent doctrine. Let us, therefore, simply *assume* there is some solution or other to it. Our remarks in this chapter will be sufficiently general that they will be consistent with just about any specification of what is meant by two worlds being indistinguishable at an instant. This is essentially what we did in Section 3.3 when we left the concept of "state" an open concept. Indeed, if we *had* the concept of "state" that would be required for a full specification of the meanings of the terms employed in the First Argument, we could easily define 'S':

$Sxy =_{df} (\exists t)$ (the state that x is in at t = the state that y is in at t).

(The *definiens* of this definition contains a specimen of a certain sort of loose talk I have indulged in before, and, owing to its convenience, shall continue to indulge in. A possible world is an abstract object, and does not change with the passage of time; or, at least, it changes only in the "Cambridge" sense. When I talk of the state that a possible world w is in at time t, I am to be taken as talking about the state that, at w, *the* world—the cosmos, the universe—is in at t.)

I must be satisfied to leave the content of the indistinguishability-at-a-time relation pretty much open, pending the formulation of a theory of properties that allows us satisfactorily to distinguish between *being grue* and *having only six days to live* on the one hand, and well-behaved properties like *being blue* and *having only six moving parts* on the other. But I offer the reader two ways of looking at this relation that seem to me to have some heuristic value.

Let us imagine a Leibnizian God, who somehow "stands outside" all possible worlds and is able somehow to "examine" them individually, *sub specie aeternitatis*. Presumably, such a God would be able to restrict his examination of a world to (focus on, as it were) the way that world is at a single instant of time. If we find this way of speaking intelligible, then we may say that the indistinguishability relation holds between two worlds if there is some instant t such that, if God were to examine each of these worlds "as it as at t", he could observe, on the basis of these examinations alone, no difference between them.

Or if we are willing to think of a possible world (strictly speaking, to think of the universe that exists in that world) as a compact sequence of instantaneous three-dimensional "slices", then we may say that the indistinguishability relation holds between two worlds just in the case that they have a slice in common—hence, the suggested English reading of 'S'.

Let us now turn to 'N'. I mean this predicate to represent the equivalence relation that holds between two worlds just in the case that the laws of nature are the same in each. An alternative reading of 'Nxy' is 'what is physically necessary and impossible in x is what is physically necessary and impossible in y', provided these modal terms are not taken as meaning 'what is *now* physically impossible or necessary, given the actual past'. (For example, it is, I suppose, *now* physically necessary that a total eclipse of the Sun be visible, weather permitting, in Siberia on 9 March 1997. But I should think there are possible worlds—though perhaps only worlds in which the "entire past" was different—that bear the relation I intend 'N' to express to the actual world, and in which no eclipse will then be visible.) Rather, these modal terms must be taken to refer to what is "timelessly" physically necessary and impossible.

Examples of worlds that do not bear this relation to the actual world would probably be controversial. But I should think that there are probably possible worlds in which the fundamental constants of nature—Planck's Constant, the speed of light, the charge on the electron, and the universal constant of gravitation—have values different from their actual values. Whether there are worlds in which the laws of nature have a different *structure* from their actual structure—worlds, say, in which the energy associated with a photon is not a function of its wavelength, or worlds in which the force of mutual gravitational attraction between two particles is inversely proportional to the cube of the distance between them—is something I should not care to speculate about. (There do seem to be deep conceptual reasons for the structure exhibited by physical law. But we view these matters through a glass darkly.)

Let us now examine our defined predicate, 'D'. This predicate represents a property of some possible worlds, the property of being deterministic, which may be informally characterized as follows: a world is deterministic if that world itself is the *only* world that both shares a slice with it and has the same laws of nature it does.

Perhaps an example will make the point of this definition clear. Let w be some possible world that shares with the actual world, A, a slice taken at the instant Harold's eye was pierced by a Norman arrow. It may share indenumerably many other slices with A; it shares at least that slice. And let us suppose that in A and w the laws of nature are the same. There are two possibilities: A and w may be the same world or they may be distinct. But A and w can plausibly be called 'deterministic' only if they are identical. For suppose they are *not* identical: let us say that w is one of those worlds in which a thermo-nuclear war was fought in 1966. If there is a world that has all the properties we have ascribed to w, it would be odd to say that anything that could reasonably be called 'determinism' is true. The actual world is a world in which a certain situation in 1066 did not precede a thermonuclear war by nine hundred years. But in w, a world having exactly the same laws of nature, precisely the same situation was followed, after nine hundred years, by a thermonuclear war. In other words, if our descrip-tion of w is consistent—that is, if w exists—then, though there was in actuality no thermonuclear war in 1966, such a war was a possibility relative to the laws of nature and the state of the world in 1066. But 'determinism' must, if violence is not to be done to every traditional association that word has, be used to refer to the thesis that there are no such alternative possibilities. Let us, therefore, understand by 'determinism' the thesis that the actual world is "deterministic": according to determinism, every world distinct from the actual world either differs from it at every instant, or, if it differs from the actual world at only *some* instants, is governed by a different set of laws of nature.

3.8 So much for determinism. Now for free will. We shall talk of a person's abilities in terms of which worlds he "has access to". (Thus, our relation *having access to* bears little re-semblance to the "accessibility" relation that figures in a Kripke-style semantics for modal logic. Our "having access" relation holds between *persons* or *agents* and worlds; the "accessibility" relation holds between worlds and worlds.) In order to show what is meant by saying that a person "has access to" some merely possible world—we may take it to be true by definition that everyone has access to the actual world —I shall first give some translations from ordinary talk about *abilities* to "access" talk. We translate, 'Napoleon could have defeated Wellington at Waterloo' as 'Napoleon had access to some possible world in which he defeated Wellington at Waterloo'. We translate 'It is within my power to keep the money I found and within my power to return it' as 'I have access to some world in which I keep the money I found and I have access to some world in which I return it'. Non-actual worlds, we remember, are unrealized possibilities. Thus "access" talk is a way of organizing our talk about unexercised abilities by reference to unrealized possibilities: an unexercised ability is treated as an ability to realize some unrealized possibility. This seems to be a harmless and quite intelligible rewriting of ordinary ability-talk. Like our earlier treatment of unexercised abilities as abilities to render true propositions false, it is somewhat artificial. The artificiality has in both cases the same excuse: if we are to investigate the conceptual relations between free will and determinism, it is hardly to be supposed that we shall succeed if the vocabulary we use to state the thesis of determinism and the vocabulary we use to state the thesis of free will have no elements in common. Therefore, if determinism is formulated as a thesis about possible worlds (or about propositions) the best plan would seem to be to try to formulate the free-will thesis as a thesis about possible worlds (or propositions). Of course one might apply this strategy in reverse: the free-will thesis might be formulated as a thesis about *acts*, and determinism as a thesis about *events*, acts being treated as a species of event. I prefer the present course. Here is a good rationalization of my choice (that is, a good reason for it that did not in fact influence my choice): the action-theory industry has generated so much controversy about acts and events that a good many philosophers would be more interested in whatever I had to say about acts and events than they would be in what I had to say about free will. But I want to talk about free will.[25]

If "access" talk is artificial, it is not therefore unusable in everyday life. The following bit of dialogue shows how our moral discourse might sound if we gave up ordinary ability-talk and adopted in its place the language of access to possible worlds.

A.   You ought not to have cut my lecture on Friday.

B.   But I did not have access to a possible world in which I attended your lecture on Friday, since I suffered an unforeseen paralysis of my legs on Thursday that mysteriously vanished on Saturday. In every possible world to which I had access, I spent Friday in bed.

A.   Have you access to a possible world in which a doctor writes me a note verifying your story?

B.   Unfortunately not: no possible world that I had access to on Friday contained a doctor in this city who makes house calls.

And so on. Perhaps the relationship between ordinary ability-talk and access-talk might best be explicated by showing the relationship between access-talk and a rather artificial near-relation of ordinary ability-talk, namely, talk of one's abilities with respect to bringing about events of some specified sort: to say that a person can bring about an event satisfying a certain description is to say that he has access to at least one possible world in which an event satisfying that description happens; and to say that a person has access to a possible world satisfying a certain description is to say that he can bring about events of a sort that happen only in worlds satisfying that description.

   In order to make this relationship intuitively more clear, I shall devise a sort of metaphor or picture that might be used as an informal model both for talk of being able to bring about events and talk of access to possible worlds. Consider a man who is walking through an infinite system of branching corridors. He has always been walking and must always keep walking, never stopping and never retracing his steps. He finds that some branches are sealed off by bars and some are not. Frequently he comes to a branching of the corridor from which at least two unbarred branches lead away, and he must make a choice about which to take.

Let us call any location within the system of corridors an *event*. Then we may say that the man *can bring about* a certain event just in the case that there is some path through the corridors leading from where he is to that event (location) without passing through any barred corridors.[26]

Let us call a *possible world* any infinitely long path through the system of corridors that does not cross itself. The *actual world* is that one path through the corridors along which the man always has walked, is walking, and always will walk. Those worlds to which the man *has access* at any given moment are just those infinite paths that do not pass through any barred corridors, and which are continuations of the path-segment along which he already walked.

This picture has its limitations as a model for talk of access to possible worlds: it is no longer applicable if we assume (as is the case) that *which* possible world the actual world is depends on the choices of more than one person. We might, of course, elaborate our imagery by assuming that there are n persons walking through the system of corridors, and call a *possible world* any n-membered *set* of infinite paths. The actual world, then would be the set of paths that *are* taken, and a person P would have access at any given moment to those possible worlds that are such that (i) they differ from the actual world by at most one member, (ii) this member is the path that P is in fact going to take, and (iii) each of them that does not contain the path that P is in fact going to take, contains instead a continuation of the path-segment that P has already walked that does not pass through any barred corridors.

But this more elaborate picture breaks down in its turn if we assume (as is the case) that persons come into and go out of existence, and that the choices they make partly determine what choices it is *possible* for their fellows to make. I do not think, however, that there is anything to be gained from constructing a yet more elaborate picture in order to accommodate these facts. We should note that the relation expressed by 'H' is, strictly speaking, a non-temporal relation between persons and possible worlds: it is not a triadic relation satisfied by ordered triples of the form ⟨person, world, instant⟩, but a dyadic relation satisfied by ordered pairs of the form ⟨person, world⟩. For example, if Tom, a doctor, once had access to a possible world w in which his profession is law, then, even if he no longer has access to w, it is true that Tom bears the relation expressed by 'H' to w. Thus, a better English reading of 'Hxy' might be 'x had, has, or will have access, at some point in his life, to y'.

It is also perhaps worth noting a respect in which the "access" idiom is unrealistic. A possible world is a very *detailed* thing. To see what I mean by this, try to name any possible world other than the actual world. Probably this cannot be done: for any predicate we might devise, this predicate will be satisfied by many non-actual worlds if it is satisfied by any. That is, while we can pick out various *sets* of non-actual worlds—for example, the set of worlds in which Napoleon won at Waterloo—we cannot pick out any single merely possible world.[27] Thus, talk of access to *particular* merely possible worlds is very likely too "fine-grained" to be a literally correct way of describing our unexercised abilities: none of my unexercised abilities is so "definite" an ability as to be correctly describable as an ability to get some *particular* possible world to be actual. No act I might have performed is such that my having performed it entails the actuality of any particular world. No act I might have performed is such that, for some world, if I had performed that act, then *that* world would have been actual. No world is the world that would have been actual if I had raised my hand one minute ago. Thus it would probably be more realistic to describe my unexercised abilities in terms of access to *sets* of possible worlds. For example, the state of affairs that consists in my having an unexercised ability to break this cup could be described as being identical with the state of affairs that consists in my having access to the set of possible worlds in which I break this cup. Moreover, the concept of access to a set of possible worlds can easily be defined in terms of the concept of the ability to render a proposition false:

> s has access to the set of worlds $x =_{df} (\exists y)$ (y is true in just exactly those worlds that belong to x and s can render the denial of y false).[28]

Despite these difficulties, I shall retain the useful fiction that a person's unexercised abilities may be described in terms of his having access to particular non-actual worlds. This will result in a very neat formal argument. It would be a simple, almost a mechanical, task to transform this argument into an argument involving access to sets of worlds, and the only expense would be some clutter. But part of the point of the Second Argument is the elimination of clutter. Those who like clutter will find all they could desire in the First Argument. My hope is that the Second Argument is unrealistic only as the Kinetic Theory of Gases (which ignores certain features of the real world, such as inter-molecular forces) is unrealistic: it makes certain simplifying assumptions, assumptions that are literally false, in order to lay bare the most important features of an interrelated family of phenomena.

3.9 Let us now return to the Second Argument. We shall call the thesis

$$(\exists x)\,(\exists y)\,(\mathrm{H}xy\ \&\ y \neq \mathrm{A})$$

the *minimal free-will thesis* (MFT). MFT is a very weak thesis. It tells us only that some person, past, present, or future, had, has, or will have access to some possible world besides the actual world. MFT is true, for example, if Julius Caesar had access to some world w in which he did not cross the Rubicon, even if no other person, past, present, or future, has access to any world besides A, and Caesar himself had access only to w and A. But if MFT is false, then any more interesting free-will thesis is false. And, therefore, if determinism is incompatible with MFT, it is incompatible with any more interesting free-will thesis.

Determinism may be represented in our present vocabulary by the simple formula 'DA'. Clearly the denial of MFT cannot be formally deduced from 'DA'. Nevertheless, there is an important sense in which determinism is incompatible with MFT. There are two theses, which I shall call 'metaphysical assumptions', each of which seems more likely to be true than either determinism or the minimal free-will thesis, such that the denial of MFT may be formally deduced from determinism and these two theses. The two metaphysical assumptions are:

MAA $(x)\,(y)\,(Hxy \supset SyA)$

MAB $(x)\,(y)\,(Hxy \supset NyA)$.

MAA asserts that every world to which any person has access must be indistinguishable from the actual world at some instant. Or, alternatively, every world to which any person has access must share a slice with the actual world. For example, however many possible worlds I have access to, surely they must all be indistinguishable from the actual world at some time in the remote past—say, 10,000 BC, or indeed, any time before I was born. In terms of the "infinite-system-of-corridors" metaphor: all the possible worlds (paths) that I have access to are continuations of the path-segment I have already travelled. MAA may be regarded as a statement of the familiar principle that no one can change the past.

MAB asserts that no person has access to any world in which the laws of nature are different from what they are in the actual world. This seems undeniable, for, as we have seen, no one can render a law of nature false. Moreover, it is clear that it is not up to anyone whether any given *true* proposition is a law of nature. Such things are not matters of human choice, any more than the theoremhood of a given mathematical proposition is a matter of human choice. It is, in my opinion, possible "in the broadly logical sense" for the laws of nature to have been different. The speed of light might have been different; Planck's constant might have been different; the charge on the electron might have been different. But if such possibilities exist, and if they are really possibilities about alternative sets of laws of nature, then it is beyond our power to realize them. And this is just another way of saying that no one has access to possible worlds in which the laws of nature are different. It may of course be true that some people have access to possible worlds in which our *beliefs* about the laws of nature are different. Perhaps if Newton or Einstein had acted differently, had done certain things they could have done but did not do, then we should now hold other beliefs about the laws of nature. But this, of course, is irrelevant to our present concerns.

The denial of MFT can easily be seen to be formally deriv-
able from 'DA', MAA, and MAB. (Here is a sketch of a proof
of this that employs techniques common to most logic texts.
Assume 'Hxy'. Universally instantiate MAA and MAB. *Modus
Ponens* yields 'SyA' and 'NyA'. From these two formulae and
the universal instantiation of the second conjunct of the formula that 'DA' abbreviates, we get, by *Modus Ponens*, 'y = A'.
Thus, by Conditional Proof and Universal Generalization, we
have, '(x) (y) (Hxy $\supset$ y = A)', which is logically equivalent to
the denial of MFT.) The argument having 'DA', MAA, and
MAB as its premisses, and the denial of MFT as its conclusion,
is the Second Formal Argument. We have already commented
upon the premisses of this argument. We may put the conclusion of the Second Argument thus: if determinism is true,
then no one has access to any non-actual world. That is, no
one has an ability that may correctly be described as an ability
to realize some in fact unrealized possibility.

3.10 The Third Argument is a modal argument; that is, it
involves a modal operator, an operator that attaches to sentences that have (or that express propositions that have) truth-
values, to form sentences that have truth-values; and the
truth-value of a sentence formed in this way is not in every
case a function of the truth-value of the sentence to which
the operator attaches. The operator is 'N'. For any sentence
p, the result of prefixing p with 'N' may be regarded as an
abbreviation for the result of flanking 'and no one has, or
ever had, any choice about whether' with occurrences of
p. Thus

N All men are mortal

is an abbreviation for

All men are mortal and no one has, or ever had, any
choice about whether all men are mortal.

'N' is a very interesting operator, and the task of constructing
a plausible and complete logic for 'N' would be an interesting
one. It would be even more interesting if the vocabulary of
this logic included the usual "alethic" modal operators. But it
will not be necessary for our purposes actually to construct

such a logic.[29] I think the following two inference rules ought to be valid rules of this logic:

(α) $\Box p \vdash Np$

(β) $N(p \supset q), Np \vdash Nq$.

I shall require no formulae that contain 'N' to be logically true other than those that these two rules allow us to deduce from the empty set of premisses. The operator '$\Box$' in Rule (α) represents "broadly logical necessity".

The Third Argument will have the following logical structure: from a logical consequence of determinism (determinism being conceived as in the First Argument), we shall deduce that no one has any choice about anything whatever.

In the Third Argument we shall once more use the symbols 'P_0' and 'L', which appeared in our statement of the First Argument. But these symbols will have a slightly different sense. In the First Argument, 'P_0' and 'L' were used as names for certain propositions. In the Third Argument, we shall use them as abbreviations for sentences expressing these propositions. Thus, in our present usage, 'P_0' and 'L' have the grammatical features of sentences and not of terms: in the usage of the First Argument, 'P_0 is true' was grammatical and '$P_0 \supset L$' was ungrammatical (for the same reason that 'Quine $\supset$ Davidson' is ungrammatical); in our present usage, '$P_0 \supset L$' is grammatical, and 'P_0 is true' is ungrammatical (for the same reason that 'All men are mortal is true' is ungrammatical).

We shall once more use the letter 'P'. This letter will serve as a dummy for which one can substitute any sentence one likes, provided it expresses a true proposition—'Quine finds quantified modal logic puzzling', say, or 'Paris is the capital of France'.

If determinism is true, then it follows that

(1) $\Box(P_0 \mathbin{\&} L. \supset P)$

is true. From (1) we may deduce

(2) $\Box(P_0 \supset (L \supset P))$

by elementary modal and sentential logic. Applying rule (α) to (2), we have:

(3) $N(P_0 \supset (L \supset P))$.

We now introduce a premiss:

(4) NP_o.

From (3) and (4) we have by Rule (β):

(5) $N(L \supset P)$.

We introduce a second premiss:

(6) NL.

Then, from (5) and (6) by (β):

(7) NP.

This deduction shows that if determinism is true, then no one ever has any choice about anything, since any sentence that expresses a truth may replace 'P' in it. Consider, for example, the question whether anyone had a choice about whether Richard Nixon would receive a pardon for any offences he might have committed while in office. Nixon did receive such a pardon. Therefore, if determinism is true,

> $\Box(P_o$ & L. $\supset$ Richard Nixon received a pardon for any offences he might have committed while in office).

Therefore, if (α) and (β) are valid rules, and if NL and NP_o, then we have:

> No one had any choice about whether Richard Nixon received a pardon for any offences he might have committed while in office.

Most of us, I presume, think this conclusion is false. Most of us think Gerald Ford had a choice about whether Nixon would receive a pardon. (Even if someone thinks that Ford's actions were wholly controlled by some cabal, he none the less thinks *someone* had a choice about whether Nixon would receive a pardon.) But the above deduction (The Third Formal Argument) shows that if we wish to accept this conclusion we must reject one of the following five propositions:

> Determinism is true;
>
> NP_o;
>
> NL;
>
> Rule (α) is valid;
>
> Rule (β) is valid.

My choice, of course, is to reject determinism. But let us examine the alternatives.

I do not see how anyone can reject 'NP$_0$' or 'NL'. My reasons are essentially those that I gave in support of MAA and MAB in the Second Argument and in support of premises (5) and (6) of the First Formal Argument. The proposition that P$_0$ is a proposition about the remote past. We could, if we like, stipulate that it is a proposition about the distribution and momenta of atoms and other particles in the inchoate, presiderial nebulae. Therefore, surely, no one has any choice about whether P$_0$. The proposition that L is a proposition that "records" the laws of nature. If it is a law of nature that angular momentum is conserved, then no one has any choice about whether angular momentum is conserved, and, more generally, since it is a law of nature that L, no one has any choice about whether L.

I do not see how anyone could reject Rule (α). If (α) is invalid, then it could be that someone has a choice about what is necessarily true. Hardly anyone besides Descartes has been willing to concede such a capability even to God. No one, so far as I know, has ever suggested that human beings could have a choice about what is necessarily true. (I take it that "conventionalist" theories of modality don't *really* imply the thesis that human beings have a choice about what is necessarily true; or, at least, not in any sense relevant to our present concerns.)

Only Rule (β) remains to be considered. The validity of (β) is, I think, the most difficult of the premises of the Third Argument to defend. How might one go about defending it? How, in general, does one go about showing that an inference rule is valid? There would seem to be two ways.

First, one might employ the methods of formal semantics. In the present case, since 'N' is a modal operator, the methods of *possible-world* semantics might seem promising. Here is a sketch of how we might apply these methods to (β).[30] We first delimit a certain set W of worlds and say that Np is true just in the case that p is true in all these worlds. This would amount to a semantical definition of 'N'. It would be a definition of the same sort as that which we give when we say that a proposition is physically necessary if it is true in all worlds in which the laws of nature hold, or when we say that a proposition is morally required if it is true in all morally permissible worlds. For example, we might say that Np is true if p is true in both the actual world and in all non-actual worlds about whose actuality human beings have, or once had, a choice. Interestingly enough, the question of the membership of W is of no *formal* significance. If we accept *any* definition of Np of the following form: 'Np is true if and only if p is true in all worlds such that . . .', where the condition that fills that ellipsis makes no mention of p, then (β) will "come out" valid. (Obviously, if p is true in every member of W, and if $p \supset q$ is true in every member of W, then q is true in every member of W.) Despite its utter triviality, this formal result is not without persuasive force. Nevertheless, it is far from decisive. It depends on the assumption that there is *some* set of worlds such that Np *can* plausibly be thought of as making the assertion that p is true in every member of that set. While this assumption seems right to me, I have no argument for it, and a person who was determined to reject (β) might very well reject the assumption.

Secondly, one might attempt to show that an inference rule is valid by "reducing" it to certain generally accepted inference rules, that is, by deducing its validity from the assumption that these generally accepted rules are valid. But it seems unlikely that this method can be used to show that (β) is valid: I can think of no generally accepted inference rules that seem relevant to (β), much less of any that it can be deduced from.

The prospect of *showing* (β) to be valid, therefore, appears to be bleak, though perhaps no bleaker than the prospect of *showing* anything of philosophical interest. I must confess that my belief in the validity of (β) has only two sources, one incommunicable and other inconclusive. The former source is what philosophers are pleased to call "intuition": when I carefully consider (β), it seems to be valid. But I can't expect anyone to be very impressed by this fact. People's intuitions, after all, have led them to accept all sorts of crazy propositions and many sane but false propositions. (The Unrestricted Comprehension Principle in set theory and the Galilean Law of the Addition of Velocities in physics are good examples of propositions in the second category.) The latter source is the fact that I can think of no instances of (β) that have, or could possibly have, true premisses and a false conclusion. Consider, for example, these two instances of (β):

> Alice has asthma and no one has, or ever had, any choice about whether she has asthma;

> If Alice has asthma, she sometimes has difficulty breathing, and no one has, or ever had, any choice about whether, if she has asthma, she sometimes has difficulty breathing;

hence, Alice sometimes has difficulty breathing, and no one has, or ever had, any choice about whether Alice sometimes has difficulty breathing.

> The sun will explode in 2000 AD, and no one has, or ever had, any choice about whether the sun will explode in 2000 AD;

> If the sun explodes in 2000 AD, all life on earth will end in 2000 AD, and no one has, or ever had, any choice about whether, if the sun explodes in 2000 AD, all life on earth will end in 2000 AD;

hence, All life on earth will end in 2000 AD, and no one has, or ever had, any choice about whether all life on earth will end in 2000 AD.

These arguments are clearly valid. There is simply no way things could be arranged that would be sufficient for the truth of their premisses and the falsity of their conclusions. Take the second. Conceivably we could do something to prevent the explosion of the sun. Then perhaps the conclusion of this argument would be false; but its first premiss would also be false. Perhaps we could erect an enormous shield that would protect the earth from the explosion of the sun; if we could do this, the conclusion would be false. But the second premiss would also be false. Perhaps we could spread a poison that would destroy all life on earth before 2000 AD; but in that case too the second premiss would be false. I cannot help feeling that the reader who makes a serious attempt at constructing a counter-example to (β) will begin to appreciate, even if he does not come to share, the intuition that I have expressed by saying, "when I carefully consider (β), it seems to be valid".[31]

It is interesting to note that rule (β) seems to figure in recent discussions of the philosophical and social implications of socio-biology and the question whether certain widespread features of human social behaviour are genetically determined. Consider, for example, the proposition (P) that there are certain jobs (jobs that both sexes are physically capable of performing) such that, in every society, these jobs devolve almost entirely upon women. Suppose a socio-biologist alleges that there is a certain fact or set of facts (F) about the evolutionary history of our species that explains why P is true. Anyone who says this is likely to be the target of some such criticism as this:

> What you are saying is that "women's role" is genetically determined, and thus that all attempts at changing the role of women in this or any other society are doomed by biology. This doctrine is pernicious. You are not a scientist but an ideologue, and the ideology you are peddling makes you a most useful prop for the existing system.

Anyone who is the target of such criticism is likely to defend himself in some way pretty much like this:

> Not so. While I believe that F explains why P is true, I do not say that F makes P *inevitably* true. Given F, there is a tendency for P to be true, but tendencies can be resisted. I do not say that "biology is destiny". It may well be that we have a choice about whether we shall behave in accordance with this tendency that our evolutionary heritage has presented us with.

Now I am not so much interested in where the right lies in disputes that take this form—after all, where it lies may depend on what is substituted for 'F' and for 'P'—as I am in its underlying logic. I believe that the logical skeleton of this dispute looks something like this:

CRITIC: It follows from your position that the premisses of the following valid argument are true:

N F obtains

N(F obtains ⊃ P is true)

hence, N P is true

SOCIO-BIOLOGIST: The first premiss is certainly true, but the second does *not* follow from my position and may very well be false.

It would probably never occur to the socio-biologist to deny that the conclusion of the argument he has been charged with endorsing actually does follow from its premisses. And if he did deny this, then the critic would rightly charge him with sophistry, for if it is granted that no one has any choice about whether, given that our history is such-and-such, we do so-and-so, and if it is granted that our history *is* such-and-such and that we have no choice about this, then it just obviously does follow that no one has any choice about whether we do so-and-so. This does not, of course, entail that (β) is valid, for it may be that while this instance of (β) is valid, other instances of (β) are invalid. But I think that anyone who said that, while the argument the critic has formulated is valid, (β) is *not* valid, would be saying something that is not on the face of it very plausible. The validity of (β), in its full generality, certainly does seem to be part of the "common ground" in the socio-biological dispute I have imagined. (Despite the fact that I have imagined it, its logical structure is typical of disputes about biological determinism.) That is, (β) seems to be accepted, and properly so, by both sides in the dispute; the dispute seems to turn simply on *what*—according to socio-biology —we have a choice about, and not on any questions about the validity of inferences involving 'having a choice about'. People who accept, or are accused of accepting, "special determinisms"—that is, theories that say, or are sometimes interpreted as saying, that some important aspect of human behaviour is determined by this or that factor outside our control—tend to find themselves embroiled in disputes about the freedom of the will. I have used a socio-biologist as an example of such a person because I am writing now, but the "biology is destiny" debate is not the only one of its type. If I had been writing a few years ago, I should have constructed an example involving a Freudian or a Marxist and the point of my example would have been the same. Anyone who denies the validity of (β), it seems to me, must react to such disputes in one of two ways. He must either call them pseudo-disputes that arise because both parties to the dispute wrongly accept (β), or he must contend that the dispute does not really involve (β) after all. In the former case, he should recommend that the socio-biologist reply to the critic like this:

> I admit that F is a fact about the history of our species and that that's something no one has a choice about. I admit *if* F is a fact about the history of a given species, then, in societies that comprise members of that species, certain jobs will devolve almost entirely upon women, and that no one has any choice about *that*. Still, we *do* have a choice about whether, in our society, these jobs will devolve almost entirely upon women.

I cannot imagine anyone saying this with a straight face. In the latter case, he owes us an account of these disputes that shows how the apparent acceptance of (β) by both parties is merely apparent.

The point of this discussion may be summed up in a question: Why is none of the participants in the debates about biological determinism a compatibilist? Perhaps the answer is that the participants in these debates take the idea of biological determinism much more seriously than philosophers are accustomed to take the idea of "universal" or "Laplacian" determinism, and that compatibilism with respect to a given type of determinism is possible only for people who do not take that type of determinism very seriously.[32]

I said above that I could think of no instances of (β) that had, or could possibly have had, true premises and a false conclusion. I meant, of course, that I could think of no instances of (β) that could be seen to have true premises and a false conclusion independently of the question whether free will is compatible with determinism. If free will is compatible with determinism, and if determinism is true, then, presumably, at least one of the following two instances of (β) has true premises and a false conclusion:

N (P$_0$ ⊃ (L ⊃ Nixon received a pardon))

N P_0

hence, N (L ⊃ Nixon received a pardon).

N (L ⊃ Nixon received a pardon)

N L

hence, N Nixon received a pardon.

But it would be nice to see a counter-example to (β) that did not presuppose the compatibility of free will and determinism. After all, the examples I gave in support of (β) did not presuppose the *incompatibility* of free will and determinism. I should think that if there are *any* counter-examples to (β), then some of them, at least, could be shown to be such independently of the question whether free will and determinism are compatible.

It may be hard to credit, but there are almost certainly philosophers who would say that the fact that determinism and compatibilism together entail that there are counter-examples to (β) shows that my use of (β) in an argument for incompatibilism is question-begging. But if this accusation were right, it's hard to see how any argument could avoid begging the question. If one presents an argument for a certain proposition, then, if that proposition is false, *some* step in the argument is wrong (I am counting the use of a false premiss as a "wrong step"); and one may believe of a particular step in the argument that *if* any step is wrong, *that one* is. But it hardly follows that one is "begging the question" by taking that step. One may be begging the question—whatever, precisely, begging the question is—but that one is begging the question is not a consequence of the mere existence of a "weakest link" in one's chain of reasoning.

Now these questions about question-begging and where the burden of proof lies, and so on, are very tricky. Let's look at them from a different angle. Suppose a compatibilist were to say something like this: "The Third Argument depends on the validity of (β). But this rule is invalid. I prove this as follows:

Compatibilism is true

hence, (β) is invalid.

You yourself admit that the conclusion of this argument follows from its premiss." (I do.) "You may not accept its premiss, but that's *your* problem, for that premiss is *true*. Moreover, you can hardly object to this little argument of mine on the ground that it begs the question. It's no worse in that respect than *your* argument, which is essentially this:

(β) is valid

hence, Compatibilism is false."

What am I to say to this? I suppose I can do no more than appeal to the intuitions of my readers. Here's how it looks to me (and doesn't it look this way to you?): Rule (β) seems obviously right and compatibilism does not seem obviously right. If two principles are in conflict and one of them seems obviously right and the other does not seem obviously right, then, if one must choose, one should accept the one that seems obviously right.

Well, suppose the compatibilist says he finds compatibilism obviously right. Presumably this assertion is either grounded in an immediate and intuitive relationship to compatibilism— he claims to *see* that it's true, just as I claim to see that (β) is valid—or it is grounded in some argument for compatibilism. Let us first look at the case of the philosopher who claims to see the truth of compatibilism intuitively. Arguments, like explanations, must come to an end somewhere. Perhaps, if there is such a philosopher, he and I constitute a genuine case of a conflict of rock-bottom intuitions. But I must say I should find any such claim as the one I have imagined incredible. Compatibilism looks to me like the kind of thing one could believe only because one had an argument for it. I simply cannot see what could be going on in the mind of someone who claimed to know it intuitively. I don't know what that would *feel* like.

The philosopher who accepts compatibilism on the basis of an *argument* is not likewise mysterious to me. But I shall want to know what the premises of his argument are. And I shall raise the following question about his premises: Are they really intuitively more plausible than (β)? I find it hard to believe that there are any propositions that entail compatibilism

that are more plausible than (β). Still, who knows? Perhaps
there are. What can we do but proceed by cases? In Section
4.3, we shall compare (β) with the premisses of a popular
argument for compatibilism, the argument I called the "Conditional Analysis Argument" in Chapter I.[33]

This completes my presentation of the Third Argument and
my defence of its premisses. I have now given three arguments
for the incompatibility of free will and determinism. If the
compatibilist wishes to refute these arguments—and, of course,
nothing obliges him to do this—here is what he will have to do:
he will have to produce some set of propositions intuitively
more plausible than the premisses of these arguments and show
that these propositions entail compatibilism, or else he will
have to devise arguments for the falsity of some of the premisses employed in the present chapter, arguments that can be
evaluated and seen to be sound independently of the question
whether free will and determinism are compatible.

3.11 Some compatibilists, when they are confronted with
arguments for the incompatibility of free will and determinism,
say something like this: "Your argument simply demonstrates
that when you use phrases like 'could have done otherwise'
or 'has a choice about', you are giving them some meaning
other than the meaning they have in our actual debates about
moral responsibility". This criticism is equally applicable,
mutatis mutandis, to all three of our arguments for incompatibilism. And my answer to it is essentially the same in each
case. But this answer can be presented very compactly and
efficiently in terms of the vocabulary employed in the Third
Argument. Therefore, I shall answer only this charge: "When
you use the phrase 'has a choice' you are giving it a meaning
different from the meaning it has in our actual debates about
moral responsibility", and I will leave to the reader the mechanical task of adapting this answer to the requirements of the
First and Second Arguments.[34] My answer consists simply in
a reinterpretation of 'N':

> $Np =_{df} p$ and, in just the sense of *having a choice* that is
> relevant in debates about moral responsibility, no one has,
> or ever had, any choice about whether p.

If there is anything to the objection we are considering, then at least one of the four propositions,

NP$_o$,

NL,

Rule (α) is valid,

Rule (β) is valid,

is false, given that 'N'—which occurs in (α) and (β)—is interpreted as above. But this does not seem to be the case. If one carefully retraces the steps of the Third Argument, one will find, I think, that no step becomes doubtful under our new interpretation of 'N'. The conclusion of the present chapter is, therefore, that if determinism is true, then no one has any choice about anything, in just that sense of *having a choice* that is relevant in debates about moral responsibility.

Chapter IV

Three Arguments for Compatibilism

4.1 If determinism is true, no one can act otherwise than he does. If determinism is true, no one has it within his power to realize any possibility that is in fact unrealized. If determinism is true, no one has any choice about anything. In short, if determinism is true, there is no free will. This was the conclusion of Chapter III.

In the present chapter, I shall examine arguments for the conclusion that free will and determinism are compatible. I shall not examine arguments that turn on the contention that a belief in the incompatibility of free will and determinism rests on some confusion or other—say, a confusion of "descriptive" with "prescriptive" laws, or a confusion of causation with compulsion. *My* belief in the incompatibility of free will and determinism rests on the arguments of Chapter III, and these arguments involve no such confusion. I shall examine only positive arguments for compatibilism, arguments that purport to establish compatibilism and not merely to expose an error that might lead one to believe in incompatibilism.

I know of only three positive arguments for compatibilism that have any currency. I shall call them 'the Paradigm Case Argument', 'the Conditional Analysis Argument', and 'the *Mind* Argument'. I have given brief descriptions of these arguments in Section 1.6.

4.2 The classical statement of the Paradigm Case Argument is due to Antony Flew.[1] Flew is primarily concerned to show that the proposition that we always freely do what is right is compatible with the proposition that God so arranged things at the first moment of creation that our always doing what is right is the inevitable consequence of the initial arrangement. But Flew explicitly says that his argument shows that freedom and determinism are compatible. If we leave aside theological considerations, we may represent part of his argument as follows:

> There are various words and phrases we use in ascribing free action to people: besides the obvious 'acted freely' and 'did it of his own free will', there are such phrases as 'could have done otherwise', 'had a choice about what she did', 'had alternatives', and 'could have helped doing what he did'. We learn these phrases by watching people apply them in concrete situations in everyday life, just as we learn, for example, colour words. These concrete situations serve as *paradigms* for the application of these words: the words mean *things of that sort*. Therefore they must apply to something; they must apply at least to the paradigmatic objects or situations. Careful investigation, philosophical or scientific, of these situations may indeed yield information about what freedom of choice really consists in, but it cannot show us that there is no such thing as freedom of choice. This is strictly parallel to the following proposition: careful investigation, philosophical or scientific, may show us what colour really consists in, but it cannot show us that there is no such thing as colour.

Well, so far so good. But this argument is not an argument for the compatibility of free will and determinism, though it may be part of such an argument; rather, it is an argument for the existence of free will. There seem to be two arguments with which Flew supplements the above argument in order to show that free will not only exists, which many incompatibilists will grant, but is also compatible with determinism.

(a) When we do carefully investigate the paradigm cases of free action, we find that their common feature is just this: we apply the word 'free' to a person's act just in the case that, "*if* he had chosen to do otherwise, he would have been able to do so; that there were alternatives, within the capacity of one of his physical strength, of his IQ, with his knowledge, and open to a person in his situation".[2] And, of course, a person's act may have this feature whether or not determinism is true.

(b) We have seen that scientific investigation could not show that none of us has free will. But scientific investigation could show that determinism is true. Hence, if free will were incompatible with determinism, scientific investigation could show that we have no free will, which is impossible.

In order the better to see the logical relationship between these two supplementary arguments, let us look at two parallel and familiar arguments about colours. Let us give the label 'hypochromatism' to the thesis that visible objects are composed entirely of tiny objects that are themselves colourless. Some philosophers have thought that hypochromatism is incompatible with the thesis that ordinary visible objects are coloured. But we may refute them as follows:

(i) When we carefully investigate the paradigm cases of coloured objects, we find that their common feature is just this: we apply the word 'coloured' to an object just in the case that, *if* that object were presented to a normal observer under standard conditions of observation, it would cause him to experience colour-sensations. And, of course, an object may have this feature whether or not hypochromatism is true.

(ii) We have seen that scientific investigation could not show that no objects have colours. But scientific investigation could show that hypochromatism is true. Hence if the existence of coloured objects were incompatible with hypochromatism, scientific investigation could show that no objects have colours, which is impossible.

Obviously, arguments (a) and (b) have mutually consistent sets of premises, and there is no reason why Flew should not employ both. Argument (a), however, is essentially what I have called the "Conditional Analysis Argument". The thesis that 'he could have done otherwise' means something like '*if* he had chosen to do otherwise, he would have been able to' is frequently employed as a premiss by compatibilists who would reject any appeal to paradigm cases in philosophical argument. Moreover, if this thesis is correct, then it can be used to show "directly" that free will is compatible with determinism, that is, it can be used to demonstrate this compatibility without the use of paradigm cases—or any other device—first to establish that there actually are occasions on which people act freely.

I shall discuss the Conditional Analysis Argument in the next section. Let us understand "the Paradigm Case Argument" to be the argument that (i) purports to establish the existence of actual occasions of free action by an appeal to the necessary correctness of applying the term 'a free act' to those acts that are used to teach the meaning of this term, and (ii) proceeds, by means of argument (b), to derive from the possibility of so establishing the existence of free action the conclusion that free will and determinism are compatible.

In calling this argument (part of) Flew's argument, I am *interpreting* Flew. There is a great deal in his paper that I do not understand, and I may simply have got him wrong. In any case, this argument is the clearest and most cogent argument I can find, or think I can find, in Flew's paper. If it is not Flew's argument, perhaps it is sufficiently similar to his argument that what I say in the sequel will be relevant to his argument.

The argument I have attributed to Flew is invalid. It is obviously possible to think of propositions that are consistent with all our observations and which have the consequence that no one can do otherwise than he does. Here is a fanciful but logically adequate example.

(M) When any human being is born, the Martians implant in his brain a tiny device—one that is undetectable by any observational technique we have at our disposal, though it is not *in principle* undetectable—which contains a "program" for that person's entire life: whenever that person must make a decision, the device *causes* him to decide one way or the other according to the requirements of a table of instructions that were incorporated into the structure of the device before that person was conceived.[3]

Now someone might object that (M) is not in fact consistent with our observations, since we can normally "feel" our decisions "flowing" naturally from our desires and our beliefs; but if (M) were true (so the objection runs), we should "feel" ourselves being interfered with. But to meet this objection we need only suppose that the Martian device causes us to have desires and beliefs appropriate to the decisions it will cause us to make. (If Davidson is right, the device could cause our decisions simply *by* causing us to have certain desires and beliefs. It makes no difference for our purposes whether this is so or whether, having caused our desires and beliefs, the device must then do something further to cause our decisions: it does *whatever* is necessary to cause our decisions.) But if the Paradigm Case Argument were valid, then it would follow that (M) was compatible with free will. If (M) were true, the world would look the way it in fact looks, and our linguistic practices would be the same—or, at least, we should emit the same sounds in the same situations, and our production of these sounds and their reception by our audience would be accompanied by the same internal sensations.

If the Paradigm Case Argument is valid, only such superficial features of people and their acts as these can be relevant to determining whether to apply the term 'free': one must be able *effectively* to compare some present act in which one is interested with the paradigms of free action that one remembers in order to see whether the present act is sufficiently similar to the remembered paradigms to be correctly called 'free'. And, obviously, one could never make an effective comparison of the present act with the paradigm if the relevant features of the paradigm were unobservable. Thus, if the Paradigm Case Argument were correct, the extension of the term 'free' could be just what it in fact is even if (M) were true, since (M) does not require any observable features of the world to be different from what they are in actuality. But (M) obviously *does* entail that no one can act otherwise than he does. If we should discover that some particular person— Himmler, say—acted as he did because a Martian device, implanted in his brain at the moment of his birth, had caused all his decisions, then we should hardly want to say that Himmler had free will, that he could have helped what he did, that he had any choice about the way he acted, or that he ever could have done otherwise. And I don't see why matters should be different if we discovered that *everyone* was "directed" by a Martian device: then we should have to make these judgements about everyone.[4]

If the proponent of the Paradigm Case Argument is to meet this objection, then, it seems to me, he must show that there is some difference between (M) and determinism that he can exploit in constructing an improved version of his argument. That is, he must delimit some class of propositions C having the following features: (i) determinism belongs to C and (M) does not, and (ii) propositions belonging to C can validly be shown to be compatible with free will by some style of argument that is recognizable as an appeal to paradigm cases, and propositions not belonging to C cannot be shown to be compatible with free will by this style of argument.

I do not think this can be done. There are, of course, all sorts of important differences between determinism and (M). (M) entails that each human being's dispositions to act are chosen for him by a non-human intelligence, and determinism does not. (M) entails that each human being's acts have among their immediate causes an object which, though it is inside that person's skull, is not a natural part of him, and determinism does not entail this. These are indeed differences between (M) and determinism that are of the highest importance: they are what makes it *evident* that (M) is incompatible with free will, while the incompatibility of determinism with free will is a matter of debate. What is hard to see is the relevance of these incontestably important facts to the Paradigm Case Argument. Indeed, it is hard to see how, if the Paradigm Case Argument is correct, *any* features of a given proposition could be relevant to the question whether that proposition is compatible with free will, other than those of its features that would make a difference in how things *appear* to us. But there just obviously *are* other features of a proposition than these that are relevant to whether that proposition is compatible with free will, or, indeed, compatible with any given proposition. It is possible to exploit this fact to construct propositions, which, while they are consistent with all of our observations, are inconsistent with the thesis that we have free will. This is how we constructed (M). The fact that we can construct such propositions shows that it is at least *possible* that certain propositions that we know of but have not ourselves constructed are also consistent with our observations but inconsistent with the free-will thesis. Perhaps determinism is such a proposition.

There seems to be no reason to think this implausible. Determinism is a very general thesis, and it essentially involves concepts (like 'law of nature') that are intimately connected with the concept of ability (since no one is able to change the laws of nature). Mightn't it simply *turn out* that determinism and free will are incompatible? How can we be sure that this isn't what careful investigation will show? I believe that this is what careful investigation *has* shown.

There are certain arguments for the compatibility of free will and determinism that are sufficiently similar to the Paradigm Case Argument that they too can be seen to be invalid by reflection on their implications for the relation between free will and propositions like (M). That is, reasoning very much like the above reasoning can be used to show that if these arguments succeeded in establishing that free will was compatible with determinism, then similar arguments would succeed in establishing the absurd conclusion that free will was compatible with (M).

Consider, for example, the following argument:

> Our everyday ascriptions of the ability to act otherwise make no reference to determinism. That is, we do not find out whether an agent's act was undetermined by past events in order to find out whether he could have acted otherwise. Therefore, the thesis normally expressed by 'he could have acted otherwise' does not entail the falsity of determinism.

I am chagrined to report that I am unable to find a clear example of this argument in print. But I have heard it many times in conversation and read it many times in correspondence. I believe, therefore, that I am justified in devoting a bit of space to it. It is not absolutely clear to me how this argument is supposed to work, but the most obvious way to read it is as an application of the rule of Universal Instantiation to the following premiss:

> The thesis normally expressed by 'he could have acted otherwise' does not entail the falsity of any general thesis to which our everyday ascriptions of the ability to act otherwise make no reference.

This principle is false. It suffices to point out that either Goldbach's Conjecture or its denial is a counter-example to it, but such counter-examples could be evaded by replacing this principle with one that refers only to contingent truths (though

I would point out that some philosophers have believed that determinism is a necessary truth) or by restricting it in some other way. It would be less easy to restrict the principle so that (M) is not a counter-example to it—which it is—but no doubt this could be done. I feel reasonably confident, however, that for any revision of the principle, I can find a counter-example to the revised principle that can be seen to be a counter-example independently of the question whether 'he could have done otherwise' is compatible with determinism. Or, at least, I feel confident of my ability to do this up to the point at which the class of general theses to which the revised principle is supposed to apply has been so restricted that the principle has become no more than a shamelessly transparent statement of compatibilism. However this may be, the argument in its *present* form is obviously invalid, since, if it were valid, an almost exactly similar argument could be used to show something false: that (M) is compatible with free will.

A second argument that can be seen to be invalid owing to the fact that its validity would entail the compatibility of (M) and free will is due to Keith Lehrer.[5] Lehrer points out that it would be easy to collect evidence on which the hypothesis that a certain agent could have acted otherwise is *highly probable*. This evidence might, for example, consist of a large body of propositions each asserting that in very similar circumstances in the past, the agent *has* acted otherwise than he did upon this particular occasion. It is this sort of evidence, after all, upon which everyone, compatibilist or incompatibilist, *does* base his judgements about people's abilities to act otherwise. But such evidence as this clearly does not render *indeterminism* highly probable. It would be absurd to argue like this: "In similar circumstances, Tom has often acted otherwise than he did upon this particular occasion, and it is therefore highly probable that determinism is false". Now consider the following theorem of the calculus of probabilities:

If H_1 is highly probable on e and H_2 is not highly probable on e, then H_1 does not entail H_2.

It follows from this theorem and what we have established above that free will does not entail indeterminism; that is, that free will and determinism are compatible.

However plausible or implausible this argument may seem at first, it is exactly as plausible as the argument that can be got by substituting '(M)' for 'determinism' in it. And that argument has an obviously false conclusion.[6]

The general lesson of the present section is this. There *are* theses that are incompatible with free will. The philosopher who attempts to show that free will and determinism are compatible should make sure that his arguments cannot be used to "show" that some thesis that is just obviously incompatible with free will is compatible with it.

4.3 In this section, I shall examine an argument for the compatibility of free will and determinism that is accepted, in one form or another, by the great majority of the present-day defenders of compatibilism. This argument rests on a theory about the meaning of ascriptions of ability. According to proponents of this theory, which I shall call *conditionalism*, ascriptions of ability are really disguised conditionals. For example, according to one version of conditionalism, what the proposition

Smith could have saved the drowning child

"really means" is

If Smith had chosen to save the drowning child, Smith would have saved the drowning child.

(If this contention is correct, then the proposition that Smith could have saved the drowning child but did not is obviously no more incompatible with determinism than is the proposition that this sugar cube would dissolve if, contrary to fact, it were placed in water.)

Conditionalism comes in a great many varieties. In one rather primitive variety, it entails that 'Smith could have saved the drowning child' means

If Smith had chosen to save the drowning child, Smith could have saved the drowning child.

This version of conditionalism, however, faces a great many difficulties that I do not propose to enumerate.[7] The only interesting varieties of conditionalism, I think, are the "would have" varieties.

One point on which conditionalists differ is that of the proper content for the antecedents of their conditionals. Where one conditionalist will say, "If Smith had chosen . . .", others will say, ". . . had willed . . .", ". . . had decided . . .", ". . . had set himself . . .", or ". . . had tried . . .". I shall discuss only certain "had chosen" and "had wanted" versions of conditionalism explicitly. But what I say will apply *mutatis mutandis* to versions involving other verbs.

If an adequate conditional analysis of ascriptions of ability is possible, it will assign at least some of them conditional paraphrases of rather more complicated forms than the form exemplified by the above paraphrase of the "drowning child" proposition. For example, it could hardly be true that

> Napoleon could have won at Waterloo

really means

> If Napoleon had chosen to win at Waterloo, Napoleon would have won at Waterloo!

I shall, however, confine my discussion to questions about our abilities to perform acts that do not involve the execution of elaborate plans or demand special knowledge or skill. Thus I can concentrate on situations in which relatively simple conditional analyses are adequate if *any* conditional analyses are.

Even in these simple cases, however, it is doubtful whether any *very* simple conditional analysis of ability is correct. R. M. Chisholm has called our attention to a fundamental difficulty facing conditionalism.[8] An example of Keith Lehrer's nicely illustrates this difficulty.[9] Consider the proposition:

> Smith could have eaten one of the red candies.

This proposition is not equivalent to

> If Smith had chosen to eat one of the red candies, then Smith would have eaten one of the red candies.

For suppose that Smith is pathologically afraid of the sight of blood, and that the candies are the colour of blood. Then it may well be that Smith was unable to *choose* to eat one of the red candies. And, in that case, he could not have eaten one of the red candies. Nevertheless, we may suppose, if he *had* chosen to eat one of the candies, he would have.

A natural reaction to this example would be to add the clause

> . . . *and* Smith could have chosen to eat one of the red candies

to the conditional proposition. But what does this second 'could have' mean? Either it means the same as the 'could have' in 'Smith could have eaten one of the red candies' or it means something else. If it means the same, the emended definition will be of no help to us, since the question we are considering is a question about the relation between 'could have' statements and determinism. Moreover, if the second 'could have' means the same as the first, and if the expanded conditional proposition really is equivalent to the proposition that Smith could have eaten one of the red candies, then the latter is equivalent to the proposition

> If Smith had chosen to eat one of the red candies, then Smith would have eaten one of the red candies, and if Smith had chosen to choose to eat one of the red candies, then Smith would have chosen to eat one of the red candies, and Smith could have chosen to choose to eat one of the red candies.

Not only does the monstrous sentence I have just written out contain an unreduced 'could have' like its "predecessor" and like all its ever more monstrous successors, but it contains the mysterious clause 'if Smith had chosen to choose to eat one of the red candies'. But what is it to choose to choose something? One can, of course, choose to choose *between* two or more things: in choosing to drink wine, I may in effect be choosing to choose between drinking claret and drinking burgundy. But that is not to choose to choose *something*; what would count as a case of choosing to choose claret? Nothing that I can see. I think we must abandon the hypothesis that the second 'could have' means the same as the original, for this hypothesis has led us into incoherency.

But if the second 'could have' is not the 'could have' of power or ability, just what is it? Let us use 'COULD HAVE' to denote the required "new" sense of 'could have', and use 'could have' only in its power-or-ability sense. The conditional analysis may now be written:

> x could have done $y =_{df}$ if x had chosen to do y, x would have done y, and x COULD HAVE chosen to do y.[10]

Whatever 'COULD HAVE' may mean exactly, there would seem to be a condition that must be met by any adequate account of its meaning: 'x COULD HAVE chosen to do y' must entail 'x could have chosen to do y'. If this condition is not met, then it will be easy enough to produce a Chisholm-style counter-example to this definition. Here is the recipe. Simply pick one of those logically possible cases in which someone COULD HAVE chosen to do something, but could not have chosen to do it (and, of course, construct the example in such a way that his choice would have been effective). This will be a case in which our imaginary person could not have performed a certain act, though, according to the proposed definition, he could have. I do not myself see any way to define 'COULD HAVE' that will meet this condition. Moreover if I knew how to do this—if I knew how to give 'COULD HAVE' a sense such that 'COULD HAVE chosen' entails 'could have chosen'—it seems likely that I should be able to give 'COULD HAVE' a sense such that 'COULD HAVE' *tout court* entails 'could have' *tout court*. And if I could do *that*, then why should I not be able to apply this insight "directly", that is, without making any use of the conditional that is the first conjunct of the *definiens* of the conditional analysis?

There is a way for the conditionalist to avoid all these difficult problems. An act of choice is, of course, an act,[11] and we may therefore raise the question whether its agent could have refrained from performing it, thus precipitating the unhappy infinite regress whose consequences we have been exploring in the preceding paragraphs. But suppose a conditionalist were to offer an analysis of 'could have' of this form:

> x could have done $y =_{df}$ if Rxy, then x would have done y, and A,

where 'Rxy' represents some condition on x and y such that it is possible that this condition hold without x's *doing* anything antecedent to his doing y. The second conjunct of the *definiens*—represented in this schema by 'A'—may be any sort of qualification. If the antecedent of the first conjunct of our *definiens* can be true even if x *does* nothing, then we shall not be able to raise Chisholm-style objections to this definition. One very simple *definiens* of this type is

> if x had wanted to do y (more than anything else), then x would have done y.

Wanting to perform an act (unlike choosing to perform an act) is not itself an act. Therefore, if someone says, for example, "If he had wanted to eat a red candy, then he would have eaten one", we may not say in response, "Yes, but could he have wanted a red candy?" Or, more precisely, we could so respond, but our words would have to mean something like "was it possible—in some unspecified sense of 'possible'—in that situation that he should have wanted a red candy?" If it was not possible that he should have wanted to eat a red candy, this does not seem to imply what 'it was not within his power to choose to eat a red candy' *does* seem to imply: that it was not within his power to eat a red candy. Suppose, for example, that Jones has been given a drug that makes one indifferent to food of any sort—not revolted by the thought of food, but simply wholly indifferent to eating. It seems to be correct to say (in *some* sense of 'possible') that it was not possible that, in that situation, Jones should have wanted to eat a red candy. Yet it does not seem to follow that Jones could not have eaten one, that it was not within his power to eat one. After all, people sometimes do what they have no particular desire to do.

But if the *definiens* we are considering is immune to Chisholm-style counter-examples, it nevertheless faces problems that are not entirely dissimilar to the problems that such counter-examples created for the "choice" version of conditionalism. Let us look once more at the "red candy" case. Note that Smith—the man who has a pathological aversion to the colour of blood, and, *per accidens*, to the colour of the candies—doesn't *want* to eat a red candy. The very sight of them, we may suppose, makes him uneasy: he feels a strong temptation to cover the dish of candies with a napkin. Now suppose he did want to eat one of the candies. Presumably he would. But also, presumably, he would not be afflicted with his curious neurosis, a neurosis which, in actuality, renders him unable to eat one of the candies. So it would seem that both the propositions

If Smith had wanted to eat a red candy, he would have

and

Smith could not have eaten a red candy

are true. Therefore, the analysis we are considering fails. The general lesson is that if a certain agent had had desires he did not in fact have, then his powers to act might also have been different, a possibility that vitiates the analysis we are considering. Here is a simpler case. Smith, considerably shaken by his experience with the candies, wanders out into traffic, is struck by a bus, and is taken to a hospital in a deep coma from which he never emerges. Consider poor Smith, comatose in his hospital bed. The two propositions

Smith cannot get out of bed

If Smith wanted to get out of bed, he would

would seem both to be true, the former because he is in a coma, and the latter because, if he *did* want to get out of bed he wouldn't be in a coma.[12] (We must also suppose, of course, that nothing keeps him from getting out of bed but unconsciousness, a state which his wanting *anything* would suffice for the absence of.)

This sort of example does not show that the sort of analysis we are considering is hopeless, but only that its *definiens* must contain some qualification, some further condition to be inserted in the space occupied by 'A' in the abstract schema above.

What should this qualification be? The best answer to this question I can think of is suggested by an analysis of 'could have' devised by Keith Lehrer.[13] If we incorporate Lehrer's idea into the analysis we are considering, we obtain:

x could have done $y =_{\mathrm{df}}$ if x had wanted to do y, x would have done y and it is false that if x had wanted to do y, *x* would have possessed some advantage with respect to doing *y* that *x* did not actually possess.[14]

This analysis does not have the consequence that Smith (our neurotic) could have eaten a red candy. For, though it is true that Smith would have eaten a red candy if he had wanted to, it is also true that if he had wanted to eat a red candy, he would have possessed an advantage with respect to eating a red candy that he did not in fact possess: freedom from his peculiar neurosis. Similarly, if Smith had wanted to get out of his hospital bed, he would have possessed an advantage with respect to getting out of bed that he did not in fact possess: consciousness.

But this analysis rules out obvious cases of ability. If I wanted to fly to Washington, I should (come to) possess a certain advantage with respect to flying to Washington: a reserved seat on a Washington-bound flight; and this advantage is one I do not actually possess. But this fact obviously does not entail that I could not fly to Washington. I am not sure how the above *definiens* ought to be rewritten to avoid this difficulty. I tentatively suggest this:

> if *x* had wanted to do *y*, *x* would have done *y* and *x*'s wanting to do *y* would not have been sufficient (in the "broadly logical" sense) for *x*'s possessing an advantage with respect to doing *y* that *x* did not actually possess.

If I wanted to fly to Washington this would perhaps be *causally* sufficient for my acquiring a reserved seat on a flight to Washington, but it would not have been logically sufficient. But if Smith had wanted to get out of bed, this would have been *logically* sufficient, in the broad sense, for his being conscious. It is not so clear whether Smith's wanting to eat a red candy would be logically sufficient for the removal or non-existence of his pathological aversion to red things, but let us suppose this is so. Better, let us suppose that we have found some sense of sufficiency—certainly stronger than causal sufficiency, possibly weaker than broadly logical sufficiency—that is "best" for our present purposes, that either makes our definition extensionally adequate or at least comes as close to satisfying this requirement as possible. Better still, let us suppose we have found the *best possible* conditional analysis of ability, or one of them if there is a tie: let us suppose we have found an extensionally adequate analysis if any such exists, or, if none exists, have found one that can't be improved by tinkering or by the addition of further clauses and is not markedly farther from extensional adequacy than any fundamentally different analysis. Call it the Analysis. The Analysis is right if any conditional analysis is right, and wrong only if no conditional analysis is right.

What does the Analysis do for us? How does it affect our understanding of the Compatibility Problem? It does very little for us, so far as I can see, unless we have some reason to think it is *correct*. Many compatibilists seem to think that they need only present a conditional analysis of ability, defend it against, or modify it in the face of, such counter-examples as may arise, and that they have thereby done what is necessary to defend compatibilism.

That is not how I see it. The particular analysis of ability that a compatibilist presents is, as I see it, simply one of his premisses; his central premiss, in fact.[15] And premisses need to be defended. I see no particular reason to think that statements of ability can be analysed as conditionals, much less that any particular conditional analysis of such statements is correct. Moreover, I see what seems to me to be a good reason to think that no conditional analysis is correct—or, at least, that no conditional analysis that supports compatibilism is correct. If any conditional analysis is correct then *ex hypothesi* the Analysis is. Let us consider the Analysis in relation to any of the arguments for incompatibilism that were presented in Chapter III. For the sake of concreteness, let us consider the First Argument. The First Formal Argument is valid. Therefore, if the Analysis is correct, at least one of the premisses of the First Formal Argument is false. (I *assume* this conditional is true. If it isn't, of course, then free will and determinism are incompatible *even if* the Analysis is correct.[16]) Conversely, if all the premisses of the First Formal Argument are true, the Analysis is incorrect. Therefore, since I have presented arguments for each of the premisses of the First Formal Argument—arguments that do not in any clear sense presuppose that statements of ability are not disguised conditionals—I have in effect presented an argument for the conclusion that the Analysis fails.[17]

Now if we had at our disposal some argument for the thesis that the Analysis was correct, we could compare this argument with my arguments for the premisses of the First Formal Argument and try to determine which side had the stronger case. But, unless there is something I'm missing in the many "conditional" defences of compatibilism to be found in the philosophical literature, no argument has ever been given in defence of the thesis that statements ascribing to an agent the power to act can be correctly analysed as conditionals. It's not that this thesis seems *inherently* implausible to me. If I consider it in isolation from the Compatibility Problem, I feel no inclination either to accept or to reject it. But when I consider the fact that it is incompatible with certain propositions—the premisses of the First Formal Argument, for example—that seem to me to be highly plausible right at the outset, then, of course, I feel very strongly inclined to reject it indeed.

These considerations are very abstract. They can be presented in a form that is more concrete. It is possible to show exactly where the Analysis comes into conflict with our incompatibilist arguments, to show just which premiss of each of the arguments must be false if the Analysis is true. And if we have located the premiss of any of these arguments that, from the compatibilist's point of view, is the crucial premiss, then we may compare that premiss and the Analysis and see which seems to be the more plausible. (Of course we don't really know what the Analysis is. Nevertheless, we know various things about it. I shall try to show that we know enough.)

It will be most convenient to apply this strategy to the Third Argument. I said in Chapter III that the crucial premiss, the premiss most in need of support, of the Third Argument was the validity of Rule (β). It therefore seems likely that if the Analysis is correct, Rule (β) is invalid. This speculation can be shown to be correct.[18] Or, at any rate, it can be shown that Rule (β) is incompatible with the conditional analyses we have actually stated, and it therefore seems likely that if the Analysis—whatever precisely it may be—is incompatible with any of the premisses of the Third Argument, it is incompatible with the validity of (β). If the Analysis is incompatible with no premisses of the Third Argument, then incompatibilism is true even if the Analysis is correct. And it is highly implausible to suppose that, whereas simpler conditional analyses of ability are incompatible with the validity of (β) and apparently compatible with the other premises of the Third Argument, the Analysis is compatible with (β) but incompatible with some other premise.

I will content myself with showing that the simplest analysis we have considered entails the invalidity of (β). I leave it as an exercise for the reader to show that the several more complex revisions of this simple analysis that we have considered also have this consequence.

Rule (β), it will be remembered, is this: $Np, N(p \supset q) \vdash Nq$, where '$Np$' abbreviates '$p$ and no one has, or ever had, any choice about whether p'. If our first conditional analysis of ability is correct, then 'Np' is equivalent to something like the following:

> p and, for every agent x, it is not the case that if x had ever chosen (or were ever to choose) to make it false that p, then x would have made (or would make) it false that p.

Let us suppose that this equivalence holds. Now consider the following instance of (β):

> N It is psychologically impossible for Smith to choose to eat a red candy;
>
> N (It is psychologically impossible for Smith to choose to eat a red candy $\supset$ Smith does not eat a red candy);
>
> *hence*, N Smith does not eat a red candy.

We may easily imagine the premises of this argument to be true and its conclusion false. Let us take our story of the neurotic Smith and add to it the following conditions. Suppose, just to simplify the example, that Smith is the only person. Suppose that if Smith were to choose to make it false that it was psychologically impossible for him to choose to eat a red candy, he would fail. Then the first premise of our argument is true. Moreover, let us suppose that something renders it impossible for Smith to eat a red candy without choosing to —perhaps a mechanism outside his control snatches the candies away if he *inadvertently* reaches for one, or something of that sort. Then, since no one does by choice what it is psychologically impossible for him to choose to do, the second premiss is true. Suppose that *if—per impossibile psychologicale* —Smith were to choose to eat a red candy, then he *would* eat a red candy. Then the conclusion is false. Since these suppositions seem consistent, we have devised a counter-example to Rule (β) that holds provided that 'Np' is interpreted according to the terms of the first conditional analysis. So much the worse for the first conditional analysis, *I* say. The thesis that Rule (β) is valid seems to me to be obviously true and the first conditional analysis does not seem to me to be obviously true. If two propositions are incompatible and one seems obviously true, then, as I said in Chapter III, if one must choose one should accept the proposition that seems obviously true.

We have been talking about the first conditional analysis, which is known to be defective on other grounds than its incompatibility with Rule (β). What about the Analysis itself? Well, as I have argued, it is certainly reasonable to believe that the Analysis is incompatible with the validity of (β). (And if it's not, the compatibilist is in deep trouble: if it's not, then either the Analysis is incompatible with some premiss of the Third Argument that is even *more* evidently true than the proposition that (β) is valid, or else the Third Argument is sound even if the Analysis is correct.) Which is it more reasonable to believe: that Rule (β) is valid or that the Analysis is correct? I believe I know enough about the Analysis to answer this question with some confidence. The Analysis, whatever its exact content may be, will almost certainly look something like the analysis in terms of "advantage" that we examined earlier in the present section. Even if it does not make use of the same "idea", it will at least be of a comparable level of complexity. When I look at philosophical analyses that are that complex, then, unless I have been shown some convincing argument for their correctness, I simply have no idea whether they are correct. My reaction to them could be expressed in these words: "Well, that *might* be right. I don't know. Why do you think it's right?" Rule (β), on the other hand, appeals immediately to the reflective intellect; like *Modus Tollens*, it can be easily grasped by the mind and *seen* to be true. But the mind is no more capable of grasping analyses of *can* that are of the order of complexity of the "advantage" analysis than it is capable of grasping the average candidate for the "fourth condition" of knowledge. One cannot—I cannot, at any rate—see them steadily and see them whole. Therefore, in making a choice between Rule (β) and the Analysis, I feel no qualms of conscience about applying the epistemic rule-of-thumb that was introduced in Section 3.10: Rule (β) seems obviously correct; the Analysis, owing to its extreme complexity if to nothing else, does not seem obviously correct; therefore, I accept Rule (β) and reject the Analysis. And for this reason I reject the Conditional Analysis Argument.

If someone produced a convincing counter-example to (β), this would vitiate my argument. If someone produced a plausible argument for the conclusion that (β) is invalid, this would vitiate my argument. If someone produced a simple, easily graspable conditional analysis of ability, and if this analysis seemed right and if there were no known counter-examples to it, this would vitiate my argument. If someone produced a plausible argument for the correctness of some conditional analysis—however complex that analysis might be—this would vitiate my argument. But none of these things has ever been produced and I do not think that any of them is ever going to be produced. I conclude that since Rule (β) is more plausible than the Analysis and, *a fortiori*, more plausible than any other conditional analysis of ability, the Conditional Analysis Argument fails.

I gather that most compatibilists think that compatibilism is an inherently plausible thesis and that incompatibilism is inherently implausible. If someone thinks this, perhaps he will regard the argument

Compatibilism is true

hence, (β) is invalid

as a "plausible argument for the conclusion that (β) is invalid". As I said in Section 3.10, I am willing to grant that this argument is valid. But why should anyone find compatibilism inherently plausible? I think there is only one possible answer to this question: because (a) the thesis that we have free will is inherently plausible, and (b) because, many philosophers think, it is inherently *implausible* to suppose that a free act involves some causally undetermined event. Why do they think this? What is implausible about it? These questions are most conveniently discussed in connection with the *Mind* Argument.

4.4 The *Mind* Argument occurs in three forms. Or, at any rate, there are three closely related strands of argument that are often twisted together and which it is important to separate. These three "forms" or "strands" have a common beginning in a certain set of reflections on what the nature of free action must be if the incompatibilist is right. I shall now set forth this common beginning. Until further notice, I shall speak *in persona compatibilistae*.

Incompatibilists maintain that free will requires indeterminism. But it should be clear even to them that not just any sort of indeterminism will do. Suppose, for example, that there is exactly one undetermined particle of matter somewhere in the universe, and that it is far from any rational agent, the rest of the universe being governed entirely by strict, deterministic laws. In that case, determinism is, strictly speaking, false. But, clearly, if determinism is incompatible with free will, so is the thesis that everything except one distant particle of matter is determined. Suppose now we assume that there are *many* undetermined particles of matter, some of them very near us. In fact, let us suppose that at every moment many undetermined events take place inside each human body. But let us also suppose that these undetermined events play no role in shaping or influencing anyone's acts. Just as clearly, if determinism is incompatible with free will, then so is the state of affairs we are imagining. If the question whether there are any undetermined events is relevant to the question whether we have free will, this can only be because the question whether there are undetermined events *that shape or influence our acts* is relevant to the question whether we have free will. Therefore, the incompatibilist must believe not only that free will entails that there are undetermined events; he must believe that free will entails that there are undetermined events that shape our behaviour. And not just any such event will do for his purposes. Among the events that have shaped my behaviour are certain events that I witnessed or experienced between the ages of, say, one and twelve, events that were central to my moral education and to the formation of my character. Suppose that these events were somehow undetermined, but that all subsequent events that made up my history were determined—or at least were determined given these earlier undetermined events. This state of affairs, too, is incompatible with my having free will, provided determinism *simpliciter* is.

It should be evident by now that there is only one point in the history of each of my acts at which the positing of an undetermined event *could* be conceptually relevant to the question whether that act was a free act: the point at which the act *itself* (or the deliberation that immediately preceded it) occurred. For if my acts and decisions and deliberations are themselves determined by earlier events or states of affairs, then these earlier states of affairs are outside my control at the time at which I must act or decide or deliberate. They are outside my control because they are in the past.

The arguments of Chapter III exploit the fact that if determinism is true, then one's acts are determined by states of affairs that obtained before one was born. Whatever dialectical advantage an appeal to this fact may win the incompatibilist, however, it has no more logical or philosophical significance than has an appeal to the fact that if determinism is true, then one's acts are determined simply by *past* events. As Agathon observed, not even the gods can change the past, and this is no *more* true of the events of a thousand years ago than it is of the events of one second ago. Therefore, if a man's acts were determined by events that occurred earlier than those acts—by *however* short an interval—then one could show that his acts were unfree using arguments essentially similar to the arguments of Chapter III. Therefore, if the incompatibilist is right, a free act must be an undetermined act, or, at least, the immediate result of undetermined deliberations.

But now let us see what an undetermined act would really be like. Let us consider the case of a hardened thief who, as our story begins, is in the act of lifting the lid of the poor-box in a little country church.[19] He sneers and curses when he sees what a pathetically small sum it contains. Still, business is business: he reaches for the money. Suddenly there flashes before his mind's eye a picture of the face of his dying mother and he remembers the promise he made to her by her death-bed always to be honest and upright. This is not the first oc-casion on which he has had such a vision while performing some mean act of theft, but he has always disregarded it. This time, however, he does *not* disregard it. Instead, he thinks the matter over carefully and decides not to take the money. Acting on this decision, he leaves the church empty-handed.

We may suppose that this decision was undetermined. That is, we may assume that there are possible worlds in which things were absolutely identical in every respect with the way they were in the actual world up to the moment at which our repentant thief made his decision—worlds in which, moreover, the laws of nature are just what they are in the actual world—and in which he takes the money.

According to the incompatibilist, this indetermination is necessary for the thief's act of repentance to have been a free act. But if we look carefully at the idea of an undetermined act, we shall see that such an act could not be a free act.

(I now revert briefly to speaking *in propria persona*. It is this argument about what the incompatibilist's account of free action is committed to that the three strands of the *Mind* Argu-ment have as their common beginning. I have no wish to dis-pute the premises of this common beginning or to question its validity. I shall now let the compatibilist set forth the three strands separately. I shall reply to them in turn.)

(i) If the incompatibilist's account of free action is correct, then a free act is an act that is undetermined by prior states of affairs. But an act that is undetermined is a mere *random* or *chance* occurrence, and a random or chance occurrence is hardly the kind of thing that could be called a free act.

Reply: The doubtful premise in this argument is the assertion that if our acts are undetermined they are mere "random" or "chance" events. What does this mean? The words 'random' and 'chance' most naturally apply to *patterns* or *sequences* of events. (If the argument is that if our acts were undetermined they would issue from us in a meaningless and incoherent jumble, as if we were perpetually deciding what to do by consulting a table of random numbers, there seems to be no

reason whatever to believe this. There are computers that
sometimes change state in ways that are not determined by
their earlier states and their input, but their output is not
random in the way in which a table of random numbers is
random.) It is not clear what 'random' and 'chance' mean
when they are applied to single events. These words *might*
simply mean 'undetermined'; but in that case we should have
no argument but only an assertion that undetermined events
are not the sort of thing that can be called free acts. A more
interesting possibility is that, in this strand of the *Mind* Argument, 'chance' and 'random' are being used, properly or not, to
mean 'uncaused'. But, as we shall discover when we discuss the
second strand, an undetermined act need *not* be an uncaused
act. Therefore, if 'random' and 'chance' mean 'uncaused' the
first strand is invalid. I know of no other things that 'random'
or 'chance' might mean,[20] and I therefore conclude that the
first strand fails to disprove incompatibilism. Let us turn to
the second strand.

(ii) If an act, or what *looks* superficially like an act, is not
determined to occur by prior states of affairs, then it is not
really an act at all. (It should be clear that something can look
like an act and yet not be an act. If a clever brain-physiologist
stimulated the motor centres of your brain in the right way,
then he might make it look as if you had raised your hand
when you had not.) This is because, whatever else an act may
be, it is a production of its agent. But if an "act" is undetermined, it is not a production of its putative agent and hence
not really his act at all. Let us consider our thief who refrained
—or so we should say if we went by outward appearances—
from robbing the poor-box. His refraining, or the event that
we should initially be inclined to call his refraining, was *ex
hypothesi* undetermined. Let us examine this event carefully.
We shall assume that some version or other of the mind-body
identity theory is true, but this assumption will be only an
aid to our intuition, and not a premiss of our argument: it is
easier to visualize changes in a material substance than changes
in a spiritual substance, but the point of our argument would
remain if it were restated on the assumption that, for example,
Cartesian Dualism provided the correct description of our

nature. On the assumption of psycho-physical identity, the thief's act of refraining was identical with a certain event in his brain. Now suppose that some event in your brain is identical with one of your acts. And suppose that this event was undetermined by earlier events in your brain. Let us call this undetermined event E. There would seem to be no reason to suppose that E or any other undetermined event is *essentially* undetermined. Suppose, for example, that a cup sitting untouched on a table suddenly breaks at t and that this event—the cup's breaking at t—is undetermined by earlier states of affairs. It would seem that it *might* have been determined by earlier states of affairs: a hammer might have struck the cup at just the proper moment that its breaking at t should have been causally determined by this blow. (Some philosophers might want to raise the question whether the event that would have occurred in such a case was numerically the same as the event that in fact happened,[21] but we need not consider this question. It will do for our purposes to note that if an undetermined event happens, it is logically possible for a *descriptively* identical determined event to have happened at the same moment.) Let us suppose that this had happened in the case of E: suppose that an event just like E and having the same consequences had happened—it may have been E itself or some other event—and that it was determined. Let us suppose that it was determined by the action of some supernatural power: a freakish demon caused it.[22] The sequence of events is this: the freakish demon performs some supernatural act such that it is causally impossible for this act to be performed and E— or an event just like E—not to occur; E is identical with the event we also call 'the thief's deliberations', under which description we include the outcome of these deliberations; this outcome then determines that the thief shall refrain from robbing the poor-box and shall depart.

Or we may describe the case as follows. In the "actual" case the thief's deliberations take a certain course that results in his refraining from stealing. These deliberations are identical with a certain rather protracted event in the thief's brain. If his act is free, and if incompatibilism is true, then this protracted brain-event is undetermined. We then imagine something that *might have* happened: a freakish demon might have done something that rendered it causally impossible for this in fact undetermined event not to occur.

Suppose the demon *had* done this. Then the thief would not really have *acted* at all, because he would not have been the *producer* of the event in his brain that initiated the bodily motions characteristic of a man leaving a poor-box empty-handed. The case is really no different from the case of the man whose brain has been "wired" by a brain-physiologist and whose arm rises whenever the physiologist presses a certain button. That man does not *raise* his arm when the physiologist presses the button; rather, his arm *rises* as a consequence of what the physiologist does.

The thief, therefore, if his (supposed) act is caused by the freakish demon, does *not* act. Now let us restore the "actual" situation: we remove from our imagined case the demon and his works, leaving an uncaused event and its consequences. Does this somehow change the "demon" story to a story in which the thief *does* act? How could that be? If a certain change in one's body is determined to occur by events that were produced at the pleasure of some rational being other than oneself, this shows that neither this change nor its consequences could be, or be a part or component of, one's act. But it shows this only by bringing into prominence the fact that the determinants of the change are not to be found within *oneself*. Now if an event is *undetermined*, then it is just as true that the determinants of that event are not to be found within oneself as it would be if these determinants were to be found in the capricious acts of a demon, for if the determinants of one's act are not to be found, then, *a fortiori*, they are not to be found within *one*. If we are asking whether a certain event is a production of *mine*, then we must admit that there is no *philosophical* difference between this event's being undetermined and its being determined by an external force, for each of these cases is quite simply a case of *interference* with my plans, desires, deliberations, and hopes. In the one case we have a causally explicable sort of interference. In both cases we have *some* sort of interference.

If this is not sufficiently obvious, perhaps we can make it so by elaborating the story of the freakish demon. Let us suppose he exercises his influence over the thief in this way: there is an invisible wire that passes through the thief's skull and into his brain (no hole is required, for the wire is made of the subtle matter that the Stoics postulated); at the other end of the wire is a sort of piano that is also made of subtle matter and upon the keyboard of which the demon plays; by what he plays, he can "direct", via the subtle wire, the motions of the atoms in the thief's brain and can thereby direct the thief's inner life, including his deliberations. And that is just what he has done in the case we have imagined: by striking the keys in a certain order, he has guided the thief's brain through just that sequence of states that correspond to the deliberations of a man who refrains from stealing. It is clear, in this case, that neither the thief's bodily motions nor the pseudo-deliberations that preceded them were things *he* produced: he was merely the demon's instrument and *acted* only in the etiolated sense in which a fiddle acts in the hands of a violinist or a scalpel acts in the hands of a surgeon.

Let us now gradually, very gradually, modify this case. Let us first suppose that the demon's actions at the keyboard are undetermined by the demon's own inner states and by any-thing else. This change in the case does not weaken the argu-ment for our earlier conclusion (that the thief did not act). Now let us remove the demon and suppose that the "sort of piano" we imagined the demon to be playing is a sort of *player* piano: let us imagine that the keyboard is worked by a mechanism internal to the piano; and let us suppose that this internal mechanism is an indeterministic one. This further change in the case does not weaken our argument for the con-clusion that the thief does not act. Now let us remove the piano and suppose that impulses simply *appear* in the subtle wire (which now protrudes from the thief's skull, its far end unattached to anything) undetermined by prior states of af-fairs. Again, this change does not weaken our argument for the conclusion that the thief did not act. Now let us imagine the wire becoming shorter and shorter till only the part inside the thief's skull remains. This change, too, does not weaken our argument: if impulses undetermined by past states of affairs appear in the wire and if these impulses determine the putative acts of the thief—determine what movements are made by his limbs and what thoughts pass through his mind—then these putative acts are not real acts, are not among the things he *does* or produces. Now let us suppose that the subtle wire is replaced by one of too, too solid flesh, by a "wire", or wire-shaped thing, made of brain cells. This change does not weaken our argument. What difference does it make *what* the wire that delivers undetermined impulses to the thief's brain is *made of*? The important thing is that the impulses of which it is the carrier should be undetermined by past states of affairs. Let us now make one final change: let us suppose that the wire-shaped thing made of brain cells is a *natural part* of the thief's brain.

Does this make a difference? It's hard to see why it should. Take any part of an agent's brain and replace it with an arti-ficially produced perfect duplicate; then, assuming the re-placed part of the brain was not something essential to the agent's *identity*, this would certainly not affect the agent's free will. If this is true, such a replacement performed "in reverse" should be equally irrelevant to the agent's free will. Our thief has a wire-shaped thing made of brain cells within his brain, in which there arise impulses, undetermined by past states of affairs, which determine his every action. If we now suppose that this thing is a *natural part* of the thief, we are making a supposition not about its momentary operations, but only about its origins. But only the present, momentary operations of the parts of one's brain should be relevant to the question whether one is *now* acting freely. Facts about the *origin* of a part of one's brain can be relevant to questions of free will only in so far as they are relevant to questions about the momentary operations of the part. Thus, to replace a part of one's brain with a perfect duplicate of different ori-gins can have no effect on one's free will—always assuming that the replacement leaves one's identity intact.

We have now got to the point of imagining our thief's "acts" being the result of undetermined impulses originating in a certain section of his brain. This section of his brain plays the same part in our final story that a freakish demon played in our original story. We moved from one point to the other by gradually modifying the freakish demon and his apparatus until we had turned them into a natural part of the thief's brain. Now in our original story, it was clear that the thief did not *act*. We have seen that none of our series of modifications introduced any "opportunity" for him to act. We must therefore conclude that in our *final* story the thief did not act. But our final story is just exactly the tale the incompatibilist tells when he is asked what goes on inside someone who acts freely. Therefore, the incompatibilist's story is incoherent.

All this window-dressing, of course, is not strictly necessary. Anyone whose "analytical imagination", as Hobart calls it, is in good working order can see right at the outset that a person whose "acts" are the consequences of undetermined events —whether these undetermined events occur within a natural part of him or not—is not really an agent at all. Such a person is not acting, but is merely being pushed about or interfered with. People whose analytical powers are modest, however, may find our technique of telling a sequence of stories, each of which is very slightly closer than its predecessor to the incompatibilist's story of the inner nature of a free act, a useful substitute for adequate analytical powers.

We have seen, therefore, that an act, and *a fortiori* a free act, cannot be an undetermined act, for an undetermined act is a contradiction in terms.

Reply. My analytical powers are apparently inadequate. The "longer story" helps me to see why someone would say that an apparent act that is undetermined is not really an act at all. This story is, of course, a "slippery-slope" argument. Such arguments are, to my mind, a useful but dangerous tool for philosophers. They are dangerous because, when they are moving briskly along, they acquire a kind of dialectical momentum that can carry the unwary audience smoothly over gaps in the argument.[23]

I think there is a gap in the argument. That is, I think there is a point at which the allegedly philosophically unimportant alteration that the proponent of the *Mind* Argument makes in his story *does* make a philosophical difference. At a certain point in the story, the reader will remember, the freakish demon and his keyboard of subtle matter have been reduced to a wire-shaped thing of brain-stuff. The next step is to suppose that this thing is a *natural part* of the thief. This next step is, in my view, the one that makes the difference. I do not, of course, say that an undetermined change in a natural part of a human being will *necessarily* have an action of that human being's among its consequences; I do say that it's not clear that it *couldn't*. If I am right in supposing this, then the *Mind* Argument—or the strand of it that we are currently investigating—errs in supposing that the step from "wire-shaped thing" to *"natural* wire-shaped thing" is an obviously harmless step. And therefore, if I am right, this strand of the *Mind* Argument does not succeed in showing that an undetermined act is a contradiction in terms.

I shall now attempt to show that it is not clear that an apparent act of a human being that was the consequence of an undetermined change in a natural part of a human being *could not* be a real act. I shall attempt to show this by constructing two "models" of human action according to which this *is* possible. Since neither of these models is known to be impossible or incoherent, it will follow that there may well be a gap in the apparently continuous progression of modifications of the "freakish demon" case that the *Mind* Argument presents us with. And if that is true, then the *Mind* Argument fails to establish its conclusion.

I shall not contend that either of the models is right. I do not know—except as we all know—what human action is. I shall not contend that either of these models entails that an undetermined *free* act is possible. (I shall presently discuss the question whether an undetermined *free* act is possible.) I shall show only that if either of these models is correct, then an undetermined *act* is possible.

The first model I shall mention only briefly, since so many philosophers are convinced of its incoherence—on what grounds, I am not clear—that it would be a tactical mistake for me to discuss it at length. The model I am alluding to is that of *immanent* or *agent* causation.

The medieval philosophers, like all theists, believed that God was the cause of all things other than himself. Unlike many theists, they—or most of them—believed that God was *changeless*. This raised a difficult philosophical problem, since the causes we observe in nature produce their effects only at the expense of some change in themselves. So far as I know, the Schoolmen never solved this problem, though they postulated a solution and gave this solution a label. They postulated a type of causation that does *not* involve a change in the cause and called it *immanent* causation. (Garden-variety causation they called *transeunt* causation.)

In our own time, this medieval idea has been revived by Roderick Chisholm and applied not to God but to the human agent.[24] More or less the same idea has been employed by Richard Taylor, who prefers the term "agent causation".[25] (Chisholm has lately come to prefer this second term himself.) According to Chisholm and Taylor, the *agent himself* is sometimes (when he acts freely) the cause of his own acts, or, perhaps, the cause of the bodily or mental changes that manifest them. This does not mean that a change in the agent causes these acts or changes; rather the agent *causes* without himself changing in any way. (Save accidentally. The human agent, unlike the God of the Philosophers, is not only mutable but is *constantly* undergoing change. But, according to the Chisholm-Taylor theory, none of these changes he undergoes is the cause of his free acts.)

Now let us ignore the contention that an immanently caused act would be a *free* act, which is not our present concern, and consider only the thesis that we are the immanent causes of at least some of our acts. If this thesis is true—and it is not my purpose here to argue that it is coherent, much less that it is true—then it is easy to see that an act can be an undetermined act. Let us return to the case of our thief. To say that it was not determined that he should refrain from stealing is to say this: there is a possible world that (a) is *exactly* like the actual world in every detail up to the moment at which the thief refrained from stealing, and (b) is governed by the same laws of nature as the actual world, and (c) is such that, in it, the thief robbed the poor-box.

It is plain that immanent causation allows for the possibility of such a world: its divergence from the actual world is possible because the immanent causation of an event does not imply that that event is determined by earlier states of affairs—if anything, the immanent causation of an event implies that that event is *not* determined by earlier states of affairs. Moreover, there is no basis for the caution implied by the use of phrases like 'what looks superficially like an act' or by writing

'act' inside scare-quotes. If the thief moves in a way typical
of a man who very nearly robs a poor-box but draws back from
doing so at the last moment, and if the same thoughts pass
through his mind that would typically pass through the mind
of a man who considers but refrains from robbing a poor-box,
and if these thoughts and movements are caused *by the agent
himself*, then it surely follows that if we say "He refrained
from robbing the poor-box", we are describing his *action* and
describing it in words that are literally correct.

Therefore, *if* immanent causation is a coherent concept,
the second strand of the *Mind* Argument fails to show that
the notion of an undetermined act is a contradiction in terms.
The proponent of the *Mind* Argument is likely to concede
this and to argue, or assert, that immanent causation is *not* a
coherent concept. I will not dispute this. I have mentioned
immanent causation because it is an idea that has won the
allegiance of highly respected philosophers and which is therefore worthy of the attention of anyone who is troubled by
the *Mind* Argument. I commend their writings to you. Let
us proceed to the second "model" of human action I have
promised.

Donald Davidson has proposed an account of human action
that is an elaboration—an elaboration constructed with great
sophistication and philosophical sensitivity—of the following
very simple idea: an act is *caused* by the very factors its agent
would adduce if asked to give his reason for performing it, to
wit, by the agent's desire that a certain state of affairs should
be realized and his belief that an act of that type was the best
—or, at least, an unsurpassed—means to realizing that state of
affairs.[26] Suppose, for example, that a certain man has raised
his hand; and suppose that, when he is asked why he raised
his hand, he says that he did this because he wanted to vote
for the measure before the meeting and believed that the way
to vote for this measure was to raise his hand. If what he says
about the reasons for his act is correct, then, according to
Davidson, the cause of his act is his desire to vote coupled
with his belief that he could realize his desire by raising his
hand.

Now this is a very sketchy and simple-minded account of
Davidson's theory. Indeed, if it were my purpose to criticize

Davidson, and if I directed my criticisms against the theory presented in the preceding paragraph, I should be guilty of criticizing a travesty. But I don't wish to criticize Davidson's account of action, but rather to draw upon it in constructing the "model" of human action I have promised. The simple-minded outline of Davidson's theory that I have presented will be useful as a first step in the construction of this model. It makes no difference, really, whether I have accurately represented Davidson, even within the broad limits of accuracy appropriate to a rough sketch. I have mentioned Davidson's name only because the model I am going to construct will immediately suggest his theory to anyone with the most superficial knowledge of the theory of action, and because I wish specifically to disclaim any intention of presenting an accurate introduction to his theory. Those who want accurate information about Davidson's views should seek it in his own writings. (Something that is well worth doing, by the way.)

We have before us now, whatever its origin may be, a theory about the causes of human action. Let us supplement this theory with a theory about causation itself. *This* theory is not even remotely inspired by Davidson; it is in fact the very antithesis of his theory of causation. Before presenting this theory, however, I wish to say a few words about the *standard* or *Humean* theory of causation, of which Davidson's theory is a version.

Many, perhaps most, philosophers believe that causes *determine* their effects. They believe, that is, that given the cause— we are talking once more about "normal" causation, a relation that takes *events* or *states of affairs* or some such, and not *persons*, as its terms—the effect *must* follow. (This 'must', of course, is the 'must' of physical, not logical, necessity.) They believe that if A is the cause of B, then, if A had happened and had *not* been followed by B, this could only have been because the laws of nature were different. Some of the philosophers I am alluding to think that laws of nature are merely exceptionless regularities; others think that only some exceptionless regularities are laws and differ as to what makes a regularity a law. These disputes are important, but they need not concern us at present. I shall count a philosopher a proponent of the standard or Humean view if he thinks that the effect is determined by the cause together with the laws of nature, however he may understand 'the laws of nature'.

Considering its vast army of adherents, the really striking thing about the standard theory is that there seems to be no reason to think it is true. (In what follows, I am indebted to Professor Anscombe's inaugural lecture,[27] though I do not claim to be saying just what she says.)

Suppose someone throws a stone at a window and that the stone strikes the glass and the glass shatters in just the way we should expect glass to shatter when struck by a cast stone. Suppose further that God reveals to us that the glass did not *have* to shatter under these conditions, that there are possible worlds having exactly the same laws of nature as the actual world and having histories identical with that of the actual world in every detail up to the instant at which the stone came into contact with the glass, but in which the stone rebounded from the intact glass. It follows from what we imagine God to have told us that determinism is false. But does it also follow that the stone did not break the glass, or that the glass did not break *because* it was struck by the stone? It is not easy to see why we should say this follows; perhaps the only reason we could have for saying this is that we accept a corollary of the standard theory of causation: that instances of causation simply *are* instances of universal, exceptionless laws, that the concept of the instantiation of an exceptionless law and the concept of causation are one and the same concept. But this proposition is very doubtful.

Let us suppose that we are watching a slow-motion film taken by a camera trained on the point at which our stone came into contact with our pane of glass. We observe the following: the stone moves through the air toward the point of impact; the stone touches the glass; the glass bends ever so slightly; cracks appear in the glass, radiating outward from the point of impact; shorter cracks appear, joining these radial cracks, thus producing detached shards of glass; the stone moves through the space formerly occupied by the unbroken pane, pushing, or apparently pushing, shards of glass out of its way; the stone continues along its path, trailing a rough cone of spinning shards. Watching this slow-motion film several times should make it very hard to believe that the stone did not break the glass. We could perhaps construct some wild hypothesis, logically consistent with our visual evidence, according to which the stone did not cause the glass to break (for example, the stone didn't touch the glass; a demon caused the pane to shatter a thousandth of a second before the stone would have touched it, carefully counterfeiting the appearance of what would have happened if things had been left to themselves). And if God revealed to us that something like this had happened, then we should have to admit that, despite appearances, the stone hadn't really caused the glass to break. But what about the revelation we earlier imagined God's having delivered? Could this revelation really lead us to say that, despite appearances, the stone didn't cause the glass to break? That this is a *logical consequence* of this revelation? Wouldn't it be more reasonable to say this: that, while the stone did cause the window to break, it was not *determined* that it should; that it *in fact* caused the window to break, though, even if all conditions had been precisely the same, it might not have?

This case convinces me that whatever the *facts* of the matter may be, it is at any rate not part of the *concept* of causation that a cause—or even a cause plus the totality of its accompanying conditions—determines its effect. (A similar case: whatever the facts of the matter may be, it is not part of the *concept* of a human being that a human being should have a liver. If a madman says he is a man who has no liver, we can't simply tell him that it's part of the concept of a human being that a human being has a liver. But just as all human beings *do* have livers, it may be that all causes *do* determine their effects.)

Suppose that some causes don't determine but merely, as we might say, *produce* their effects. Suppose that our simple-minded version of Davidson's theory of the causes of human action is correct. Suppose that among the causes that merely produce their effects are (some of) the "Davidsonian" causes of action. This is our "second model". Let us look once more at our thief. If the model of the causes of action we are considering is correct, then his refraining from robbing the poor-box (R) was caused but not necessitated by his desire to keep the promise he made to his dying mother coupled with his belief that the best way to do this would be to refrain from robbing the poor-box (DB). Let us suppose that the second model is correct: R was caused by DB and DB did not *have* to cause R; it just *did*. We may suppose that God has thousands of times caused the world to revert to precisely its state at the moment just before the thief decided not to steal, and has each time allowed things to proceed without interference for a few minutes, and that DB caused R on about half these occasions. On the other occasions, we may suppose, DB did *not* cause R: instead the thief's desire for money, coupled with his belief that the best way for him to get money was to rob the poor-box, caused him to rob the poor-box. (If we are right in supposing that causes may *produce* their effects without *determining* them, then our supposition about the distribution of outcomes that results from God's thousands of "resettings" of the world is a perfectly possible one.)

Does it follow that the thief *didn't* refrain from robbing the poor-box? I don't see why it should be supposed to follow. The thief's act—or what looks very much like his act—was *caused* by his desires and beliefs, after all. What more do we want?[28] (Remember, I am not saying that the thief acted freely in refraining from taking the money but only that he *acted*.)

I do not know what to say about this case to make it more persuasive. It seems to me to be at least possible that some sort of Davidsonian theory of the causes of action is correct. It seems to me to be at least possible that some causes do not determine their effects. If these two things could be severally true, then I do not see anything to prevent their being jointly true. If they could be jointly true, then the case we have presented seems to show that it is possible for an agent's *act* to be undetermined by antecedent states of affairs. We can now see why the compatibilist's move from 'wire-shaped thing made of brain cells' to 'natural part' was not so innocent as he alleged. A change in a natural part of one may well be identical with one's coming to have a certain desire or with one's acquiring a certain belief. But a change in something that is *not* a part of one—even if it is inside one's head and made of brain cells—could not possibly be identical with either of these things.[29]

We have examined two "models" of the causation of human action, neither of which, I maintain, is known to be conceptually incoherent. Each has the feature of permitting the existence of acts that are truly the productions of their agents and which are nevertheless undetermined by antecedent states of affairs. I do not know whether either of these models is correct. I do not know where the springs of action rise. But I need not know what human action is in order to show, by means of these models, that the second strand of the *Mind* Argument does not, as it stands, prove that the idea of an undetermined act is self-contradictory. I have not proved that this idea *is* an internally consistent idea, of course. But I do not think the burden of the proof lies with me. It is generally pretty difficult to show that a concept is internally consistent. In fact, it is not clear what would count as showing such a thing. But I will make a conditional promise to anyone who says I should show that the idea of an undetermined act is consistent: I will do it if he will show that the idea of a determined act is consistent.

Let us now turn to the third strand of the *Mind* Argument. This strand does not purport to show that the idea of an undetermined *act* is inconsistent but rather that the idea of an undetermined *free* act is inconsistent. In broad outline, the argument is this: a free act is an act one has a choice about; but no one has any choice about that which is undetermined.

(iii) Let us imagine a mechanism the salient features of which are a red light, a green light, and a button. If one presses the button, we'll suppose, then exactly one of the two lights must flash, but it is causally undetermined *which*. (If currently accepted physical theory is correct, it would be easy to construct such a mechanism.) Now suppose that you must press the button on this mechanism. Have you any choice about which of the lights will flash? It seems obvious that you have no choice about this. It is, of course, very likely that if the mechanism were not truly indeterministic but merely extremely complex—if it contained something like a tiny roulette wheel the motion of which was "in principle" determined— you would have no choice about whether the light flashed red or green. But this would not follow *logically* from the description of the mechanism. Though you or I might have no choice about the result of pressing the button on the mechanism that is "extremely complex but determined in principle", another being might. Consider, for example, the Intelligence imagined by Laplace in his *Essai philosophique sur les probabilités*. The Intelligence might very well know that if he were to shake the mechanism *just* so, then the red light would be the next to flash, or something of that sort. And, in virtue of his having knowledge of this kind, he might well have a choice about what light would flash when he pressed the button. But even the Laplacian Intelligence could have no choice about the response of the truly undetermined device, since, in a situation involving true indetermination, there is nothing that the Intelligence can apply his remarkable predictive talents *to*.

We may now follow a path that was laid out for us in our presentation of the second strand of the *Mind* Argument. Let us imagine that our red-green device is "hooked up" to our thief's brain in such a way that, if it flashes green he will steal the money and if it flashes red he will repent and depart; and we may suppose that his coming to be in a state of uncertainty about whether to steal or to repent has the effect of pressing the button. It should be clear that the thief has no choice about whether to steal or to repent (even supposing that the case we have imagined is consistent with the supposition that he *do* either of these things). We may now, by a sequence of minute alterations, turn this case into one in which the red-green device is replaced by a "functionally equivalent" natural part of the thief's brain. The technique will be familiar from our earlier discussion, and there is probably nothing to be gained by actually rehearsing the sequence of alterations. We must, of course, have some reason to be sure that we could construct a sequence in which no step allowed the incompatibilist to contend that, at that point, the possibility of the thief's having a choice was introduced. But it would seem that this requirement will be satisfied provided only that our successive modifications of the original case preserve this feature of it: that there be a truly *undetermined* link in the chain that binds deliberation to action. We were able to achieve this in the "demon" case, and it is evident that the "red-green device" case is not essentially different.

We shall therefore "end up with" a situation that would seem to be just the situation that the incompatibilist sees as a typical case of free action. And we have seen that in this situation, the agent has no choice about the action that will follow upon his deliberations. Therefore, free action is impossible if incompatibilism is true: the very essence of the incompatibilist's theory of free action—indeterminism—ensures that the agent who performs a "free" act has no choice about whether he performs it, and thus ensures that the act is not free after all. Therefore, free action entails determinism and, since free action is *possible*, free action is *a fortiori* compatible with determinism.

This conclusion cannot be evaded by any argument that exploits the two models of the causal antecedents of action that were considered above. Let us look at the second of these models, which most philosophers will probably find more plausible than the first. Suppose that one's acts are caused by a "mixture" of desire and belief, as the second model requires; and suppose that this causation is indeterministic, as the second model requires. We may concede that if the thief's apparent act of repentance is caused in the normal way by his desires and beliefs, then this apparent act was not merely apparent but real, even if the sequence of causation is indeterministic. But it does not by any means follow that it was a free act, for it does not follow that the thief had any choice about whether to steal or to repent. Let us use the symbols 'R' and 'DB' once more. Since DB caused R, it may be correct to say that the thief acted. But note that DB did not *have* to cause R. Moreover, since DB did not have to cause R, and since DB *alone* caused R, R did not have to occur. But then did the thief have any choice about whether R would occur? A principle we have already established entails that he did not: namely, the principle that no one has any choice about the occurrence of an undetermined event. And this general principle does not look any less plausible when we examine the details of the present case. Once DB has occurred, then *everything* relevant to the question whether R is going to happen has occurred. After that we can only wait and see. In a perfectly good sense, it is going to be a matter of *chance* whether R occurs, whatever sophistical difficulties some philosophers may raise about defining this notion.

Thus the "second model" of action cannot be used to show

that the present argument for the incompatibility of free will
and indeterminism is invalid. Let us briefly turn to the first
model, the model involving immanent causation. According
to this model the thief himself is the cause of R. (Or, if this
seems to imply that the thief's beliefs and desires are causally
unrelated to R, we could employ the language of "causal contribution". A flame, the presence of oxygen, and the dryness
of a certain stick may be said each to *contribute causally* to
the stick's catching fire, though none of them is sufficient for
the stick's catching fire. If we accept the idea of immanent
causation, there would seem to be no reason to reject the idea
of *immanent causal contribution*. If we have *this* idea, then
we may say that DB contributed causally to R though it was
not sufficient for R, and that the thief himself also contributed
causally to R.[30]) But it is far from clear that an appeal to immanent causation does any more than sweep the incompatibilist's problem under the carpet. It is evident that the
thief must have become the cause of R at a certain moment.
Consider this event, the thief's acquisition of the property
being the cause of R. This event is undetermined according
to the theory of immanent causation, for if it were determined
R would be determined. If it is undetermined, then the thief
cannot have a choice about whether it obtains. Or if the thief
can have a choice about whether it obtains, if, in general, an
agent can have a choice about an undetermined event, then
one might as well say right at the outset that the thief had a
choice about R and not bring the mysterious notion of immanent causation into the discussion at all.

Reply: I begin with an artless question. Given that the thief
had no choice about whether R followed DB, why couldn't
someone who accepted the second model say that he nevertheless had a choice about whether R occurred? More generally: suppose that s was the "inner state" of a certain agent
that was the cause of some act a of his (s might have been a
Davidsonian mixture of belief and desire, or anything you
like); suppose that, while s caused a, and caused a in the "normal" or in a "non-deviant" way,[31] s did not *determine* that a
should occur; suppose the proponent of the *Mind* Argument
is right in thinking that it follows from these two suppositions

that the agent had no choice about whether, *if s* occurred, *a* followed; why couldn't one say that, despite all this, the agent had—or at least might have had—a choice about whether *a* occurred?

Here is the obvious reply to this artless question.

"But that would be possible (in the case of the thief) only if the thief had a choice about whether DB occurred, and (in the general case) only if the agent had a choice about whether *s* occurred. While we may sometimes have a choice about the inner states that precede our acts, very often we don't. For example, it is unlikely that our thief had any choice about whether DB occurred; and even if he did, this could only be because he had a choice about some earlier states of affairs of which DB was a consequence; if so, the questions we are asking about DB could be asked about those earlier states of affairs. If someone maintained that *those* states of affairs, too, were states of affairs about which the thief had a choice, we could point out that they resulted from still earlier states of affairs, and this process could, in principle, be carried on till we reached the thief's 'initial state' about which he certainly had no choice. So let us assume at the outset that the thief had no choice about whether DB occurred, for we should sooner or later have to make an assumption that would have the same philosophical consequences. But if the thief had no choice about whether DB occurred, and had no choice about whether, *if* DB occurred, *then* R followed, in that case, surely, the thief had no choice about whether R occurred."

This reply to my artless question is, in my opinion, unanswerable. I have asked the artless question and have imagined this obvious and unanswerable response, in order to make explicit a premiss of the third strand of the *Mind* Argument: the validity of the inference rule (β). For it is (β) that the proponent of the *Mind* Argument appeals to in the preceding paragraph. If he refuses to countenance (β), then his elaborate examination of the internal "workings" of the thief perhaps establish that N DB occurs and that N(DB occurs $\supset$ R occurs). But these two propositions do not entail that N R occurs unless (β) is valid.[32] Or so it would seem. There are, of course, other inference rules than (β) that would support the contention that this entailment holds. Any argument that is an instance of one valid rule of inference is an instance of many. But I should like to see a rule other than (β) that licenses the inference of 'N R occurs' from 'N DB occurs' and 'N(DB occurs ⊃ R occurs)' that is anything other than an *ad hoc* restriction of the general rule (β) to some special subject matter, such as the causation of human action.

The third strand of the *Mind* Argument, therefore, depends on rule (β) no less than do our arguments for incompatibilism. (Of course, only the Third Argument of Chapter III explicitly involves (β). But I am confident that since the "point" of the three arguments is essentially the same, the First and Second arguments would be unsound if (β) were invalid.) We might, in fact, think of the answer that the proponent of the third strand of the *Mind* Argument has given to the "artless question"—and this answer is an essential part of the third strand of the *Mind* Argument—as being, like the arguments of Chapter III, a defence of an argument in the logic-text sense. More specifically, we might think of it as being a defence of the premisses of this argument:

(1) The thief's repentance was caused but not determined by DB, and nothing besides DB was causally relevant to the thief's repentance [assumption for conditional proof]

(2) N DB occurred [premiss]

(3) If (1) is true, then N(DB occurred ⊃ the thief repented) [premiss]

(4) No one (including, of course, the thief) had any choice about whether the thief repented

(5) If the thief's repentance was caused but not determined by DB, and nothing besides DB was causally relevant to the thief's repentance, then the thief had no choice about whether he repented.

In this argument, (4) follows from (1), (2), and (3) by elementary logic and (β); assuming the validity of (β), (5) then follows by the principle usually called Conditional Proof. It seems, therefore, that the third strand of the *Mind* Argument invokes a rule of inference the validity of which is the only doubtful premiss of one of our arguments for incompatibilism. It follows that if the third strand of the *Mind* Argument is valid, then free will is incompatible with determinism! Therefore, the compatibilist had better not endorse the third strand of the *Mind* Argument after all. And, therefore, the compatibilist is left without any argument with which to support his position.

But am I any better off than the compatibilist? Suppose a compatibilist were to reply to the argument of the preceding paragraph as follows:

> I see now that the whole trouble was with (β). I ought not to have accepted any argument that depended on it. But neither should you! For if (β) *were* valid, then the third strand of the *Mind* Argument *would be* sound! And that's certainly a conclusion you don't want to accept. Therefore, you too should reject (β) and with it your arguments for incompatibilism.

This compatibilist is certainly right in his contention that I don't want to accept the third strand of the *Mind* Argument. Though I have been treating this argument as an argument for the compatibility of free will and determinism, it is, strictly speaking, an argument for the *incompatibility* of free will and *indeterminism*. Therefore, if it were sound, then either free will would be compatible with determinism or else free will would be incompatible with both determinism and indeterminism and hence impossible. Moreover, as we have seen, if it were sound free will would be incompatible with determinism (since, if it were sound, (β) would be valid and the Third Argument sound); hence if it were sound, free will would be impossible. Therefore, anyone who believes in free will must reject the third strand of the *Mind* Argument. And anyone who believes in free will and who accepts the arguments of Chapter III must reject it on some ground other than the fact that it depends upon (β). On what ground should the incompatibilist who believes in free will reject the third strand of the *Mind* Argument? I think there is no general answer to this question. Different incompatibilists who held different theories of action might answer it in different ways. And I, as I have said, do not know what the right theory of action is. But I shall give an example of how an incompatibilist who accepted a particular theory of action might respond to the challenge offered by our imaginary compatibilist: I shall show

how a compatibilist who accepted the second model of action might respond to this challenge. As a matter of literary convenience, I shall talk as if I accepted this model (which I certainly don't *reject*).

Since I accept the arguments of Chapter III and believe in free will, I must reject the contention of our imaginary compatibilist that if (β) were valid the third strand of the *Mind* Argument would be sound. Since I accept the second model of action, I must therefore reject (3), the second premiss of the formal argument given above. More generally, I must reject the following proposition:

> If an agent's act was caused but not determined by his prior inner state, and if nothing besides that inner state was causally relevant to the agent's act, then that agent had no choice about whether that inner state was followed by that act.

I must admit that I find it puzzling that this proposition should be false. But if the second model of action is correct, then the alternative to supposing that this proposition is false is to suppose that one of the following propositions is false:

> Free will is possible;
>
> (β) is valid;
>
> Every true proposition about the way things were before there ever had been any rational beings is such that no one has, or ever had, any choice about whether it is true;
>
> Every law of nature is such that no one has, or ever had, any choice about whether it is true;
>
> Every necessary truth is such that no one has, or ever had, any choice about whether it is true.

And the falsity of any of these propositions, it seems to me, is not simply puzzling but inconceivable.

Now I wish I knew *how it could be* that, for example, our thief had a choice about whether to repent, given that his repenting was caused, but not determined, by his prior inner states, and given that no other prior state "had anything to do with"—save negatively: in virtue of its non-interference with—his act. I have no theory of free action or choice[33] that would explain how this could be.[34] But then neither have I, and neither has the compatibilist, any theory of free action or choice that would explain how any of the propositions in the above list could be false. Moreover, it is certainly not unheard of in philosophy for an incontrovertible argument to force upon one a puzzling conclusion that one has no theoretical account of. Consider, for example, the case of the man who has been elected President and who is just mounting the platform to give what everyone except him believes will be his victory speech; but suppose that *he*, owing to some operatic misapprehension, believes that his hated opponent has been elected and that the audience expects to hear him concede defeat. Bitter words burst from his lips: "Everything your new President will say to you tonight is false". Now I wish I knew *how it could be* that this man did not tell his audience that everything their new President would say to them that night was false. I have no theory of truth or assertion that would explain how this could be. But, as a familiar sort of argument shows, to suppose that he did tell them this commits one to accepting something inconceivable.

I must choose between the puzzling and the inconceivable. I choose the puzzling. At the end of Section 4.3, I raised the question why anyone should think that incompatibilism was inherently implausible. Perhaps this puzzle that I am unable to resolve is what leads people to think that incompatibilism is inherently implausible.[35] If so, I continue to be convinced that incompatibilism, however implausible it may be, is on balance far more plausible than compatibilism. There are, after all, arguments for incompatibilism that depend upon nothing more implausible than the validity of (β). And we have seen in the present chapter that the most promising arguments for compatibilism turn out to be invalid (the Paradigm Case Argument), or to depend upon premises that lack the "luminous evidence" of (β) (the Conditional Analysis Argument), or to be refutable on certain special grounds (the first and second strands of the *Mind* Argument), or to be more damaging to the position of the compatibilist than to that of the incompatibilist (the third strand of the *Mind* Argument).[36]

4.5 This completes my examination of those arguments for compatibilism that seem to me to be worth discussing at length. In this final section of Chapter IV, I wish to tie up a loose end.

I said in the preceding section that I had no theory of action or choice that would explain how it could be that the crucial premiss of the third strand of the *Mind* Argument was false. The friends of immanent causation may want to remind us that they do have a theory that purports to explain this.

Consider our thief. His desire to obey his mother's final injunction and his belief that he could best achieve this end by repentance cause or contribute causally to his repentance. Moreover, no "deviant causal chains" are involved in this episode, and his desire and his belief, we may suppose, though they cause or contribute causally to his repentance, do not *determine* it. Given that he had no choice about the occurrence of the inner state DB, he could have a choice about repenting only if he has a choice about the truth of this conditional: if DB occurs then R occurs. But how can he have a choice about whether R follows DB if DB is insufficient for R, and nothing else is even causally relevant, save negatively, to R? This is our problem. The solution according to the doctrine of immanent causation is a simple one: "It is false that nothing besides DB is causally relevant to R. What is true is that no other prior *event* or *state of affairs* is causally relevant to R. But there is another sort of causation than "event causation": there is *agent* causation. We may therefore suppose that the thief himself, the man, the substance, the continuant, is "causally relevant" to R. That is, we may suppose that the thief was the immanent cause of—or, at any rate, contributed immanent-causally to—his repentance."

This is a "simple" solution to our problem in the sense that it is not very complex. But it is hardly unproblematic. I find the concept of immanent or agent causation puzzling, as I suspect most of my readers do (those who don't find it downright incoherent). In fact, I find it more puzzling than the problem it is supposed to be a solution to. *Obscurum per obscurius*!

There is a way in which the idea of immanent causation can be made no *more* puzzling than the problem it is supposed to be a solution to. Roughly speaking, the thesis of immanent causation may be regarded as the conjunction of the free-will thesis and the second model. I offer a definition, rather in the style, and very much in the spirit, of Roderick Chisholm:

s is the immanent cause of $a =_{df}$

(i) a is an act that s performs;

(ii) a is caused ("transeuntly") by a prior inner state of s; this causation is not "deviant";

(iii)   This prior inner state does not *determine* that a shall occur, and no other state, unless it is a cause or an effect of that inner state is causally relevant to a (except negatively);

(iv) s has a choice about whether that inner state shall be followed by a.

This definition does not remove all obscurity from this idea of immanent causation. I have not said whether the acts and events that the *definiens* talks of are universals or particulars, and I have not said anything about distinguishing negative from positive causal relevance. Still, it seems to me that this definition is intelligible in a rough-and-ready sort of way. It at any rate leaves the idea of immanent causation less mysterious than it found it. Given this definition I have at least some sort of understanding of immanent causation and, what is more, I can see that it exists if and only if we have free will and some indeterministic causal theory of action along the lines of the second model is correct. But, of course, if this is what immanent causation is, then immanent causation cannot figure in a solution to the puzzle with which the third strand of the *Mind* Argument presents us. For, in the present sense of 'immanent causation', that puzzle just *is*, "How can there be such a thing as immanent causation?"[37]

Chapter V

What Our Not Having Free Will Would Mean

5.1 If the arguments of Chapters III and IV are correct, then we cannot consistently believe both in free will and in determinism. In Chapter VI, I shall argue that anyone who accepts my arguments for incompatibilism should reject determinism and accept the free-will thesis. In the present chapter, I shall set the stage for the argument of Chapter VI by examining the possibility of rejecting the free-will thesis. I wish to see what such a rejection would involve.

I shall approach this problem from two angles. I shall first ask what rejecting free will would mean for us who reject it, without attempting to answer the question, "What does the denial of free will logically entail?" That is, I shall not ask what we should be logically or rationally committed to believing if we gave up a belief in free will, but, rather, what effects such a rejection would have on our lives *whether or not* we accepted all those propositions to which the rejection of free will committed us. I shall then go on to ask what rejecting the free-will thesis would logically commit us to.

5.2 Many people have said that there is no such thing as free will. Baron Holbach, for example, writes:

Man's life is a line that nature commands him to describe upon the surface of the earth, without his ever being able to swerve from it, even for an instant . . . Nevertheless, in spite of the shackles by which he is bound, it is pretended he is a free agent . . .[1]

One might wonder how Holbach found this out, just as one might wonder how Mark Twain, Clarence Darrow, and Freud discovered the truth of the very similar propositions that are to be found in their writings. But these thinkers, and many others, certainly do reject the free-will thesis, at least verbally, however shy they may be about giving arguments in support of this rejection.[2]

Does it follow that they do not believe—that is, fail to have the belief—that there is such a thing as free will? This follows only on two assumptions: (i) that they mean what they say, and (ii) that their beliefs are consistent. These are assumptions I am not willing to make. I think, in fact, that it can be shown that we all believe in free will and that, as a consequence of their sharing this universal belief, Holbach *et al.* either do not mean what they say or are inconsistent.

The argument I shall give in support of this contention is adapted from an argument of Richard Taylor's,[3] though, I believe, it is importantly different from Taylor's argument. This argument proceeds from the fact that we deliberate. To deliberate is to try to decide between (or, it may be, among) various incompatible courses of action.[4] Some philosophers, like Hobbes, believe that deliberation, while it ends in activity, is not itself an activity but rather a state in which the agent is a passive arena within which various hopes, fears, and desires contend for the prize of causing his next action. Other philosophers see deliberation as activity *par excellence.* But all philosophers who have thought about deliberation agree on one point: one cannot deliberate about whether to perform a certain act unless one believes it is possible for one to perform it. (Anyone who doubts that this is indeed the case may find it instructive to imagine that he is in a room with two doors and that he believes one of the doors to be unlocked and the other to be locked and impassable, though he has no idea which is which; let him then attempt to imagine himself deliberating about which door to leave by.) Different accounts have been given of why this is so. I believe the reason is a very straightforward one. Almost any piece of human behaviour manifests certain beliefs of the agent who performs it. One very special case of behaviour that manifests its agent's beliefs is verbal behaviour: if I say, "The cat is on the mat", then, in the normal case, my utterance manifests a belief that the cat is on the mat, and, I should think, various other beliefs, such as a belief that someone may care whether the cat is on the mat, and a belief that someone may not know that the cat is on the mat. But one's beliefs may also be manifested in one's non-verbal behaviour. If I throw my forearm across my eyes, then, in the normal case, this behaviour manifests a belief that my eyes are in danger; if someone arranges for his wife to be followed by private detectives, this act manifests a belief that she is untrustworthy; if someone edges carefully away from every cat he sees, this habit manifests a belief that cats are best avoided. These pieces of behaviour could, of course, be devices for pretending to the beliefs they are normally manifestations of, just as is the case with verbal behaviour.

Deliberation, *pace* Hobbes, is a species of behaviour, and it would therefore not be surprising if deliberation manifested certain beliefs of the deliberator. I think that this is indeed the case. In my view, if someone deliberates about whether to do A or to do B, it follows that his behaviour manifests a belief that it is *possible* for him to do A—that he *can* do A, that he has it within his power to do A—and a belief that it is possible for him to do B. Someone's trying to decide which of two books to buy manifests a belief with respect to each of these books that it is possible for him to buy *it* just as surely as would his holding it aloft and crying, "I can buy this book". (More surely, in fact, for "trying to decide" is at least partly a description of the book-buyer's unobservable, inner behaviour. What would be strictly analogous to *saying* "I can buy this book" would be *appearing* to be trying to decide which book to buy.) I do not mean to deny that people sometimes deliberate *hypothetically*. Someone may deliberate, for example, about whether to break off his lecture if the audience should become unruly, or about whether to cut down his intake of gin if the doctor should order it. More to the present point, someone may deliberate about whether to marry if anyone should ask her, or about whether to buy a certain painting if it should come on the market. That is, someone may deliberate about whether to perform a certain act *if he can*. But the woman who deliberates about whether to marry if she should be asked, or who deliberates about whether to buy a certain painting if it should come on the market, is not an example of someone whose deliberation about a certain course of action fails to manifest a belief that it is within her power to pursue that course of action. This is true simply because to deliberate about whether to marry if one should be asked is not to deliberate about whether to marry, and to deliberate about whether to buy a certain painting if it becomes available is not to deliberate about whether to buy that painting. I do not know how to convince someone who denies this that he is wrong. I suppose I might ask him to consider the following two propositions, which seem to me to be both true and analogous: to order the guard to shoot the prisoner if he should try to escape is not to order the guard to shoot the prisoner; to believe that Smith will help us if he can is not to believe that Smith will help us.

If I am right about deliberation, then there is a very simple reason why one cannot deliberate about what one does not believe (i.e. fails to believe) is possible: when one deliberates, one's behaviour manifests a belief that what one is deliberating about is possible. But couldn't one's behaviour manifest a belief that one doesn't have? This strikes me as a very queer question. To ask it is like asking whether a person's frown might be a manifestation of an emotion he is not experiencing. Well, a person can pretend to feel a certain emotion he does not in fact feel, and can frown "insincerely" as part of this pretence, can't he? This is certainly the case, but we should not say in such a case—if we knew what was going on— that the person's frown was a manifestation of, for example, anger; we should say that it wasn't a manifestation of any emotion at all but was merely meant to look as if it were. Well, couldn't a person's deliberative behaviour fail to be a manifestation of any belief? If by 'deliberative behaviour' is meant the outward and visible signs of deliberation, of course. If by 'deliberative behaviour' is meant deliberation, of course not.

Let us now return to Baron Holbach. What did he believe? What he *said* is clear enough: that there is no free will: that of any two incompatible courses of action, at most one is within the agent's power to carry out. Did he believe what he said? There is at least some reason to suspect that he did not believe that *he* lacked free will. I have given arguments above for the conclusion that no one could deliberate about whether to perform an act that he does not believe it is possible for him to perform. Even if these arguments are wrong, their *conclusion* has been accepted by everyone I know of who has thought about deliberation. It would seem to follow from that conclusion, a proposition as near to being uncontroversial as any philosophically interesting proposition could be, that either Holbach never deliberated or else he believed in the case of some pairs of incompatible courses of action that each was within his power. Did he deliberate? Well, of course he did. If he hadn't, he would be as notorious as Pyrrho. A man who didn't deliberate would either move about in random jerks and scuttles, or would withdraw into catatonia.[5] (That some catatonics are people who have ceased to believe in their own free will is an interesting hypothesis.) Therefore he believed in free will, or, at least, in his own free will. Were his beliefs therefore inconsistent? Or should we say that he didn't really believe that there is no free will, but merely said he did?

I am not sure what to say about this. Let us consider a more homely story that poses the same puzzle and see what we are inclined to say about it. Suppose there is a man who goes to great lengths to praise his wife's fidelity and to express his absolute confidence in her devotion to him and him alone. And let us suppose that the belief in her fidelity that he continually and stridently professes is perfectly sincere in this sense: if he were filling out a questionnaire about current sexual mores, and was perfectly convinced of the anonymity of his answers, he would check the "absolutely certain" box beside the question, 'Is your spouse faithful to you?' But let us also suppose that he becomes upset if he discovers that she has been alone with another man, even under the most innocuous and socially acceptable of conditions; that he opens her letters; that he attempts to eavesdrop on her telephone conversations; that, in fact, he hires private detectives to report on her every move. What should we say about this man's beliefs? It seems clear that he manifests in his behaviour a belief that his wife is unfaithful to him, or is at any rate likely to be. Whatever he may *say*, his behaviour shows "what he really believes". But what about what he says? Does his verbal behaviour also manifest his beliefs? There are two ways in which we might describe his "doxastic situation". We might say he *lacks* the belief that his wife is faithful and that his frequent utterance of sentences that express the proposition that his wife is faithful is a sham. Or we might say that his utterances *do* manifest the belief that his wife is faithful and that his beliefs are simply inconsistent. I do not know which of these is the right thing to say—though I favour the second of them—and I have no idea of how to go about finding out. I can say no more than this about Baron Holbach. I do not know how to describe his doxastic situation. Does he *lack* the belief that he has no free will? Is his frequent utterance of sentences that express the proposition that he has no free will a sham? Or do his utterances manifest the belief that he has no free will? Are his beliefs simply inconsistent? While again I favour the second alternative, I have no idea of how to go about finding out which alternative is right.

But perhaps there is no need for us to find out which alternative is right. Suppose we were to bring to the attention of Holbach—or of anyone else who denies the existence of free will—the fact, for fact it is, that in deliberating one manifests in one's behaviour a belief in one's free will with respect to the act under deliberation. Suppose we were able to convince him of this. What should he do? This, I think, is the important question.

There would seem to be two courses open to him (besides changing his mind about free will): he might cease to deliberate or he might simply decide to "live with" having irremediably inconsistent beliefs. The former course is unattractive, implying as it does a life spent in catatonic withdrawal or purely random activity. What about the latter? What precisely is wrong with having inconsistent beliefs? It's obviously not a wholly good thing, but is it a very bad thing? I think that Professor Geach has given the right answer: "The trouble about inconsistency is that if our factual statements are inconsistent, one or the other of them is going to be false, and we often wish statements made by or to ourselves to be true".[6] That is to say, having inconsistent beliefs is not "in itself" a bad thing. What is bad in itself is having *false* beliefs. Having inconsistent beliefs is bad only because having inconsistent beliefs ensures having at least one false belief.

Why is this point important? Well, it *could* be very important. Suppose one had a certain belief that one found one couldn't rid oneself of, however much one tried. And suppose one had indisputable evidence—and regarded it as indisputable evidence—for the falsity of that belief. If it were true that there was something "intrinsically" bad about having contradictory beliefs, then it might well be—depending on how bad it was—that what one should do is to (attempt to) stop having any beliefs that contradict one's "immutable" belief. But if the only thing wrong with having contradictory beliefs is that being in that state ensures believing a falsehood, then there would seem to be no reason to attempt to arrange one's other beliefs in such a way as to avoid conflict with the immutable belief. After all, that belief is *ex hypothesi* in conflict with one's evidence. In all probability, therefore, it is false. If one's other beliefs are supported by one's evidence, then one might as well hold on to them, even though this would ensure that one have at least one false belief, for the immutable belief is very likely false and thus one's having at least one false belief is highly probable in any event. Why give up any *true* beliefs simply to achieve consistency?

The argument of the preceding paragraph was very abstract. Let us underscore its point by looking at a particular case:

I once heard a story of a Japanese astronomer who seemed to succeed very well in treating the sun alternately as an inanimate natural body whose properties can be investigated by the techniques of mathematical physics, and as a divinity, the ancestress of the Japanese imperial dynasty; when challenged about the matter by a European colleague, he said 'Here in Europe I know it's all nonsense, but in Japan I believe it'.[7]

Let us interpret this story as entailing that the Japanese astronomer simply has not got it within his power to stop believing that the sun is a divinity. What should he do? If his highest value is consistency, then, clearly, he should give up his western heliological beliefs, despite the fact that the evidence on which they are based is as impressive as the evidence for the thesis that the Japanese emperor is descended from the sun is unimpressive. But if the *only* thing wrong with having inconsistent beliefs is that inconsistent beliefs ensure false beliefs, then his best course of action is to continue to believe that the sun is a divinity *and* to believe that the sun is an inanimate object. Following this course of action ensures his having a false belief, but since, we are supposing, he can't give up his belief that the sun is a divinity, he is going to have a false belief whatever he does. By retaining his western beliefs, however, he gains the advantage of having a body of true belief about the sun that, no doubt, is often useful to him.

I think that this is the way Holbach should look at his

doxastic situation. He has, or thinks he has, overwhelming evidence for the thesis that he has no free will. Yet he repeatedly engages in behaviour that is a sufficient condition for his believing he has free will, behaviour that he would have to be literally mad to give up. Moreover, he sees, or thinks he sees, that there is no evidence whatever in favour of the thesis that he has free will. The best thing for him to do would seem to be simply to say something like, "I have inconsistent beliefs, but that doesn't trouble me. The only way for me to achieve consistency would be for me to give up my assent to the obviously true proposition that we lack free will. This is too large a price to pay for consistency, the only virtue of which, after all, is that it does not logically necessitate having a false belief. But, apparently, I must have a false belief whatever I do, so this feature of consistency, though a virtue in the abstract, would not benefit *me*."

I said earlier that in the present section I should ask what rejecting free will would mean for us without asking what the denial of free will logically entails. The answer is: to reject free will is to condemn oneself to a life of perpetual logical inconsistency. Anyone who rejects free will adopts a general theory about human beings that he contradicts with every deliberate word and act. This perhaps sounds worse than it is. We have seen that it is the best course to adopt for one who is convinced that he is in the possession of evidence that proves that we have no free will. When described abstractly, the man who rejects free will may seem rather a comic figure, a sort of metaphysical version of our suspicious husband. And indeed we do generally regard the man whose acts belie his words as comic. But this is partly because we suppose that the contradiction of word by act is not an inevitable feature of life. This supposition is sometimes not unreasonable. The suspicious husband might have been different. It might have been the case that his words and his acts did not manifest contrary beliefs about his wife's fidelity. There is nothing impossible in this; in fact, it would seem to be the normal case. But anyone who denies the existence of free will must, inevitably, contradict himself with monotonous regularity. Far from finding such a person comic, one might very well see him as a kind of philosophical hero, particularly if one approves of his *reasons* for rejecting free will. He is certainly likely to see himself that way.

I now turn to the question, "What does the thesis that we have no free will logically commit its adherents to?"

5.3 The answer to this question is a philosophical commonplace. If we do not have free will, then there is no such thing as moral responsibility. This proposition, one might think, certainly deserves to be a commonplace. If someone charges you with, say, lying, and if you can convince him that it was simply not within your power *not* to lie, then it would seem that you have done all that is necessary to absolve yourself of responsibility for lying. Your accuser cannot say, "I concede it was not within your power not to lie; none the less you ought not to have lied". *Ought*, as the saying goes, implies *can*. (Of course, it is unlikely that anyone would believe you if you said that it was not within your power not to lie, but that is not the point.) Similarly, if someone charges you with *not* having done something he maintains you ought to have done, he must withdraw his charge if you can convince him that you couldn't have done it. If, for example, he charges you with not having spoken up when a word might have saved Jones's reputation, he must withdraw his charge if you can convince him that you were bound and gagged while Jones was being maligned. (These simple facts are actually a bit too simple. An agent may have been unable to perform a certain act at a certain time, but—owing to his abilities with respect to acts that were or might have been performed at earlier times—he may once have been able so to arrange matters that he would have been able to perform that act at that time. For example, I may have been unable to contribute to a certain charity yesterday because I was locked in a bank vault that can't be opened from the inside. But if it should transpire that I had shut myself into the vault in order to avoid the representatives of the charity, few people would regard my having been locked in the vault as providing me with an adequate excuse for not contributing. The reason is easy to see: though there may be a sense in which it is true that I couldn't have contributed to the charity, there was none the less a time—before I shut myself in—at which I could so have arranged matters that I should have been able to contribute to it when the time to do so rolled round. In the sequel, I shall ignore the possibility of cases like the "bank vault" case in order to avoid unnecessary detail in the statement of my argument.)

It would seem to follow from these considerations that without free will there is no moral responsibility: if moral responsibility exists, then someone is morally responsible for something he has done or for something he has left undone; to be morally responsible for some act or failure to act is at least to be able to have acted otherwise, whatever else it may involve; to be able to have acted otherwise is to have free will. Therefore, if moral responsibility exists, someone has free will. Therefore, if no one has free will, moral responsibility does not exist.

It would be hard to find a more powerful and persuasive argument than this little argument. Or so one would have thought. In a remarkable recent essay, however, Harry Frankfurt has cast grave doubts upon it.[8] Frankfurt's reasoning is essentially this. He points out that it depends essentially on the premiss:

> A person is morally responsible for what he has done only if he could have done otherwise.

(Frankfurt calls this proposition the Principle of Alternate Possibilities.) He then shows how to construct counter-examples to it. Here is a "Frankfurt counter-example" to the Principle of Alternate Possibilities. The example is my own, but it does not differ in any important way from Frankfurt's own examples.

Suppose there is a man called Gunnar who has decided to shoot his colleague Ridley. Suppose a third man, Cosser, very much desires that Gunnar shoot Ridley. Cosser is naturally delighted with Gunnar's present intention to shoot Ridley, but he realizes that people sometimes change their minds. Accordingly, he devises the following plan: if Gunnar should change his mind about shooting Ridley, Cosser will *cause* Gunnar to shoot Ridley. We may suppose that Cosser is able directly to manipulate Gunnar's nervous system, and is thus able, in the fullest and strongest sense of the word, to *cause* Gunnar to act according to his wishes. Let us suppose, moreover, that there is nothing Gunnar can do about Cosser's intentions or about the power Cosser has over his acts. It would seem therefore, that Gunnar has no choice about whether he shoots Ridley. If he does not change his mind, he will shoot Ridley. If he does change his mind, he will shoot Ridley. Every possible future that is open to him is a future in which he shoots Ridley. These futures, it is true, are of two sorts: those in which he shoots Ridley without having been caused to do so by Cosser and those in which he shoots Ridley only because Cosser caused him to. And perhaps he has a choice about which of these sorts the actual future will belong to. But he has *no* choice about whether the actual future will belong to one of these two sorts, and hence has no choice about whether he shoots Ridley.

Time passes, we suppose, and Gunnar does not change his mind and does shoot Ridley without having been caused to do so by Cosser. Could he have done otherwise than shoot Ridley? Obviously not: before he shot Ridley he had no choice about whether he would shoot Ridley, and so we may now say, after the fact, that he couldn't have done otherwise than shoot him. Is he responsible for having shot Ridley? It would certainly seem so, at least if anyone is ever responsible for anything. Let us suppose, for the moment, that Cosser had not devised his plan for ensuring that Gunnar shoot Ridley. Let us consider Gunnar's wicked act and let us "build into" our description of the circumstances under which it was performed *whatever* may be necessary for Gunnar's being responsible for it. (Someone might, for example, want us to include in our description of the act that Gunnar was its *immanent cause, à la* Chisholm.) Now let us consider adding to this description of the circumstances of Gunnar's act the statement that Cosser *would have* caused him to perform it if he had changed his mind. Does this statement alter the fact of Gunnar's responsibility? How could it? It is no more than a statement about certain of the unrealized causal dispositions of the objects that constituted Gunnar's environment during some short period that immediately preceded his act. No act, no intention, no disposition of Cosser had the slightest effect on Gunnar's act or on the deliberations that led up to it. The causal history of his act is just what it would have been if

Cosser had never existed. Now it would seem to be undeniable that if there are two possible worlds in each of which the same agent performs the same act, and if the causal history of this act is the same in every detail in both worlds, then it cannot be that the agent is responsible for that act in one world and not responsible for it in the other. If this general principle is correct, however, then Cosser's unactualized disposition to cause Gunnar to shoot Ridley does not relieve Gunnar of his responsibility for having shot Ridley. It is doubtless true that if Gunnar had changed his mind about shooting Ridley, and had, as a consequence, been caused to shoot Ridley, he *would not* have been responsible for shooting Ridley. But this proposition is consistent with the proposition that Gunnar *is* responsible for shooting Ridley.

It seems we must conclude that we have a genuine case in which an agent is morally responsible for having shot a certain man even though he could not have done otherwise than shoot that man. This case shows that the Principle of Alternate Possibilities is probably false. (I shall later explain why I say 'probably'.) Let us suppose that the Principle of Alternate Possibilities is indeed false. What follows? It does not follow that we might be morally responsible for our acts even if we lacked free will; it follows only that the usual argument for the proposition that moral responsibility entails free will has a false premiss. But might there not be other arguments for this conclusion? Might there not be other premisses from which this entailment could be derived? I shall argue that there are. I shall exhibit three principles that, I shall argue, have the following features: (i) they entail that free will is necessary for moral responsibility; (ii) though they are clearly in some sense "similar to" or "variants on" the Principle of Alternate Possibilities, they are nevertheless immune to Frankfurt-style counter-examples. (I shall call counter-examples to principles that are similar to but distinct from the Principle of Alternate Possibilities, and which are as strategically similar to Frankfurt counter-examples as possible, Frankfurt-*style* counter-examples. I shall reserve the term 'Frankfurt counter-example' for counter-examples to the Principle of Alternate Possibilities.)

The Principle of Alternate Possibilities concerns *performed* acts (things we have done). In Section 5.4, I shall consider a principle about *unperformed* acts (things we have left undone). In Sections 5.5 and 5.6, I shall consider two principles about the consequences of what we have done (or left undone). In Section 5.7, I shall argue that if these three principles are true then moral responsibility requires free will.[9]

5.4 Consider the following principle (the Principle of Possible Action):

PPA   A person is morally responsible for failing to perform a given act only if he could have performed that act.

This principle is intuitively very plausible. But the same might have been said about the Principle of Alternate Possibilities. Can we show that PPA is false by constructing a counter-example to it that is like Frankfurt's counter-examples to the Principle of Alternate Possibilities? An adaptation of Frankfurt's general strategy to the case of unperformed acts would, I think, look something like this: an agent is in the process of deciding whether or not to perform a certain act *a*. He decides not to perform *a*, and, owing to this decision, refrains from performing *a*.[10] But, unknown to him, there were various factors that *would have* prevented him from performing (and perhaps even from deciding to perform) *a*. These factors would have come into play if he had shown any tendency towards performing (perhaps even towards deciding to perform) *a*. But since he in fact showed no such tendency, these factors remained mere unactualized dispositions of the objects constituting his environment: they played no role whatever in his deciding not to perform or in his failure to perform *a*.

Putative counter-examples to PPA prepared according to this recipe produce, in me at least, no inclination to reject this principle. Let us look at one.

Suppose I look out the window of my house and see a man being robbed and beaten by several powerful-looking assailants. It occurs to me that perhaps I had better call the police. I reach for the telephone and then stop. It crosses my mind that if I do call the police, the robbers might hear of it and wreak their vengeance on me. And, in any case, the police would probably want me to make a statement and perhaps even to go to the police station and identify someone in a line-up or look through endless books of photographs of thugs. And it's after eleven already, and I have to get up early tomorrow. So I decide "not to get involved", return to my chair, and put the matter firmly out of my mind. Now suppose also that, quite unknown to me, there has been some sort of disaster at the telephone exchange, and that every telephone in the city is out of order and will be for several hours.

Am I responsible for failing to call the police? Of course not. I couldn't have called them. I may be responsible for failing to *try* to call the police—that much I *could* have done— or for refraining from calling the police, or for having let myself, over the years, become the sort of man who doesn't (try to) call the police under such circumstances. I may be responsible for being selfish and cowardly. But I am simply not responsible for failing to call the police. This "counter-example", therefore, is not a counter-example at all and PPA is unscathed.

It is, of course, proverbially hard to prove a universal negative proposition. Perhaps there are Frankfurt-style counter-examples to PPA. But I don't see how to construct one. I conclude that Frankfurt's style of argument cannot be used to refute PPA.

5.5 Both the Principle of Alternate Possibilities and PPA are principles about acts, performed or unperformed. But, in fact, when we make ascriptions of moral responsibility, we do not normally say things like 'You are responsible for killing Jones' or 'He is responsible for failing to water the marigolds'. We are much more likely to say 'You are responsible for Jones's death' or 'He is responsible for the shocking state the marigolds are in'. That is, we normally hold people responsible not for their acts or failures to act (at least explicitly), but for the results or consequences of these acts and failures. What, ontologically speaking, are results or consequences of action and inaction? What sorts of thing are Jones's death and the shocking state the marigolds are in? The general terms 'event' and 'state of affairs' seem appropriate ones to apply to these items. But what are events and states of affairs? This question, like all interesting philosophical questions I know of, has no generally accepted answer. Philosophers do not seem even to be able to agree whether events and states of affairs are particulars or universals. In order to avoid taking sides in the debate about this, I shall adopt the following strategy: I shall state a certain principle about excuse from responsibility that seems to me to be plausible, provided the events or states of affairs we hold people responsible for are particulars; and I shall state a similar principle that seems to me to be plausible, provided the events or states of affairs we hold people responsible for are universals; for each of these principles, I shall argue that it cannot be refuted by Frankfurt-style counter-examples. The first of these principles, which I shall call principles of possible prevention, is:

PPP1 A person is morally responsible for a certain event-particular only if he could have prevented it.

This principle is about events; but if we were to examine a principle, otherwise similar, about "state-of-affairs-particulars" (for example, the way secondary education is organized in Switzerland),[11] we could employ arguments that differ from the following arguments only in verbal detail.

What are events if they are particulars? They are items that can be witnessed, at least if they consist in visible changes in visible particulars, remembered, and reported.[12] They are typically denoted by phrases like 'the fall of the Alamo', 'the death of Caesar', 'the unexpected death of Caesar', and 'what Bill saw happening in the garden'.[13] How shall we identify and individuate event-particulars (hereinafter, "events")? Individuating particulars, whether events, tables, or human beings is always a tricky business. (Consider the Ship of Theseus.) As Davidson says,

Before we enthusiastically embrace an ontology of events we will want to think long and hard about the criteria for individuating them. I am myself inclined to think we can do as well for events generally as we can for physical objects generally (which is not very well) . . .[14]

In a later paper than the one this quotation is taken from, Davidson tries to "do as well". He tells us that finding a satisfactory criterion of individuation for events will consist in providing "a satisfactory filling for the blank in:

If x and y are events, then $x = y$ if and only if —."

The "filling" he suggests for this blank is (roughly) 'x and y have the same causes and effects'.[15] The biconditional so obtained, is, I have no doubt, true. But this biconditional will not be "satisfactory" for our purpose, which is the evaluation of PPP1. What we want to be able to do is to tell whether some event that *would* happen if what we earlier called "unactualized dispositions of the objects constituting the agent's environment" were to come into play, is the same as some event—the event responsibility for which we are enquiring about—that actually *has* happened; that is, we want to know how to tell of some given event whether *it*, that very same event, would nevertheless have happened if things had been different in certain specified ways. (For when we ask whether an agent could have prevented a certain event *e* by doing, say, *x*, we shall have to be able to answer the question whether *e* would *none the less* have happened if the agent had done *x*.)

To see why Davidson's criterion cannot be used to answer our sort of question about event-identity, consider the following formally similar criterion of individuation for persons: '*x* and *y* are the same person if and only if *x* and *y* have the same blood relatives, including siblings'. This criterion, while true, does not help us if we are interested in counter-factual questions about persons. For, obviously, any given man might have had different relatives from those he in fact has; he might have had an additional brother, for example. Davidson's proposed criterion is of no help to us for what is essentially the same reason: any given event might have had different effects from the effects it has in fact had. For example, if an historian writes, "Even if the murder of Caesar had not resulted in civil war, it would nevertheless have led to widespread bloodshed", he does not convict himself of conceptual confusion. But he is certainly presupposing that the very event we call 'the murder of Caesar' might have had different effects.[16]

The above considerations are not offered in criticism of Davidson's criterion, which is, after all, true, and may be a very useful criterion to employ, say, when we are asking whether a given brain-event and a given mental event are one event or two. But Davidson's criterion is not the sort of criterion we need. We need a criterion that stands to Davidson's criterion as '*x* and *y* are the same human being if and only if *x* and *y* have the same causal genesis' stands to the above criterion of personal identity. I use 'causal genesis' with deliberate vagueness. A necessary condition for x and y having the same causal genesis is "their" having developed from the same sperm and egg.[17] But this is not sufficient, or "identical" (monozygotic) twins would be *numerically* identical. This criterion can be used to make sense of talk about what some particular person would have been like if things had gone very differently for him.[18] Can we devise a "counter-factual" criterion for events that is at least no worse than our criterion for persons? I would suggest that we simply truncate Davidson's criterion: x is the same event as y if and only if x and y have the same causes. That is to say, if x is the product of certain causes, then, necessarily, an event y is the product of *those* causes if and only if y is x. (Note the similarity of this criterion to the causal-genesis criterion of personal identity.)

I do not know how to justify my intuition that this criterion is correct, any more than I know how to justify my belief in the causal-genesis criterion. But, of course, arguments must come to an end somewhere. I can only suggest that since substances (such as human beings and tables) should be individuated by their causal origins, and since we are talking about events that, like substances, are particulars, the present proposal is plausible. Moreover, I am aware that this proposed criterion is vague. It is not clear in every case of, say, a story about the events leading up to Caesar's murder, whether it would be correct to say that the murder had "the same causes" in the story that it had in reality. But I think the notion of *same event* is clear just in so far as the notion of *same causes* is clear. And this latter notion is surely not hopelessly unclear: if Cleopatra had poisoned Caesar in 48 BC, then, clearly, there would have happened an event that has not in fact happened, an event it would have been correct to call 'Caesar's death', and which would have had different causes from the event that *is* called 'Caesar's death'. And, just as clearly, we cannot say of the event we in fact call 'Caesar's death', "Suppose *it* had been caused four years earlier by Cleopatra's poisoning Caesar in Alexandria". Moreover, it is hardly to be supposed that we should be able to devise a criterion that will resolve all "puzzle cases", since we are unable to devise such a criterion for people, mountains, or tables.[19]

While I think this criterion of counter-factual event-identity is *true*, I think it is worth pointing out that the argument of the sequel will require only a certain principle that is entailed by but does not entail this criterion: if x is the product of certain causes, then, necessarily, an event y is the product of *those* causes *if y is x*. This weaker principle may also be stated in these words: no event could have had causes other than its actual causes. The criterion I have proposed is equivalent to the conjunction of this weaker principle with the proposition that if a certain chain of causes and that chain alone has produced a certain event as its effect, then no other event could have been the effect of that chain of causes and that chain alone. While I think that this proposition is true, we shall not need to make any use of it.

Let us now return to PPP1. Can we devise a Frankfurt-style counter-example to this principle? Let us try.

Gunnar shoots and kills Ridley (intentionally), thereby bringing about Ridley's death, a certain event. But there is some factor, F, which (i) played no causal role in Ridley's death, and (ii) would have caused Ridley's death if Gunnar had not shot him—or, since factor F might have caused Ridley's death *by* causing Gunnar to shoot him, perhaps we should say, "if Gunnar had decided not to shoot him"— and (iii) is such that Gunnar could not have prevented it from causing Ridley's death except by killing, or by deciding to kill, Ridley himself. So it would seem that Gunnar is responsible for Ridley's death, though he could not have prevented Ridley's death.

It is easy to see that this story is simply inconsistent. What is in fact denoted by 'Ridley's death' is not, according to the story, caused by factor F. Therefore, if Gunnar had not shot Ridley, and, as a result, factor F had caused Ridley to die, then there would have been an event denoted by 'Ridley's death' which had factor F as (one of) its cause(s). But then this event would have been an event other than the event in fact denoted by 'Ridley's death'; the event in fact denoted by 'Ridley's death' would not have happened at all. But if this story is inconsistent it is not a counter-example to PPP1. And I am unable to see how to construct a putative Frankfurt-style counter-example to PPP1 that cannot be shown to be inconsistent by an argument of this sort.

5.6 Let us now turn to a principle about universals:

PPP2 A person is morally responsible for a certain state of affairs only if (that state of affairs obtains and) he could have prevented it from obtaining.[20]

The states of affairs "quantified over" in this principle are universals in the way propositions are universals. Just as there are many different ways the concrete particulars that make up our surroundings could be arranged that would be sufficient for the *truth* of a given proposition, so there are many different ways they could be arranged that would be sufficient for the *obtaining* of a given state of affairs. Consider, for example, the state of affairs that consists in Caesar's being murdered. This state of affairs obtains because certain conspirators stabbed Caesar in Rome in 44 BC,[21] but, since it is a universal, *it*, that very same state of affairs, might have obtained because, say, Cleopatra had poisoned him in Alexandria in 48 BC. But this is a bit vague. In order the better to talk about "states of affairs", let us introduce "canonical" names for them. Such names will consist of the result of prefixing 'its being the case that'—hereinafter, 'C'—to "eternal" sentences.[22] Thus a canonical name for the state of affairs referred to above would be 'C (Caesar is murdered)'. And let us say that the result of flanking the identity-sign with canonical names of states of affairs expresses a truth just in the case that the eternal sentences embedded in these names express equivalent propositions, where propositions are *equivalent* if they are true in just the same possible worlds. I shall assume that every proposition is equivalent to and *only* to itself. This assumption could be dispensed with at the cost of complicating the syntax of the sequel. A state of affairs will be said to *obtain* if the proposition associated with it—that is, the proposition expressed by the sentence embedded in any of its canonical names—is true. Thus C(Caesar is murdered), C(Caesar is stabbed), and C(Caesar is poisoned) are three distinct states of affairs, the first two of which obtain and the last of which does not. To *prevent* a state of affairs from obtaining is to prevent its associated proposition from being true, or to see to it that or ensure that that proposition is not true.

Let us now, so armed, return to PPP2. Can we show that

PPP2 is false by constructing Frankfurt-style counter-examples to it? What would an attempt at such a counter-example look like? Like this, I think: Gunnar shoots Ridley (intentionally), an act sufficient for the obtaining of Ridley's being dead, a certain state of affairs; but there is some factor, F, which (i) played no causal role in Ridley's death, and (ii) would have caused Ridley's death if Gunnar had not shot him (or had decided not to shoot him), and (iii) is such that Gunnar could not have prevented it from causing Ridley's death except by killing (or by deciding to kill) Ridley himself. So it would seem that Gunnar is responsible for Ridley's being dead, though he could not have prevented this state of affairs from obtaining.

This case seems to show that PPP2 is false. But in fact it does not. Let us remember that if this case is to be a counter-example to PPP2 and not to some other principle, some principle involving particulars, the words 'Ridley's being dead' that occur in it must denote a universal. What universal? Presumably, C(Ridley dies). But while it is indeed true that Gunnar could not have prevented C(Ridley dies) from obtaining, I do not think it is true that Gunnar is responsible for C(Ridley dies). Why should anyone think he is? Well, Gunnar did something—shooting Ridley—that was sufficient for C(Ridley dies). What is more, he performed this act intentionally, knowing that it was sufficient for that state of affairs. This argument, however, is invalid. For consider the state of affairs C(Ridley is mortal). When Gunnar shot Ridley, he performed an act sufficient for the obtaining of this state of affairs. But it would be absurd to say that Gunnar is responsible for C(Ridley is mortal). God, or Adam and Eve jointly, or perhaps no one at all, might be held accountable for Ridley's mortality; certainly not his murderer. (Unless, of course, Ridley would have lived forever if he hadn't been murdered; let's assume that this is not the case.) We might even imagine that Gunnar was a madman and *believed* that Ridley would live forever if he did not shoot him. In that case, Gunnar performed a certain act intentionally, knowing that it was sufficient for C(Ridley is mortal), and we may suppose, *in order to* bring about C(Ridley is mortal). Even in this case, however, Gunnar is not responsible for C(Ridley is mortal).

In fact, it is arguable that C(Ridley dies) is the very same state of affairs as C(Ridley is mortal). Given our principle of identity for states of affairs, these "two" states of affairs are one if the two eternal sentences 'Ridley dies' and 'Ridley is mortal' express the same proposition. And what proposition could either of them express but the proposition also expressed by 'Ridley does not live forever' and 'Ridley dies at some time or other'? So, it should seem, Gunnar is not responsible for C(Ridley dies), and the attempted counter-example to PPP2 fails.

Nor do matters go differently if, somewhat implausibly, we think of 'Ridley's being dead' as denoting some more "specific" state of affairs, such as C(Ridley is killed by someone). If Gunnar is indeed responsible for C(Ridley is killed by someone), we shall nevertheless have a counter-example to PPP2 only if Gunnar could not have prevented this state of affairs from obtaining. Let us flesh out "Factor F" with some detail to ensure that this is the case: suppose there is a third party, Pistol, who would have killed Ridley if Gunnar had not; and suppose Gunnar was able to prevent Pistol's killing Ridley only by killing Ridley himself. By these stipulations, we ensure that Gunnar could not have prevented C(Ridley is killed by someone). But do we, in making these stipulations, absolve Gunnar from responsibility for this state of affairs, or is his being responsible for it at least consistent with our stipulations?

It seems evident to me that we absolve him. C(Ridley is killed by someone) would have obtained *no matter what* Gunnar had done, and the principle, 'If a certain state of affairs would have obtained no matter what x had done, then x is not responsible for it' seems, to say the least, highly plausible. Are there any features of the case that should lead us to reject this highly plausible principle? It would seem not. The only reason the case presents us with for thinking that Gunnar is responsible for C(Ridley is killed by someone) is this: Ridley performed an act sufficient for the obtaining of this state of affairs. But, as we have seen, this reason is not good enough; if it were, then Gunnar would be responsible for C(Ridley is mortal).

Now it is possible to flesh out "Factor F" in a way that

evades this reply. We need only suppose that Factor F "works through" Gunnar. That is, suppose Factor F, instead of involving a third party, involves some mechanism that has the following property: *if* Gunnar had decided not to shoot Ridley, this mechanism would have caused him to change his mind and shoot Ridley despite his earlier decision. This stipulation, like our earlier stipulation about Pistol, will ensure that Gunnar could not have prevented C(Ridley is killed by someone). Moreover, this revision will not allow us to argue that Gunnar is absolved from responsibility for this state of affairs because it would have obtained no matter what he had done. For, in the revised case, C(Ridley is killed by someone) would *not* have obtained no matter what Gunnar had done: it would not have obtained if Gunnar had not shot Ridley. We can, however, use a similar principle to the same purpose: 'If a certain state of affairs would have obtained no matter what choices or decisions x had made, then x is not responsible for it'. This principle seems at least as evident as the "no matter what he had done" principle, and it obviously entails that, in the revised case, Gunnar is not responsible for C(Ridley is killed by someone). Moreover, this second principle could be applied in the third-party case that we considered in the preceding paragraph, in case anyone wanted to split hairs about 'no matter what he had done' like the hairs that were split in Chapter II, note 3.

If we had chosen to examine instead of C(Ridley is killed by someone) some even more specific state of affairs, such as C(Ridley is shot to death at 3.43 p.m. 12 January 1949 in Chicago), this would have made no difference to our argument, which in no way depended on the "degree of specificity"—whatever, precisely, that might mean—of C(Ridley is killed by someone). If we attempt to construct a Frankfurt-style counter-example to PPP2, we must construct it in such a way that the agent who figures in it could not have prevented a certain state of affairs. In a Frankfurt-style counter-example, this feature is achieved by the positing of an "unactualized disposition of the agent's environment", which, if the agent had acted (or had decided or chosen) differently, would have brought about that state of affairs independently of his will, or else would have affected his will in such a way as to cause *him* to bring it about. That is to say, in a Frankfurt-style counter-example to PPP2, the agent's inability to prevent a certain state of affairs is secured by so constructing the case that that state of affairs would have obtained no matter what he had done—or, at least, would have obtained no matter what choices or decisions he had made. But then, according to our two "no matter what" principles, the agent will not be responsible for the state of affairs.

It occurs to me that someone might object to our employment of these principles on the ground that they "presuppose" PPP2. This, however, would be a mistake, since 's would have obtained no matter what x had done' and 's would have obtained no matter what choices or decisions x had made' are stronger statements than (i.e. neither one is entailed by) 'x could not have prevented s'. Suppose, for example, that Swallow is a dipsomaniac: he cannot refrain from drinking if drink is present. Suppose drink *is* present; then Swallow cannot prevent C(Swallow drinks). But it is not true that this state of affairs would have obtained no matter what Swallow had done, or true that it would have obtained no matter what choices or decisions he had made. If he had not drunk, it would not have obtained; if he had steadfastly *chosen* not to drink it would not have obtained. But if 'x could not have prevented s' does not entail (is a weaker statement than) either 's would have obtained no matter what x had done' or 's would have obtained no matter what choices or decisions x had made', then it would seem that neither of our two principles "presupposes" PPP2.

These two principles may be false, but they certainly *seem* to be true. If someone were to construct a Frankfurt-style example in which an agent was *clearly* responsible for a state of affairs that would have obtained no matter what he had done or had chosen or had decided, then, of course, we should have to reject our two principles, plausible though they may be. But none of the Frankfurt-style examples we have considered, or any other that I know of, has this feature. The Gunnar-Ridley examples—and I know of no Frankfurt-style putative counter-examples to PPP2 that are essentially different from the Gunnar-Ridley examples—may initially impress one as implying that Gunnar is responsible for some baneful state of affairs that would have obtained no matter what he had done or chosen or decided. This impression, however, seems to depend on the assumption that if an agent performs a certain act (and is responsible for performing it) and if that act is sufficient for the obtaining of a certain state of affairs, and if the agent performs that act knowing it is sufficient for the state of affairs (or perhaps even performs it *in order to* cause that state of affairs to obtain), then that agent is responsible for that state of affairs. But, as we have seen, this assumption is false, for, if it were true, Gunnar would be responsible for its being the case that Ridley is mortal.

It seems, therefore, that Frankfurt's ingenious style of argument, however effective it may be against the Principle of Alternate Possibilities, cannot be used to refute PPP2. This result is not implausible. Its intuitive plausibility can be seen if we think in terms of the following picture: in attempting to construct Frankfurt-style counter-examples to PPP2, we have been imagining cases in which an agent "gets to" a certain state of affairs by following a particular "causal road", a road intentionally chosen by him in order to "get to" that state of affairs; but, because this state of affairs is a *universal*, it can be reached by various causal roads, some of them differing radically from the road that is in fact taken; and, in the cases we have imagined, *every* causal road that *any* choice of the agent's might set him upon leads to this same state of affairs. This is why the agent in our attempts at Frankfurt-style counter-examples always turns out not to be responsible for the state of affairs he is unable to prevent.

Perhaps the point of this fanciful talk about "causal roads" will be clearer if we look at a case in which an agent is unable to prevent a certain state of affairs that involves roads *secundum litteram*. Suppose Ryder's horse, Dobbin, has run away with him. Ryder can't get Dobbin to slow down, but Dobbin will respond to the bridle: whenever Ryder and Dobbin come to a fork in the road or a crossroad, it is up to Ryder which way they go. Ryder and Dobbin are approaching a certain crossroad, and Ryder recognizes one of the roads leading away from it as a road to Rome. Ryder has conceived a dislike for Romans and so, having nothing better to do, he steers Dobbin into the road he knows leads to Rome, motivated by the hope that the passage of a runaway horse through the streets of Rome will result in the injury of some of her detested citizens. Unknown to Ryder, however, all roads lead to Rome: Dobbin's career would have led him and Ryder to Rome by *some* route no matter what Ryder had done. Therefore, Ryder could not have prevented C(Ryder passes through Rome on a runaway horse). Is Ryder responsible for this state of affairs? It is obvious that he is not. And it seems obvious that he is not responsible for this state of affairs just because it would have been the outcome of *any* course of action he might have elected. Our conclusion—that PPP2 cannot be refuted by Frankfurt-style counter-examples—is therefore not only true but intuitively plausible.

The universals that PPP2 is "about" are states of affairs; but if we had examined a principle, otherwise similar, about "event-universals" (for example, "its coming to pass that Caesar dies"), we could have employed arguments that differed from the above arguments only in verbal detail.

It has been suggested to me[23] that these arguments appear less plausible if one reflects on the fact that essentially similar arguments could be used to show that Gunnar did not *bring about* C(Ridley is killed) and that Gunnar's pulling the trigger did not *cause* this state of affairs. It is certainly true that if the above arguments are sound, then similar arguments can be used to show that Gunnar did not bring about C(Ridley is killed) and that his bodily movements did not cause this state of affairs to obtain. But these conclusions appear to me to be simply true. Let us concentrate on

(I)   Gunnar did not bring about C(Ridley is killed).

Why should anyone think (I) is false? It would clearly be invalid to argue that (I) is false because Gunnar did something logically or causally sufficient for C(Ridley is killed), for by the same argument we could establish the falsity of the (true) proposition that Gunnar did not bring about C(Ridley is mortal). Or consider the case of Ryder and Dobbin. In turning into a certain road, Ryder did something causally sufficient for his passing through Rome on a runaway horse, but would anyone want to say that Ryder *brought about* the (for him inevitable) state of affairs C(Ryder passes through Rome on a runaway horse)?

The states of affairs we have been considering are universals. There are *many* ways the concrete particulars that make up our surroundings could be arranged that would be sufficient for their obtaining. What Gunnar and Ryder can bring about is *which* of these possible arrangements of particulars—which murderer, which road—the universals will be "realized in"; that some arrangement or other of the particulars will realize these universals in something totally outside their control; it is not something they bring about. Here is an analogy involving another sort of universal, properties: Chisel is a sculptor, we suppose, and sculpts the heaviest statue that ever was or will be, *The Dying Whale*; thus Chisel brings it about that a certain particular, *The Dying Whale*, exemplifies the property of being the heaviest statue;[24] but he does not bring it about that this property is exemplified, since, no matter what he had done, this property would "automatically" have been exemplified by something or other. He causes something to exemplify this property, but he does not cause this property to be exemplified.

In affirming (I), I do not mean to affirm the falsehood

(II) Gunnar did not bring about Ridley's death,

where 'Ridley's death' denotes an event-particular (the identity of which is determined by its causal antecedents), one that is also perhaps denoted by 'Ridley's untimely death', 'the only death Gunnar ever caused', and so on. Anyone who feels inclined to reject (I) should make sure that this inclination does not arise from a failure to distinguish between (I) and (II). To revert to our sculpture example, (I) and (II) stand to each other roughly as do the following:

> Chisel did not cause the property of being the heaviest statue to be exemplified

and

> Chisel did not cause (the particular thing that is) the heaviest statue to exist.

The former is, as I argued above, true, and the latter false.[25]

So, it would seem, we are unable to devise a Frankfurt-style counter-example either to PPP1 or to PPP2. If our attempts at counter-examples looked initially plausible, this, I think, was due to a confusion. When we hear the Gunnar-Ridley story, it seems correct to say that it follows from the story that Gunnar is responsible for Ridley's death and that Gunnar could not have prevented Ridley's death. But 'Ridley's death' is ambiguous. If we are using this phrase to denote a universal, then we may say that Gunnar could not have prevented Ridley's death, but not that he was responsible for Ridley's death. If we are using this phrase to denote a particular, then we may say that Gunnar was responsible for Ridley's death, but not that he could not have prevented it.

This result might lead us to wonder whether Frankfurt's counter-examples to the Principle of Alternate Possibilities rest on a similar confusion. Suppose we were to split the Principle of Alternate Possibilities into two principles, one about "act-particulars" (event-particulars that are voluntary movements of human bodies) and one about "act-universals" (that is, things that could be done by distinct agents, such as murder, prayer, or killing Jones at noon on Christmas Day, 1953); should we then see that Frankfurt's alleged counter-examples to the Principle of Alternate Possibilities depend for their plausibility on treating one and the same act as a particular at one point in the argument and a universal at another?

I do not think that Frankfurt is guilty of any such confusion. The "acts" that figure in his counter-examples seem to me to be treated consistently as universals. If this is the case, it raises two questions. Let us split the Principle of Alternate Possibilities into two principles in the way suggested in the preceding paragraph: PAP1 (about particulars) and PAP2 (about universals). The first question: if indeed Frankfurt's "acts" are universals, he is arguing against PAP2; can his argument be met by considerations like those we raised in defence of PPP2? The answer seems to me to be "No", but I am not at all sure about this. The considerations raised in defence of PPP2 depended on our having at our disposal a fairly precise notion of "state-of-affairs universal", and I am not at present able to devise an equally precise notion of "act-universal" that I find satisfactory. The second question: what about PAP1? I do not find this question interesting, since I do not think that "event-particulars that are voluntary movements of human bodies" are what we are talking about when we talk about one's responsibility for one's acts. I shall not, however, defend this thesis here. An adequate defence of it would be fairly complex, and I do not think my reasons for thinking what I do on this matter are worth developing merely to establish a negative conclusion, a conclusion, moreover, upon which none of our arguments depends.

5.7 We have seen that three principles relating ability and responsibility cannot be refuted by Frankfurt-style counter-examples:

> A person is morally responsible for failing to perform a given act only if he could have performed that act;

> A person is morally responsible for a certain event-particular only if he could have prevented it;

> A person is morally responsible for a certain state of affairs only if (that state of affairs obtains and) he could have prevented it from obtaining.

I shall argue that these three principles entail that moral responsibility requires free will. That is, I shall deduce from these three principles the following conclusion: the thesis that there is such a thing as moral responsibility entails the free-will thesis. By 'the thesis that there is such a thing as moral responsibility', I mean the thesis that *someone* is morally responsible for *something*—for some act, some event, some state of affairs, the publication of some scurrilous pamphlet, the currency of some malicious rumour, or the decline of classical studies at some university. By 'the free-will thesis', it will be recalled, I mean the thesis that most people, if not all people, are very often, if not always, in the following position: when they are faced with having to choose among various incompatible courses of action, *each* of these courses of action is such that they can (are able to, have it within their power to) choose *it*.

In order to deduce the free-will thesis from the thesis that
there is such a thing as moral responsibility we shall need two
premisses in addition to our three principles.

The first of these is:

> If (i) no one is morally responsible for having failed to
> perform any act, *and* (ii) no one is morally responsible
> for any event, *and* (iii) no one is morally responsible for
> any state of affairs, then there is no such thing as moral
> responsibility.

This premiss is not a tautology, for there are arguably other
things for which one can be held morally responsible than
unperformed acts, events, and states of affairs. There are, if
nothing else, *performed* acts. (Of course, these may be a
species of event, but I should not want anything I say to
depend on the premiss that acts are simply a type of event.)
Could it not perhaps be that Gunnar is responsible for having
shot Ridley, though he is responsible for no event or state of
affairs? It might be thought that if he is responsible for having
shot Ridley, then it follows that he is responsible for C(Gunnar
shoots Ridley). But this does not follow. For suppose that
Gunnar has shot Ridley and is responsible for having done so,
but suppose that if Gunnar had decided not to shoot Ridley,
something outside his control would have caused him to shoot
Ridley. Then in every future that is open to him, Gunnar
shoots Ridley, and, as we have seen, is therefore not responsible for its being the case that he shoots Ridley. Even in this
outré case, however, it would seem that Gunnar is responsible
for *some* state of affairs: he is responsible for C(Gunnar shoots
Ridley without having been caused to do so by something
outside his control), for example. Moreover, he would seem
to be responsible for the event-particular, Ridley's death. I
am unable to construct a case in which it seems plausible to
say that an agent is responsible for some act but not for *any*
state of affairs, and *a fortiori*, I am unable to construct a case
in which it seems plausible to say that an agent is responsible
for some act but not for *any* state of affairs *or* any event *or*
any unperformed act. I conclude that our first premiss is true
and in fact necessarily true.

The second premiss we shall need is:

If (i) someone could have performed (i.e. had it within his power to perform) some act he did not in fact perform, *or* (ii) someone could have prevented some event that in fact occurred, *or* (iii) someone could have prevented some state of affairs that in fact obtains, then the free-will thesis is true.[26]

This premiss would be hard to deny. If any of the disjuncts of its antecedent is true, then, surely, someone has been faced with incompatible courses of action that were severally open to him. Consider, for example, the first disjunct. Suppose that Gunnar could have shot Ridley but didn't; then the course of action *shooting Ridley* was open to him owing to the fact that he could have shot Ridley; and the course of action *not shooting Ridley* must have been open to him since he took that course of action. Similar arguments could be given for the other two disjuncts.

It is easy to see that our two premises and our three principles together entail the proposition that the existence of moral responsibility entails the free-will thesis. I am aware that the argument of the present section that is intended to establish this thesis is trivial and might even be described as pedantic. It has, however, one interesting feature: it does not rely on the Principle of Alternate Possibilities but only on "similar" principles that cannot, so far as anyone knows, be refuted by Frankfurt-style counter-examples. Therefore, we may conclude that even if Frankfurt has shown that the Principle of Alternate Possibilities is false, it is nevertheless true that moral responsibility requires free will.

Our "philosophical commonplace", then, retains its status, and a major part of the answer to the question, "What would our not having free will mean?" must be: our not having free will would mean that moral responsibility does not exist.

5.8 To this argument someone might reply as follows:

You have shown at most that *in one sense* of 'free will', moral responsibility requires free will. But that is not very interesting unless it is supplemented by an argument for the conclusion that this sense of 'free will' is the sense this term has in other parts of your book. Mightn't it be that some key term that figures in the definition of 'free will'—'could have done otherwise', say—has more than one sense? And mightn't it be that you have shown that determinism entails that one "couldn't have done otherwise" in sense A and that moral responsibility requires that one "could have done otherwise" in sense B?

In Section 3.11 I briefly considered what was essentially this objection. I attempted to meet it by the following device. I invited the reader to consider the Third Argument—the First Argument would have done as well—and to consider the phrase 'No one has a choice about whether p', which occurs in that argument. I asked the reader to substitute the phrase 'No one has a choice about whether p, in just the sense of *having a choice* that is relevant to questions of moral responsibility' at each occurrence of the former phrase in the premises of the Third Argument. I then asked the reader to consider carefully whether any of these premises appeared less plausible on this new interpretation. It was my contention that the "new" premises appeared no less plausible than the "old".

In the present section, I shall attempt to meet this charge of possible equivocation in another way. I shall argue "directly" for the incompatibility of determinism and moral responsibility. That is, I shall argue that determinism is incompatible with responsibility, and my argument will make no mention whatever of free will: notions like *could have done otherwise* and *had a choice about* will play no part in the argument of the present section. This argument will indeed be *formally* identical with one of our arguments for the incompatibility of free will and determinism—the Third Argument of Chapter III—but the *concept* of free will will not figure in it. Now if I am successful in showing that moral responsibility is incompatible with determinism and if my argument for this conclusion does not make any use of the concept of free will, it will not *follow* from my success in this undertaking that my earlier arguments about "free will" and determinism, on the one hand, and about "free will" and responsibility, on the other, involve the *same* concept of free will. Nevertheless, it would be highly implausible to suppose otherwise and I doubt whether anyone who accepted the argument I am about to give for the incompatibility of responsibility and determinism would feel any temptation to think that the term 'free will' has been used in the earlier sections of the present chapter in a sense different from the sense in which it was used in earlier chapters.

The argument, pretty clearly, is sound if and only if the Third Argument is sound. We shall proceed by redefining the modal symbol 'N' that figured in that argument. 'Np' was read 'p and no one has, or ever had, any choice about whether p'. We shall now read 'Np' as 'p and no one is, or ever has been, even partly responsible for the fact that p'.[27] Our argument will depend upon two inference rules that are inscriptionally identical with the rules (α) and (β) of Section 3.10:

(A) $\Box p \vdash Np$

(B) $N(p \supset q), Np \vdash Nq$.

The validity of Rule (A) seems to me to be beyond dispute. No one is responsible for the fact that $49 \times 18 = 882$, for the fact that arithmetic is essentially incomplete, or, if Kripke is right about necessary truth, for the fact that the atomic number of gold is 79. (Doubtless it is true in some sense of 'because' that (A) is valid *because* (α) is valid; doubtless the fact that no one has any choice about the truth-value of a necessary truth is the *reason* no one is responsible for the truth-value of a necessary truth. But whatever the *reason* for the validity of (A) may be, it is unquestionably valid.) The validity of (B) is a more difficult matter. Let us return to (B) after we have presented our analogue of the Third Formal Argument.

This argument will require two premises, 'NP_0' and 'NL'. (As in Section 3.10, the symbol 'P_0' abbreviates a sentence that describes the state of the world at some time before there had ever been any human beings, and the symbol 'L' abbreviates a sentence that expresses the conjunction into a single proposition of the laws of nature.) The former of these premises is obviously true, since no human being is morally responsible for anything that occurred before any human beings had ever been. The latter is obviously true, since no human being is responsible for the laws of nature. (For example, if it is a law of nature that nothing travels faster than light, then no human being is morally responsible for the fact that nothing travels faster than light.) Our argument is inscriptionally identical with the Third Formal Argument. We begin with the consequence of determinism with which the Third Formal Argument began:

(1) $\Box(P_0 \mathbin{\&} L. \supset P)$.

('P', we remember, is a dummy letter for which any sentence expressing a truth may be substituted.) From (1) we may deduce

(2) $\Box(P_0 \supset (L \supset P))$

by elementary modal and sentential logic. Applying rule (A) to (2), we have

(3) $N(P_0 \supset (L \supset P))$.

We now introduce a premiss:

(4) NP_0.

From (3) and (4) we have by rule (B)

(5) $N(L \supset P)$.

We introduce our second premiss:

(6)   NL.

Then, from (5) and (6) we have by (B)

(7)   NP.

I have called this an argument. More precisely it is an argument-form. We may derive indefinitely many arguments from it by substituting arbitrary sentences for 'P'. If the sentence substituted for 'P' is a truth, and if determinism is true, the substitution-instance of (1) so obtained will be true and the argument so obtained will be sound (assuming, of course, that it is valid). This fact about our argument-form amounts to a proof of the following proposition: substitute any *truth* you like for 'P' in the following schema

> If determinism is true, then no one is, or ever has been, morally responsible for the fact that P

and you will get a truth. For example, if you substitute 'Kennedy was assassinated', 'The US used atomic weapons against Japan', or 'Nixon received a pardon' for 'P', you will get a truth. This result, I think, may be properly summarized in these words: determinism is incompatible with moral responsibility.

We have proved this result provided that the reasoning employed in our argument-form is valid; that is, provided that both (A) and (B) are valid; that is—since the validity of (A) is beyond dispute—provided (B) is valid. Let us now turn to the question of the validity of (B).

Since (B) is formally identical with (β), we might expect that anyone who attempted to answer this question would encounter obstacles similar to those we encountered in our attempt in Section 3.10 to answer the question whether (β) is valid. This is indeed the case.

The purely formal argument for the validity of (β) presented in 3.10 will, of course, apply to (B): if there is any set of possible worlds W such that 'Np' can be thought of as making the assertion that p is true in every member of W, then (B) will "come out" valid; if there is any set of worlds that stands to 'Np' as the set of all worlds in which the laws of nature hold stands to 'it is physically necessary that p' and as the set of all morally permissible worlds stands to 'it is morally required that p', then the validity of (B) follows. And it is not wholly implausible to suppose that there is such a set; perhaps the set containing the actual world and all and only those worlds such that human beings can be held morally responsible for their non-actuality. But I have no way of showing that there is some set of worlds—whether it is the one mentioned in the preceding sentence or some other—that bears the required relation to 'Np'. It seems to me obvious that there *must* be some such set, whether or not I have correctly named it, but the compatibilist will presumably deny that there is any such set, and I have no argument to use against him.

The prospect of showing (B) to be valid by reducing it to generally accepted inference rules seems, if anything, even bleaker than the prospect of showing (β) to be valid by that method. It is hard to see how an inference rule essentially involving the concept of moral responsibility could be reduced to inference rules involving only non-moral concepts. And it is hard to think of generally accepted rules of inference that essentially involve moral concepts. The familiar principle that *ought* implies *can* may be such a rule, but there are few if any others. And while this familiar principle might be of some use in proving the validity of (B) if we were allowed to assume the validity of (β), this is not something we can properly assume.

I think the only thing I can do to persuade the reader that (B) is valid is to ask him to consider carefully such instances of it as

> N John was bitten by a cobra on his thirtieth birthday
>
> N (John was bitten by a cobra on his thirtieth birthday⊃ John died on his thirtieth birthday)
>
> *hence*, N John died on his thirtieth birthday

and

> N Plato died in antiquity
>
> N (Plato died in antiquity⊃ Plato never met Hume)
>
> *hence*, N Plato never met Hume

and to attempt to construct counter-examples to it. (I am asking, of course, for counter-examples that can be seen to be such without assuming that determinism is compatible with moral responsibility.) I believe that the plausibility of (B), like the plausibility of (β), is best appreciated by someone who has made a serious and sustained attempt to show that it is invalid.[28]

One might at this point want to raise the question whether my use of (B) begs the question against the proponent of the compatibility of moral responsibility and determinism. But what I should say in response to this question so perfectly parallels what I have said in response to the question whether my use of (β) begs the question against the proponent of the compatibility of free will and determinism, that I shall simply refer the reader to Section 3.10 and ask him to read it *mutatis mutandis*. I will, however, risk wasting space and write out the result of making a certain set of mechanical substitutions in the final paragraph of 3.10. I have now given an argument for the incompatibility of moral responsibility and determinism. If the compatibilist (sc. with respect to responsibility and determinism) wishes to refute this argument—and, of course nothing obliges him to do this—here is what he will have to do: he will have to produce some set of propositions intuitively more plausible than the validity of (B) and show that these propositions entail the compatibility of moral responsibility and determinism, or else he will have to devise a counter-example to (B), a counter-example that can be evaluated independently of the question whether moral responsibility and determinism are compatible.

5.9 I take the arguments of Sections 5.3 through 5.8 to establish that moral responsibility requires free will in just that sense of *free will* in which it was argued in Chapters III and IV that free will is incompatible with determinism.

The main conclusion of the present chapter, then, is that our not having free will would mean that we are morally responsible for nothing. The strongest argument for the existence of free will seems to me to be this: moral responsibility requires free will and we *are* responsible for at least some of the things we have brought about. In Chapter VI, I shall argue that this is the *only* strong argument for the existence of free will. But we have also seen that free will is incompatible with determinism. Suppose there were arguments for determinism that were rationally more compelling than this argument for free will. If this were so, then we should be rationally compelled to reject the thesis of the reality of moral responsibility. Such a conclusion might lead us to reopen the question of the compatibility of free will and determinism. For, it might be argued, however plausible the premises of our various arguments for incompatibilism may be, their denials are not nearly so implausible as the thesis that there is no such thing as moral responsibility. But this consideration should lead us to reopen the question of compatibilism only if we can discover arguments for determinism whose premisses are more plausible than the premisses of our arguments for incompatibilism.

In Chapter VI, we shall take up the question "What arguments can be given in support of determinism?" and we shall compare the premisses of these arguments with the premisses from which we have deduced incompatibilism, and with the proposition that there is such a thing as moral responsibility. If we do not reject the reality of moral responsibility, then we shall have to reject either incompatibilism or determinism. I shall try to discover which of these courses is the best.

Chapter VI

The Traditional Problem

6.1 In Chapter I, I argued that the problem of free will and determinism was best looked upon as two problems: the Compatibility Problem and the Traditional Problem. Chapters III and IV were devoted to the Compatibility Problem and its ramifications. That is, in those two chapters we attempted to answer the question whether free will and determinism are compatible. We concluded that they are in fact incompatible. This conclusion has the consequence that the Traditional Problem exists, a proposition that all the most acute thinkers about free will, from the seventeenth century to the present, have been at great pains to deny. (I am not happy about enlisting in a war in which the enemy forces are commanded by Hobbes and Hume and Mill. But I must follow the argument where it leads.) In the present chapter I shall do what I can about the Traditional Problem. I do not know how to *solve* it. That is, I do not know how to find out whether we have free will. There is, I believe, one good argument for the existence of free will, and no good argument against it unless there should be some good argument for determinism. I believe, moreover, that there are no good arguments for determinism and that there are some rather good arguments against it. The preceding two sentences sum up what I believe to be the "dialectical situation" in which the philosopher who confronts the Traditional Problem finds himself. The body of this chapter will be a defence of the thesis that this description of such a philosopher's dialectical situation is an accurate one.

6.2 Let us turn to the question of determinism. That is, let us ask what reasons there are for thinking that determinism is true and what reasons there are for thinking that determinism is false. Determinism, we remember, is the thesis that the past and the laws of nature jointly determine a unique one among the possible or internally consistent futures to be *the* future, the actual future. (Let us remember that determinism must

be carefully distinguished from the thesis of universal causation, the thesis that every event—or state of affairs or what
have you—has a cause. Even if I am wrong in my belief that
universal causation does not entail determinism,[1] that this
entailment holds is certainly a substantive philosophical thesis.
And I doubt whether anyone would think that universal
causation was incompatible with free will unless he thought
that universal causation entailed determinism.) It will be convenient to present our enquiry as a commentary on two assertions: 'Science shows determinism to be true' and 'Reason
shows determinism to be true'.

(i) *Science shows determinism to be true.* This simply does
not seem to be the case. If anything, quite the opposite is
true, since the standard interpretation of quantum mechanics
is indeterministic. This bald statement requires a variety of
qualifications and comments.

(a) One sometimes hears it said that quantum-mechanical
indeterminacy applies only to unobservable, submicroscopic
events and not to the observable events of everyday life. This
is quite false: quantum mechanics is a *physical* theory—as
opposed, say, to a biological or geological theory—and is thus
as legitimately applied to the behaviour of an elephant or a
glacier as to the behaviour of a neutrino or a positron. It is
true that the predicted indeterminacy in the behaviour of an
elephant or a glacier is smaller by many orders of magnitude
that anything that could be measured by the most marvellous
instruments that are dreamt of in our science fiction. Nevertheless, it is *there.*

More important than this, however, is the fact that the
domain of the submicroscopic and the domain of the observable are not causally isolated from each other. This is, in a
sense, a truism, since the behaviour of the observable presumably supervenes on the behaviour of the submicroscopic.[2]
But there is a stronger and more interesting sense in which
these two domains are not isolated from each other: *individual*
submicroscopic events can "trigger" observable events. One
device that actually effects such a "triggering" is a Geiger
counter. The passage of a single alpha particle or electron or
burst of high-energy electromagnetic radiation through a tube

of gas can sufficiently ionize the gas in the immediate vicinity of the path of the intruder to produce an effect that—after suitable amplification, which a Geiger counter is designed to provide—registers as an audible click; and any such particle or burst will have been produced by a change in the nucleus or the orbital electrons of a single atom. These facts may, I think, be fairly summarized by saying that an individual submicroscopic event is the cause of the click that the Geiger counter produces. Given this feature of Geiger counters, it would be easy enough to construct devices whose behaviour is undetermined (provided, of course, that the quantum theory is actually right). We might, for example, build a time bomb incorporating a radioactive source, a Geiger counter, and a firing mechanism designed to take a Geiger counter's "output"—clicks or whatever—as "input". Such a bomb might be designed to explode if the counter, for example, clicked five times within any ten-second interval. Suppose we were to build such a bomb and arm it; suppose the obliging God of the Philosophers were to provide us with a thousand perfect duplicates of it—the finest duplicates that omnipotence could contrive, this duplication, of course, being understood to include the setting of the arming mechanism. What would happen? What would *not* happen, save on the barest chance, is the simultaneous explosion of all the bombs. Or at least this would not happen unless the very basis of current physical theory is a ghastly illusion. To say this is not to place limits on the possible accomplishments of omnipotence, or not unless one would place such limits if one said that even an omnipotent being could not make a functional aeroplane entirely out of cheese and whipped cream. For just as cheese and whipped cream are materials intrinsically unsuited to the needs of aeronautical engineering, *any* physically possible material is intrinsically unsuited to the task of building a time bomb that is both deterministic and constructed in the way specified earlier in this paragraph. Actual matter, matter that obeys the rules of quantum mechanics, is intrinsically incapable of carrying within itself the perfectly determinate dispositions to future behaviour that strict determinism requires.

It would seem then, that the truth of quantum mechanics is incompatible not only with determinism generally, but even with the more modest doctrine that the past states of the universe, whether observable or unobservable, determine a unique succession of future *observable* states.

(b) In classical physics, the momentary state of a physical system (or, at any rate, of a point mass) is represented by a set of vectors—say, the set containing the position and momentum vectors of the system. In quantum physics, however, the momentary state of a system is represented by a *function*, the ψ-*function* of the system. Just as the laws of classical mechanics determine the way in which a classical system will change its state with the passage of time (in response to impressed forces), so the laws of quantum mechanics determine the way in which a quantum-mechanical system will change its state with the passage of time. I use the word 'determine' quite deliberately: given the quantum-mechanical state of a closed system (such as the entire physical world) at a given time, only one "future"—one sequence of quantum-mechanical states—is possible for that system.[3] Thus, it would seem, quantum mechanics is a deterministic theory.

There is some sense in describing matters this way. But if we describe them this way, then we must distinguish between the question whether quantum mechanics is a deterministic theory in the sense of the preceding paragraph and the question whether quantum mechanics entails determinism in the sense of Chapter III. Though quantum mechanics may be a deterministic theory, it seems to me to be wholly implausible to suppose that its truth entails determinism. This would be a plausible supposition if *all* the properties of a physical system at a moment were determined by its quantum-mechanical state at that moment. This, however, does not seem to be the case, since the properties a macroscopic object can actually be *observed* to possess at a given moment do not in general follow from the quantum-mechanical state of that object (that is, the sum of the ψ-functions of all its constituents) at that moment. Rather, there is in general only a *statistical* correlation between an object's being in a certain quantum-mechanical state—whether that object is an observable or a submicroscopic object—and its possessing a determinate observable or measurable property. Consider Laplace's omniscient Intelligence. Even if it were possible for this Intelligence to know the quantum-mechanical state of the entire world at the present moment, the most that follows from the fact that quantum theory is a deterministic theory is this: the Intelligence would know the quantum-mechanical state of the world at all future moments. But from the supposition that the Intelligence will know the quantum-mechanical state of the world in, for example, the year 2000, one cannot infer that the Intelligence will know whether I shall be alive or dead in that year or where I shall be or what philosophical problems will be exercising me. At most, I think, the Intelligence would be able to assign probabilities to various alternative hypotheses about my condition in that year. As to whether any given reasonably specific hypothesis would receive a significantly higher probability-assignment than those equally specific hypotheses with which it is in competition, I have no idea. Certainly the Intelligence could not make any very detailed predictions about the undetermined time bombs we considered earlier; he would be able to tell us only things like this: "The probability that the bomb will explode within the next hour is .7362". Thus even the Intelligence who Laplace thought would have no use for the concept of probability would, in a world that quantum mechanics gives a correct description of, find this concept indispensable.

That is to say, he would find this concept indispensable if he were interested in properties other than those that belong to a system in virtue of its quantum-mechanical state. It is just possible that someone might maintain that, in some sense, only quantum-mechanical properties are "real": that a correct picture of ultimate reality would have room only for quantum-mechanical properties and must exclude any such properties as *being red, being in motion*, or *thinking about quantum mechanics*. A philosopher who took this position could consistently say that quantum mechanics is a correct theory of physical reality and that determinism is true. But such an extreme position is unlikely to win many followers, and I shall not discuss it further.

(c) Many philosophers and many scientists have had a hard time accepting quantum mechanics as anything more than a stopgap, a theory that works well and is certainly better than nothing, but which somehow *must* eventually be superseded by a deterministic theory. (Einstein, for example, felt this way.) There are two ways in which such a supersession might come about.

First, quantum mechanics might be superseded by some theory that is incompatible with it. Presumably this would have to be a novel and revolutionary theory, the postulates of which were unlike those of quantum mechanics "from the ground up". No one, of course, can say that this couldn't happen. But it is worth noting that no such theory has appeared; quantum mechanics has no serious competitor.[4]

Secondly, quantum mechanics might be superseded by some theory that is compatible with it but more comprehensive. Einstein's treatment of the statistical theory of Brownian motion provides an example of the sort of possibility I am thinking of. In a classic paper, Einstein showed that the statistical laws describing the odd path (a "drunkard's walk") taken by a dust particle suspended in a fluid (Brownian motion) could be derived from certain plausible theses concerning the agitation of the particle by the thermal motion of the molecules that fluid was composed of; he showed this, moreover, quite independently of the question whether these thermal motions were themselves deterministic. In this sense, then, Einstein showed how a statistical theory could be "embedded in" a deterministic theory (the essentially Newtonian theory of the mechanics of thermal motion). Cases of this sort might lead one to wonder whether something of the same sort might be the case with quantum mechanics. Might there not be a deterministic micro-microcosm that underlies the apparently indeterministic behaviour of the microcosm in a way analogous to the way in which molecular motion, which may be presumed for the sake of the example to be deterministic, underlies the apparently indeterministic Brownian motion? Or, to put the question more formally, might it not be possible to embed quantum mechanics in some deterministic theory,[5] in a way analogous to the way in which Einstein embedded the statistical theory of Brownian motion in classical mechanics? (Deterministic theories in which quantum mechanics might be embedded are often called "hidden variable" theories, the "hidden" variables being the variables of the theory that represent the underlying deterministic features of a physical system that go unrepresented in quantum mechanics.)

The issues this question involves are very difficult. As I understand them—and I understand them hardly at all—the answer seems to be "Probably not". Von Neumann was once widely believed to have shown that the mathematical structure of quantum theory—unlike the mathematical structure of the statistical theory of Brownian motion—is such as to prevent its being embedded in a deterministic theory. That is, he was widely believed to have shown that any theory treating of the same subject-matter as quantum mechanics, that *could* be embedded in a deterministic theory, must make different predictions about observables from quantum mechanics, predictions that are known empirically to be false. The history of the reception of von Neumann's argument has been a tortuous one, which I shall not attempt to summarize.[6] The argument was never accepted by Einstein or by de Broglie, and has often been received with rather more rhetoric than is usual with a piece of mathematics. The following passage by two disciples of de Broglie

... the great mathematician von Neumann ... even produced a theorem stating that it would be impossible to picture any hidden determinism which would reproduce the statistical laws of [quantum] mechanics. This strange theorem claims that theory will not only explain all the observed phenomena, but will also, by way of its own internal logic, preclude any other explanation. However, de Broglie carried out a critical analysis, and showed that von Neumann's theorem was based upon an *ad hoc* hypothesis which in itself rendered the whole theorem valueless. We still cannot rule out the possibility of a hidden determinism.[7]

represents an extreme but far from unique reaction. (I doubt that many of the people competent to judge these issues would agree without reservation with the claim the authors make on behalf of the analysis carried out by their *maître*.)

Current thinking on these matters is hard to pin down. I *believe* it comes to something like the following: (i) there are mathematical *lacunae* in von Neumann's argument; (ii) other, rigorous arguments for the same conclusion have been constructed;[8] (iii) even the most rigorous of these arguments necessarily depends upon certain assumptions about measurement and about the nature of the "hidden variables" whose possible existence is being investigated. The assumptions that have been made are attractive and seemingly self-evident; but attractive and seemingly self-evident assumptions have had to be rejected on several notable occasions in twentieth-century physics. But even if it is possible to embed quantum theory in a deterministic theory, no one at any rate *has* done this in any way that is generally agreed by experts in quantum theory to be both logically satisfactory and "of physical interest". Therefore, it would seem, the most reasonable thing for the non-expert to believe at the present time is that it is at least unlikely that quantum mechanics will be embedded in a deterministic theory, and that it may well be impossible for this to happen.

These qualifications and comments having been made and duly noted, it still seems reasonable to say that science shows determinism to be false and it seems plainly impossible to say that science shows determinism to be true. But some philosophers depreciate this conclusion. I have heard philosophers argue more or less as follows:

> Quantum mechanics is all very well. But no one seriously suggests that "trigger" mechanisms like your time bombs are among the antecedents of human action. And if no such mechanisms are parts of us, then the degree of indeterminacy that quantum mechanics assigns to human thoughts, words, and deeds is so small as to be experimentally meaningless. A human being might, therefore, be as much a deterministic system as, say, a digital computer, even if quantum mechanics is correct and essentially indeterministic. And a computer (unless its designers deliberately incorporate a randomizing mechanism into it) is certainly the sort of thing that is "for all practical purposes" deterministic, albeit it may, for theoretical reasons, be held to be subject to some immeasurably small degree of indetermination. But surely the great achievements of brain physiologists in understanding the functioning of the brain (our "hardware") and the equally great achievements of psychologists in understanding our cognitive functioning (our "software") make only one conclusion possible: a human

being, like a computer, is "for all practical purposes"
a thing whose future behaviour is wholly determined by
its past states and its current "input".

I accept, and regard as important, the distinction between
strict determination and determination "for all practical
purposes". And I have no doubt that if strict determination
is, as I have argued, incompatible with free will and moral
responsibility, then determination in this very slightly weaker
sense is also incompatible with them. It would, in fact, be an
easy task to adapt the arguments of Chapter III to show that
"near determinism" is incompatible with free will, though
the adapted arguments would be comparatively untidy. But
as for the "great achievements" argument, I can only call it
a bluff. I have a very hard time seeing why so many philosophers seem to think that the results of the empirical study of
human beings lend support to the hypothesis that human
behaviour is determined. (In the sequel, I shall use 'determined'
to mean 'always determined, for all practical purposes, by past
states and present stimuli'.) I do not mean that I believe that
empirical investigations have shown that human behaviour is
not determined. My difficulty is simply this: the human
organism and human behaviour are such terribly complex
things, and so little is known about the details of that terrible
complexity (in comparison with what there is to be known),
that it is hard to see why anyone should think that what we
do know renders a belief that human behaviour is determined
reasonable. I can only conclude that these philosophers are
convinced on *a priori* grounds, or perhaps on no real ground
at all, that human behaviour is determined, and, owing to this
conviction, are predisposed to regard very nearly anything as
evidence in support of it. (If this is so, it should not surprise
us. Similar cases abound. Many theists are predisposed to
overrate the evidential value of apparent design in nature, and
many atheists to overrate the evidential value of pain and
suffering.)
   Let us look at it this way. There are various theses, which,
if they were to turn out to be true, could only lead the edu-
cated person to protest that the world was, epistemically
speaking, very unfairly arranged. Astrology is a good example

of such a thesis. If astrology should turn out to be true, then the world would have to be a very different sort of world from the world that science forces those of us who attend to it to think it is. (I am not talking about the possibility that there might turn out to be a grain of truth in astrology; I am talking about its turning out to be true that there is nothing but truth in astrology.) The ultimate truth of astrology is a possibility that is perhaps logically consistent with the totality of my sensory experience to date; nevertheless, if astrology should turn out to be true, then I could only say that the world was an *epistemic cheat*, a world that had been rigged, like a crooked roulette wheel or a magician's props, to effect a most unfair divorce of appearance from reality. But suppose it should turn out that the behaviour of human beings is not determined. Should we have any reason to regard the world as a cheat? Suppose, to make this question a bit less abstract, that it turns out that the electrical resistances across certain synapses in the brain occasionally change in undetermined ways and that these changes are of sufficient magnitude and sufficiently frequent to render false the hypothesis that human behaviour is determined.[9] What physiological theories would have to be discarded? What well-established experiments would have to be regarded as having produced misleading results? What parts of our textbooks on the structure and functioning of the brain would have to be rewritten? The answer, it seems to me, is that the discovery I have imagined would reveal no defects whatever in our theories and our textbooks, simply because no scientist has ever claimed to be able to predict the actual course of events in a living brain, just as no meteorologist has ever claimed to be able to predict next week's weather in complete detail.

Let us consider an analogy. Suppose we should somehow find out that demons have for centuries been influencing human behaviour by introducing minute changes in human brains—by introducing, in fact, changes in the electrical resistances across certain synapses. I think it should be pretty clear that none of our investigations into the functioning of the brain renders this supposition in the slightest degree improbable. If we learned this we should indeed know something new about the sources of human behaviour, but none of our painfully gathered information about the functioning of the brain would have to be discarded or have to be modified in any way. No one would have any right to exclaim, "But this goes contrary to what we believed we had discovered about the brain!" Now it is doubtless true that we are perfectly well justified in assigning a negligible subjective probability to the hypothesis that demons have been affecting our brains in the way I have imagined. But this justification does not rest on our *empirical* discoveries about the brain. (The question "Where *does* it rest, then?" is one I shall leave to epistemologists.) If we should learn that there are many intelligent races in the universe, exactly half of which are afflicted with manipulative demons, all our enormous learning about the structure and functioning of the brain would be of no help whatever to us in deciding whether our own race was so afflicted, for the proximate effects of the demons' manipulations would be lost in the immeasurably vast living wilderness of the brain.

Surely the case is the same if we are asking not about demonic influence but about undetermined change. Suppose God were to tell us that the brains of half the races in the universe were determined and that the brains of the other half were subject to minute undetermined changes of the sort I have imagined. How should we find out which sort of race *we* were? There seems to be no *a priori* reason to think that there would be any difference between the brains of the two sorts of race that could be detected in practice. It therefore seems quite unreasonable to say that we have any empirical reason for saying that we are determined.

I do not say that we have no reason of any sort for saying we are determined. I am saying that any reason we do have must be at least partly an *a priori* or conceptual reason. For example, someone might say that we are determined because, if we weren't, our behaviour would be a meaningless, random series of jerks and jumps and our speech mere babble. I have said in Chapter IV why I think this contention is wrong. My present point is that it is not based upon any empirical investigation of our functioning, but rather upon an identification of an undetermined sequence with a random sequence that is, presumably, made on purely conceptual grounds. This argument is no better and no worse today than it was in, say, the seventeenth century: all the gleanings of the empirical sciences of man are simply irrelevant to the question whether it is a cogent argument.

I do not say that in no case could we have decisive empirical evidence for the thesis that a thing was "for all practical purposes" determined. If I had never before seen a watch and one day pitched my foot against one when crossing a heath, I daresay I could easily enough discover that its behaviour was determined by its prior states and the momentary external influences to which it was subject. I should think that the results of such an investigation would be as reliable as any results ever are that require high-level abstractions like 'determination' and 'state' for their statement, and that they could be called *empirical* investigations with complete propriety. But we are not watches. Determined or not, we are too complicated for our internal workings to be surveyed like those of a watch.

I do not say that we could not have empirical evidence for the thesis that a *man* was "for all practical purposes" determined. Perhaps in the future it will be possible to construct computer models of particular brains that will enable us to predict how a particular person will react to various stimuli. If these stimuli were of complexity comparable with that of the stimuli we encounter in everyday life, and if the predictions were always, or almost always, right, then we should have very good reason indeed to believe that human beings were determined. And, of course, there are almost certainly other sorts of evidence, sorts of evidence I cannot imagine, that would render highly probable the hypothesis that we are determined. But no such evidence ever has been collected, and, even if human beings are determined, it looks like being a very long time before anyone ever does collect it.

To recapitulate: there would seem to be two ways in which scientific evidence could convince us that we are determined; first, we might believe this, as Laplace did, on the basis of our most general physical theories (which apply to all physical systems and hence to us); secondly, we might believe this on the basis of the empirical study of man. But our most general physical theories are no longer deterministic. And the empirical study of man has a long way to go before it will be in a position to tell us anything about whether we are or are not determined.

(ii) *Reason shows determinism to be true.* There are philosophers who believe that determinism is a truth of reason. That is, there are philosophers who claim to see, by some sort of conceptual or ontological insight, that the laws of nature *must* be sufficiently "tight" that, at any given moment, there is only one physically possible future. I do not share this insight and I doubt whether it really exists. Moreover, I know of no very plausible argument that proceeds from premises known *a priori* to the conclusion that the world is wholly determined.[10]

There is one principle from which determinism can be deduced, however, about which I have something more useful to say than "I don't believe it". This is the famous Principle of Sufficient Reason (PSR):

> For every state of affairs that obtains, there is a sufficient reason for its obtaining.

(In this principle, 'state of affairs' is to be understood in the sense of Section 5.6.) This principle may plausibly be held to entail determinism. For suppose determinism is false. Then there is a time following which there are at least two physically possible futures. But one of these must eventually come to pass; and it is hard to see what the "sufficient reason" could be for the coming to pass of *that* particular future. Now this reasoning is far from being watertight. Someone might suggest, for example, that the actual future became actual not for any reason to be found in the natural world but rather because God chose that it should, God's choice being in that case the sufficient reason demanded by PSR. It is clear, therefore, that we should need certain supplementary premises to deduce determinism from PSR. However this may be, PSR must be rejected, for it has an absurd consequence: the collapse of all modal distinctions.

In order to see this, we must take a brief look at the concept of a sufficient reason. I do not know how to give an adequate account of this concept—if indeed any concept attaches to the words 'sufficient reason'—but I think I can see certain features that any coherent concept that could reasonably be called by this name must have. First, if x is a sufficient reason for y, then x must entail y. That is, it must be impossible for x to obtain without y's obtaining. For if it were *possible* for x to obtain and y to fail to obtain, how could the obtaining of x be a *sufficient* reason for the obtaining of y?[11] Secondly, no *contingent* state of affairs may be its own sufficient reason. This would seem to be an essential feature of the concept of a sufficient reason. (I introduce the qualification 'contingent' in order to accommodate those who hold that a necessary state of affairs is its own sufficient reason. Whether or not this is so will make no difference to our argument.)

We may now show that PSR leads to the collapse of all modal distinctions. Let P be the conjunction of all contingently true propositions into a single proposition.[12] (In what follows, I shall use 'P' indifferently to denote the conjunction of all contingently true propositions and the state of affairs that consists in the truth of this proposition. In the language of Section 5.6, this vast state of affairs would be denoted by the result of prefixing 'its being the case that' to some sentence expressing P. This state of affairs is what Plantinga calls 'the actual world'. What I call 'the actual world' in Section 3.6 is the possibility that P be true.) It is evident that P itself is a contingent proposition, for a necessary proposition may not have even a single contingent conjunct. Now, according to PSR, there exists a state of affairs S that is a sufficient reason for P. S must be contingent or necessary. But it cannot be either. It cannot be necessary, for, if it were necessary then P (which, by our first principle, is entailed by S) would be necessary. It cannot be contingent, for if it were contingent, it would be a conjunct of P; and if it were a conjunct of P it would be entailed by P; and if it were entailed by P, it would both entail and be entailed by P; and if it both entailed and were entailed by P, it would *be* P (by the criterion of identity for states of affairs given in Section 5.6[13]); and if S *were* P, then a contingent state of affairs would be its own sufficient reason, contrary to our second principle. Since S cannot be either necessary or contingent, it cannot exist, and PSR is false.

This result follows provided we assume that there is such a thing as P—that is, the conjunction of all contingently true propositions. And there is such a thing as this if there are *any* contingently true propositions. Hence if PSR is true, there are no truths but necessary truths: there is no distinction to be made between truth and necessity.[14] Now many great philosophers have believed this—Spinoza, for example. But I doubt whether many present-day philosophers could bring themselves even to consider this thesis seriously. I know I couldn't. (For one thing, given the rule of inference that was called (α) in Section 3.10, it would entail that no one had free will.) We must therefore reject PSR, and with it the only plausible attempt to show that determinism is a truth of reason.

Since, as we have seen, neither empirical science nor pure reason shows determinism to be true, or even provides us with any good reason for thinking determinism true, we can only conclude that a belief in determinism is—at least at the present time—wholly unjustified.

6.3 What reasons are there for thinking that we have or that we lack free will?

I do not think that there is any way we can simply *find out* whether we have free will in the sense in which we can find out whether there is life on Jupiter. Some philosophers believe that it is possible to find out whether we have free will by *introspection*. But this seems just obviously wrong, since, if it were right, we could find out by introspection whether we were fitted out with Martian devices like those we imagined in our discussion of the Paradigm Case Argument in Chapter IV. And, of course, we cannot do this.

It is certainly true that most of us are perfectly certain that we have free will. But there is no reason to think that our perfect certainty on this matter derives from our having, in some sense, "direct access" to the springs of action in the way some philosophers believe we have direct access to our own mental states. It rather derives, I should think, from our knowledge, in most cases inarticulate, that one cannot deliberate without believing in one's own free will. It seems to me to be reasonable to suppose that for any race of rational beings, and for any type of activity that is inextricably entwined with very nearly every aspect of their lives—as deliberation about future courses of action is inextricably entwined with very nearly every aspect of *our* lives—if there is some

proposition the unthinking acceptance of which is a presupposition of that activity, then reflective, theoretical assent to
that proposition will be common, if not universal, among the
members of that race. Philosophers belonging to that race
may, consistently with my thesis, occasionally raise questions
about how these propositions that are presupposed by very
nearly every aspect of their lives are to be justified; some
philosophers may even, consistently with my thesis, *verbally*
reject these propositions.[15]

It is because the proposition that we have free will is insep-
arably bound up with our deliberative life, in my view, that
most of us are certain we have free will. But if this is indeed
the correct explanation for our certainty, then this certainty
is without evidential value. Our certainty about our own conscious mental states may proceed from the fact that each of
us is, necessarily, in a privileged position in any dispute about
his mental states; but no one is necessarily in a privileged
position in a dispute about whether he has free will. If each
of us has implanted in his brain a Martian device like the one
we have imagined, then it is the Martians, and not we, who
are the experts on the question whether we have free will.

Is there any way other than introspection for us to find
out whether we have free will? Well, if determinism is true,
then we might find out that we have *no* free will by finding
out that we are determined. But the difficulties that attend
finding out whether we are determined have already been
discussed. Moreover, even if determinism is false, it seems to
be mere wishful thinking to suppose that we shall find out
that we have free will by finding out that determinism is false.
First, it is unlikely that we ever shall find out that we are
undetermined (in the sense of Section 6.2), even supposing
that we are undetermined: we are simply too complicated for
such a discovery to be likely. Secondly, if we *did* find out
that we were undetermined, this discovery would not show
that we have free will. I have argued in various parts of this
book that our being undetermined is a necessary condition
for our having free will and is not a sufficient condition for
our not having free will. But I have never said that our being
undetermined is a sufficient condition for our having free will.
I have not said this because it is false: the proposition that it

is undetermined whether I shall raise my hand at a certain time does not entail the proposition that I have it within my power to raise my hand at that time. Suppose, for example, that it is physically possible that I shall raise my hand one minute from now. Suppose also that I am tied to an undetermined time bomb of the sort we considered in the previous section. Suppose the bomb is in fact going to go off in 30 seconds. Then, though there are futures consistent with both the present state of the world and the laws of nature in which I shall raise my hand one minute from now, I have no choice about whether I shall raise my hand one minute from now, since I shall be in bits one minute from now and have no choice about this.[16]

So, it would seem, there is no hope of finding out whether we have free will by finding out whether determinism is true. And there is no way other than this (and introspection) that I can think of that even seems relevant to the question whether we have free will. Is our position therefore hopeless? I think not. Let us return for a moment to the consequences of rejecting the free-will thesis, a subject we discussed at length in Chapter V. We saw in that chapter that the denial of the free-will thesis entails that there is no such thing as moral responsibility. And this was hardly a surprising conclusion: there is hardly anyone who has supposed that we could be held morally accountable for what we do if we have no choice about what we do. But if the reality of moral responsibility entails the existence of free will, then, I would suggest, we have a perfectly good, in fact, an unsurpassably good, reason for believing in free will. For surely we cannot doubt the reality of moral responsibility?

There are, perhaps, people who not only doubt but reject the thesis that *they* are morally responsible agents. (I am thinking of psychopaths. I say 'perhaps' because it is not clear to me what goes on in the mind of, say, the man who rapes and murders a little girl and afterwards feels no remorse.) But few people if any will react to an act of gratuitous injury deliberately done them by a human being in the way that they would react if that same injury were caused by a bolt of lightning or a bough broken by the wind. When some *person* injures *us*—at least if we believe he knew what he was doing and that he could have helped doing it—we react in certain characteristically human ways: we blame, we remonstrate, we hate, we reflect on the futility of hate, we plan revenge, we remind ourselves that the desire for revenge is a desire to usurp God's prerogative. Which among these things we do will presumably be partly a function of our constitution and our education. That we shall do at least some one of them follows from our being human, if not simply from our being rational beings. And to react in any of these ways is to demonstrate more surely than any high-minded speech ever could that we believe in moral responsibility.

I have listened to philosophers who deny the existence of moral responsibility. I cannot take them seriously. I know a philosopher who has written a paper in which he denies the reality of moral responsibility. And yet this same philosopher, when certain of his books were stolen, said, "That was a *shoddy* thing to do!" But no one can consistently say that a certain act was a shoddy thing to do *and* say that its agent was not morally responsible when he performed it: those who are not morally responsible for what they do may perhaps deserve our pity; they certainly do not deserve our censure.

What I have said in the last few paragraphs about our belief in moral responsibility is in some respects similar to what I said in Chapter V about deliberation and our belief in free will. But there is a difference. The philosopher who denies free will continually contradicts himself because his non-verbal behaviour continually manifests a belief in free will. But, I would suggest, the philosopher who denies moral responsibility speaks *words* that contradict his theories, words like "That was a shoddy thing to do". It is not only that his deeds belie his words (though of course that is true too), but that his words belie his words. I suggested in Chapter V that it would be impossible for us to cease behaving in ways that manifest a belief in free will. But I don't think it is *impossible* for us to cease talking in ways that manifest a belief in moral responsibility. It would be merely very, very difficult. I ask you to try to imagine what it would be like never to make judgements like 'What a perfectly despicable way for him to behave' or 'You'd think a person with her advantages would know better than that' or 'I can never think of what I did without feeling sick'. If you try to imagine this, perhaps you will experience what I do when I try the experiment. I find that one difficulty I anticipate in giving up making such judgements is very much like a difficulty I should anticipate in giving up making judgements like 'That car is dangerous because of its bad brakes' and 'The mushrooms growing under that tree are poisonous'. This difficulty arises from two facts: such judgements are often *right* and they are extremely important for getting along in the world. Think of some piece of behaviour you have witnessed that you really would call 'perfectly despicable'. Isn't that the right thing to call it? Doesn't it *describe* it? Isn't it just as "objective" a description (whatever that means) as 'dangerous' or as 'poisonous'?

Many philosophers, I suspect, will say that they use such words as these to describe people's behaviour, but that in doing so they are not ascribing to those people moral responsibility for that behaviour. This seems to me to be wrong. Suppose that there is a certain man who did a thing that led us to say, "That was a perfectly despicable thing for him to do". Suppose that we later discover that he did that thing shortly after he had been given, without his knowledge or consent, a drug that is known to alter human behaviour in radical and unpredictable ways. Suppose this discovery led us to decide that he had "not been responsible for what he was doing" at the time he performed the act. It seems to me that we could not then go on saying, "That was a perfectly despicable thing for him to do", not even if we qualified this assertion by adding, "though he wasn't responsible for his acts when he was doing it". That additional clause, in fact, does not seem to me to be a coherent qualification of the original assertion (unless, perhaps, 'That was a perfectly despicable thing for him to do' is taken to mean, '*Normally* what he did would be a perfectly despicable thing for someone to do'; but that is not the case we are considering). The reason is simple. To call an act 'despicable' is to censure its agent for performing it, while to say of an agent that he was not responsible for what he was doing when he performed an act is to excuse him for performing it; and one cannot simultaneously excuse and censure.

We all, therefore, believe that people are sometimes morally responsible for what they do. We all believe that responsibility exists. And, I think, if we examine our convictions honestly and seriously and carefully, we shall discover that we cannot believe that this assent is merely something forced upon us by our nature and the nature of human social life, as our behavioural manifestations of assent to the proposition that we have free will are forced upon us by the sheer impossibility of a life without deliberation. I think that we shall discover that we cannot but view our belief in moral responsibility as a justified belief, a belief that is simply not open to reasonable doubt. I myself would go further: in my view, the proposition that often we are morally responsible for what we have done is something we all know to be true.

That we are convinced that we know something does not, of course, prove that we do know it or even that it is true. But it *is* true that we are morally responsible, isn't it? And we *do* know it to be true, don't we?

If we do know that moral responsibility exists, then we should have no doubt about whether we have good reason to believe we have free will. It is this and only this, I think, that provides us with a reason for believing in free will. It may well be that, ironically enough, we believe that we are free because we have no choice about what we believe about this (owing to the necessity, for one's deliberations, of a belief in one's own free will). But this fact cannot be anyone's *reason* for believing in free will: at most it could be someone's excuse if he were charged with believing in free will without having any reason that supported his belief. If someone were asked to *defend* his belief in free will, he could not reply by saying that neither he nor anyone else had any choice about what he believed about free will. But it is as adequate a defence of the free-will thesis as has ever been given for any philosophical position to say, "Without free will, we should never be morally responsible for anything; and we are sometimes morally responsible".

I will now consider an objection to this argument (or, more exactly, an objection to the employment of this argument by an incompatibilist) which, in some moods, I find very powerful and which, I suspect, many philosophers find absolutely convincing:

If what you say is correct, then, because we know that moral responsibility exists, we know that we have free will. But, according to you, the free-will thesis entails indeterminism. And, presumably, you think that your arguments present the attentive philosopher with a good reason for believing that the free-will thesis entails indeterminism. Therefore, if all your arguments are correct, then our (alleged) knowledge of the existence of moral responsibility, coupled with certain arguments *a priori*, can constitute a good reason for believing that determinism is false. But these things are not the *sorts* of things that can be a good reason for believing in indeterminism. Indeterminism is, to put it bluntly, a thesis about the motion of particles of matter in the void; the more special thesis that *we* are undetermined (in the sense of Section 6.2) is a thesis about the structural details and the minute workings of our nervous systems. Only scientific investigations are relevant to the truth or falsity of such theses. (This assertion is true even if you are right in saying that it is unlikely that science will be able to show that we are undetermined.) Therefore, your arguments represent just one more attempt by a philosopher to settle by intellectual intuition and pure reason a question that should be left to empirical science. And if it should prove that this question *can't* be settled by empirical science, owing perhaps to "the obscurity of the matter and the shortness of human life", then we should simply elect to have no opinion about the right answer to it.

I have said that in some moods I find this argument very powerful. Nevertheless, my considered opinion is that it ought to be rejected. Its weak point can best be brought out by comparing it with a certain argument that often figures in discussions of scepticism. Here is a version of this argument. The sceptic speaks:

You say that most of the propositions we unreflectively assume we know to be true *are* true. You, say, moreover, that we know this, or, at least, have good reason to believe it. But we can deduce from this thing you say we have good reason to believe that there exists no Cartesian Universal Deceiver—no being who deceives us all about almost everything. (For if there were such a being, then almost every proposition we think we know to be true would be false.) Now the obvious validity of the parenthetical deduction clearly provides the attentive philosopher with a good reason to accept its corresponding conditional:

If most of the propositions we think we know to be true *are* true, then there exists no Universal Deceiver.

But if we have good reason to accept both this conditional and its antecedent, then we have good reason to accept its consequent; that is, we have good reason to accept the proposition that there exists no Universal Deceiver. But these considerations are not the *sorts* of considerations that can provide us with good reasons for believing that there is no Universal Deceiver. The thesis that there is no Universal Deceiver is, to put it bluntly, a thesis about the features of a part of the world that is inaccessible to any possible human investigation. Your contention that we have good reason to believe that most of our knowledge-claims are correct is just another case of a philosopher claiming to have good reason to believe something no one could possibly have good reason to believe.

The anti-sceptic who replies to this argument has, I think, two types of response available to him.

First, he can simply reply that the deduction the sceptic has presented—coupled with his own thesis about the general correctness of our claims to knowledge—*does* show that he has good reason for believing that there is no Universal Deceiver. This might be a surprising result, he will concede, but the argument seems quite inescapable. As to the sceptic's contention that the thesis of the non-existence of a Universal Deceiver is not the sort of thesis that human beings *could* have good reason to accept (the anti-sceptic continues), the sceptic's deduction shows this initially plausible contention to be false.

Secondly, the anti-sceptic can point out that the sceptic's

argument depends essentially on the rule of inference

Rp
$R(p \supset q)$
hence, Rq

(where 'R' stands for 'one has good reason to believe that') and deny that this rule is valid.

I myself favour the first response. But this is not a book about epistemology, and I shall say no more about the question of the proper response to the sceptic's argument. My purpose in setting forth the sceptic's argument is to compare it with the argument about determinism that is our present topic. These two arguments are very much alike. They are so much alike, in fact, that the philosopher who rejects the conclusion of the argument about determinism has two types of response available to him that are exactly parallel to the two types of response available to the anti-sceptic.

First, he can simply reply that the incompatibility of moral responsibility and determinism—coupled with his thesis that we know, and hence have good reason to believe, that moral responsibility exists—*does* show that he has good reason to believe that determinism is false. As to the contention that determinism is not the sort of thesis that we could have good reasons for thinking false unless those reasons were provided by empirical science, he can reply that the arguments he accepts for the incompatibility of determinism and moral responsibility show this initially plausible contention to be false.

Secondly, he can point out that the "determinism" argument depends essentially on the inference rule displayed above, and deny that this rule is valid.

I favour the first response, but I shall not directly defend the thesis that this response is the better of the two. I shall instead argue that any philosopher who rejects the sceptical argument we have examined should also reject the argument we are considering, and for the same reason, whatever that reason may be. Any philosopher who rejects the sceptic's argument on the ground that 'one has good reason to believe that' does not behave like a necessity operator, should, of course, reject the "determinism" argument, since that argument depends on the same assumption about the logic of good reasons. And any philosopher who is willing to say that, since he has good reason to believe that our knowledge-claims are generally correct, he therefore has good reason to believe that there is no Universal Deceiver, should feel no qualms about saying that since he has good reason to believe that moral responsibility exists, he therefore has good reason to believe that determinism is false. Moreover, any philosopher who accepts the "determinism" argument will be hard-pressed to find a way consistently to reject the sceptic's argument. Assume that this philosopher accepts the rule of inference 'Rp, $R(p \supset q) \vdash Rq$', which is common to the two arguments; how then is he to reply to the critic who takes him to task as follows:

> You say that our having good reasons for believing in moral responsibility is not the sort of thing that could provide us with good reasons for believing that determinism is false. But you *also* say that our having good reasons for believing that our knowledge-claims are generally correct *is* the sort of thing that can provide us with good reasons for believing that there is no Universal Deceiver. But isn't it true that you are responding to philosophical problems that are essentially the same in arbitrarily different ways? If reflection on human knowledge can provide us with good reason for accepting a thesis about what goes on beyond the limits of any possible observation, then why can't reflection on human moral responsibility provide us with good reason for accepting a thesis about the motion of particles of matter in the void?

I can see no very convincing response to this. I conclude that the incompatibilist who believes that the existence of moral responsibility is a good reason for accepting the free-will thesis ought not to be troubled by the charge that his views commit him to the thesis that the existence of moral responsibility is a good reason for believing in indeterminism. Or, at any rate, he ought to be no *more* troubled by this charge than he is troubled by "Universal Deceiver" arguments for scepticism.

6.4 We have seen that there is every reason to think determinism false, and no good reason to think true the weaker thesis that our behaviour is determined in the way the be-haviour of computers is determined. We have seen that there is at least one excellent reason for believing that we have free will: that we are at least sometimes morally responsible. We have seen that free will is incompatible with determinism. We are therefore in a position to put forward, tentatively perhaps, an answer to the question, "Do human beings have free will or are they determined?" Human beings have free will and they are not determined.

This answer may be difficult for some people to accept. (I am not, of course, saying that it is so obviously the right answer that it should be accepted without argument. But I have given arguments. They are this book.) I am thinking of people who find this answer so initially implausible, so in-trinsically incredible, that they will respond to the arguments I have given either by ignoring them or by setting out to find something wrong with them. (And, of course, a philosopher who sets out to find something wrong with an argument will generally find some feature of it that he will consider a mistake. If he finds nothing else, he can always point to the fact that the premisses of the argument entail its conclusion and charge the argument with begging the question.)

This book is not really addressed to such philosophers as these. It is addressed to those who have kept an open mind about the question of free will and determinism and who would like to see what the arguments are. I am not one of those people who regards "keeping an open mind" as, *per se*, a virtue. To have kept an open mind about Nazi racial theories or about astrology would not be a mark of virtue, either intel-lectual or moral. But, it seems to me, the course of the free-will debate since the seventeenth century has been sufficiently confusing, and twentieth-century physics and psychology, and investigations of the human nervous system, have been suf-ficiently complex, that having kept an open mind about free will and determinism has indeed been consistent with the dictates of virtue. Why, then, do some philosophers feel com-pelled to react to the thesis of the last paragraph but one by calling its proponents "superstitious" or "believers in magic" or "armchair physiologists"?

Perhaps there is no general answer to this question. But

I am convinced that in a large number of cases the answer is that the people who regard my central thesis as simply incredible are victims of scientism. Scientism, as I use the word, is a sort of exaggerated respect for science—that is, for the physical and biological sciences—and a corresponding disparagement of all other areas of human intellectual endeavour. It hardly need be pointed out that scientism is the primary ideology of our age. It hardly need be pointed out that the illusions scientism engenders are so pervasive and so insidious that it is practically impossible to get anyone who is subject to them to consider the possibility that they might be illusions.[17] (I *hope* the following disclaimer is unnecessary: if I deprecate scientism, I do not thereby depreciate science. To deny that Caesar is due divine honours is not to belittle his generalship.)

Now it is not my purpose to enter into an extended discussion of or to offer an analysis of scientism. I wish only to call attention to two effects of scientism on contemporary philosophical thought.

The first of these effects might be described as a revolt against holism. The following sort of reasoning is common enough:

> A human being is, in the last analysis, a system of atoms, an enormously complex material thing the properties of which supervene entirely upon the properties of the individual atoms that are its parts and upon the arrangement of these individual atoms. But the kind of indeterminism you ascribe to human beings could not supervene upon the properties of a system of atoms. To say that if all the parts of a system are determined then the whole system is determined is not to commit the fallacy of composition, for determination is clearly the sort of property that "carries over" from parts to whole. Admittedly the case is complicated by the fact that the individual atoms *are* undetermined in some respects owing to quantum-mechanical considerations. But quantum mechanics has nothing whatever to do with free will, and hence you must be postulating some other source of indetermination, one having no basis in the behaviour of atoms and thus one that can have no place in a scientific world-view.

I really don't know what to say about this sort of argument, except that there must be something wrong with it. It proceeds from certain premisses (such as anti-holism and the thesis that quantum-mechanical indeterminacy has nothing to do with free will) and these premisses must be examined for plausibility. I myself am inclined to think that the two premisses I have mentioned are quite plausible. I don't think that it is very likely that we have any properties that don't in *some* sense supervene upon the properties of atoms of which we are composed; I am certainly not much tempted to think that quantum mechanics has anything to do with free choice.[18] But even if these were the only two premisses of the argument, and even if the argument were absolutely clear in its terminology, and indisputably logically valid, I should not find the argument convincing. Its premisses may be plausible, but I regard them as far less plausible than the proposition that we are sometimes morally responsible for our acts and the proposition that rule (β) is valid. And if the argument of this book is correct, then it follows from these two premisses that there is something wrong with the argument we are considering.

I should like to know just what *is* wrong with it, but I don't. I have never pretended to understand "how free will works". If I knew I would tell you, but I don't know. The questions raised by the above argument are deep ones that I have no way of answering, just as I have no way of answering the questions that I confessed myself puzzled by in Section 4.4. I have no liking for unresolved mysteries in philosophy. But it is no good trying to pretend that mysteries do not exist if they quite plainly do exist. Moreover, I prefer small mysteries to large mysteries. One way to look at this book is as an attempt to present a position on free will that commits its adherents to smaller mysteries than does any available competing position. Anyone who rejects the central theses and arguments of this book—I include under this heading the theses of the present chapter, including the thesis that we are not determined—must, if he has any well-worked-out theory of free will, determinism, and moral responsibility, accept at least one of these three propositions:

Moral responsibility does not exist;

Moral responsibility exists even though no one ever has any choice about anything;

There exist true propositions p and q such that someone has no choice about whether p is true and has no choice about whether if p is true, then q is too, and yet *has* a choice about whether q is true.

If any of these propositions were true, that, in my view, would be a very great mystery indeed, a mystery much greater than that which would attend the truth of either

We have properties that do not supervene upon the properties of the atoms that we consist of

or

Free will involves quantum-mechanical indetermination.

Those under the influence of scientism will doubtless not see it that way. In their view, no mystery could be greater than the truth of a proposition that is in conflict with "the scientific world-view". And at least the former of these two propositions is in conflict with that world-view, since it denies the anti-holism that is an essential part of the "scientific world-view".[19]

Here, I think, those philosophers whom I describe as victims of scientism and I have reached bedrock. We have nothing more to say to each other; or, at any rate, though we may call each other names we have no more arguments.

The second effect that scientism has on some philosophers is to produce in them a profound fear of being caught out by the progress of science.[20] I believe that many philosophers would find the following words an accurate expression of their thought. "Suppose I were to accept the argument that since moral responsibility exists, determinism is false, and then suppose the physicists were to decide that determinism is true after all. Or suppose the neurophysiologists or the cognitive psychologists or someone should provide us with a really good reason for believing that we're deterministic systems in at least as strong a sense as the sense in which computers are deterministic systems. I should look pretty silly then, shouldn't I? I should be laughed at for the same

reason we laugh at Hegel, who deduced the necessary existence of exactly six planets *a priori*. My argument and I should
be mentioned in the same breath as Kant and Euclidean
geometry or Paley and the Argument from Design. Well, that's
not for me.''

Perhaps I am being unkind; perhaps the words I have attributed, or nearly attributed, to "many philosophers" could be
replaced with nobler-sounding words. But I do think that the
ideas expressed in this imaginary quotation have more influence than has been generally recognized, and I do not consider
this influence a healthy one. While it would be silly for philosophers—or for anyone else, including scientists—to *set out* to
predict the future course of the sciences, I see no reason for
philosophers to shrink from holding positions that entail that
science will never be able to do this or that. Such theories
would be empirically refutable, of course, but I see no reason
to regard that as a bad thing. If a philosophical theory is
empirically refutable and gets empirically refuted, then there
will be one fewer philosophical theory about, and that would
be no bad thing.

Now some philosophers may say that a theory that calls
itself philosophical ought not to be empirically refutable, since
any theory that is empirically refutable is "automatically"
not philosophy but science. According to this view, Kant and
Paley—I pass over the fib about Hegel[21]—were, when they were
discussing geometry and design in nature, doing science (very
bad science, incidentally) rather than philosophy. According
to this view, I too am guilty of presenting science in the guise
of philosophy. This meta-philosophical thesis seems to me to
have nothing whatever to recommend it. The theories and
arguments of this book are paradigmatically philosophical,
whatever else they may be. If someone wants to say that
they're also "scientific", that's a matter of indifference to me.
Of course I should not want anyone to say that my theories
and arguments were *bad* science. Or not unless it is possible
for bad science to be good philosophy, something that seems
to me to be highly improbable. I think that what I have produced is good philosophy, and what I should like to see from
my adversaries is *arguments* for the conclusion that it is bad
philosophy.

Despite what I have said, there is one question I shall very likely be asked by philosophers who think I have overstepped the bounds of philosophy that I think is a good question and which I am bound to answer. That question might be put like this:

> Very well. You admit that your theory is in principle empirically refutable. If physics were to become once more deterministic, or if the empirical sciences of man were to provide us with really good reasons for believing that a human being is a deterministic system, then (you concede) your rejection of determinism would be rendered untenable by science. Well, suppose this *did* happen despite your prediction that it won't. What would you say then?

I am not quite sure what I would say, but I believe I would say that (β) was, after all, invalid. (I shall presently touch on the reasons for my hesitation on this point.) This response is not purely *ad hoc*; I have not simply picked some one of the possible reactions to a scientific validation of determinism and then arbitrarly embraced that reaction. Consider the following list of propositions:

(1) We are sometimes morally responsible for the consequences of our acts;

(2) The validity of (β) entails that our having free will entails indeterminism;

(3) If (1) is true, then we have free will;

(3a) We have free will;

(4) (β) is valid;

(4a) Our having free will entails indeterminism;

(5) Indeterminism is true.

In this book I have argued for, or, at any rate, asserted each of these propositions. Nevertheless, I do not regard them as equally well established. Though all of them are, in my view, very likely true—I mean I regard their conjunction as very likely true, and *a fortiori* I regard them individually as very

likely true—some of them seem to me to be what I shall call
preferable to others. (Let us say that a person regards *p* as
preferable to *q* if (i) he believes that it is much more likely
than not that both *p* and *q* are true, and (ii) he believes that
if either *p* or *q* *is*, after all, false, then *p* is true and *q* is false.)
I have indicated my preferences among these propositions by
the way I have numbered them: I regard (1) as preferable to
(2), (2) as preferable to (3), and so on. (But I regard neither
of (3) and (3a) as preferable to the other and neither of (4)
and (4a) as preferable to the other.) Why do I have this set of
preferences? Well, there are certain purely formal constraints
at work. For example, since (1) and (3) jointly entail (3a),
and since I know this, it would be rather odd of me to regard
both (1) and (3) as preferable to (3a). But, mainly, this just is
the preference-ordering I find myself with. I do not know
how to defend it, though, of course, I should be willing to
consider carefully any argument for the conclusion that I
ought to order my preferences differently. I do not, of course,
think that my ordering of preferences is entirely arbitrary.
I suppose I think that it is based on various conceptual insights
and that if you do not share my preferences you lack my
insights.

I am not in the least embarrassed by admitting this. Every
philosopher's positions, however much he may argue, must
ultimately be based on certain propositions that simply *seem*
to him to be true. There is no way round this; it is a simple
consequence of the fact that every argument has a finite
number of steps. Moreover, every philosopher must think
that those of his colleagues whose "ultimate premisses" are
incompatible with his own have either not considered those
premisses with sufficient care or else lack some sort of insight
into how things are. What else is he to think? If he thinks
that the ultimate premisses of those who disagree with him
are "just as good" as his own, then he should admit that he
has no business holding his own premisses and should, at the
very least, retreat to a position in which he accepts nothing
stronger than the disjunction of his former premisses with all
those propositions that are "just as good".

One more meta-philosophical point is in order. Given that
a philosopher must have a set of "ultimate premisses", there

would seem to be no reason to suppose that he should regard none of them as preferable to the others. There is no reason why a philosopher should not say something of this form: "Propositions A and B at present constitute the foundations of my philosophy; I have no argument for either, but I believe I can simply *see* that they're true. Nevertheless, if either of them is false, it's B."

Now given that the above list accurately represents the ordering of my preferences, it is easy for me to say what I should do if science were to provide me with an indisputable reason for believing in determinism: I should have to reject (5). But (5) is entailed by (3a) and (4a), so I should have to reject either (3a) or (4a). Since I prefer (3a) to (4a), I should therefore have to reject (4a). But (4a) is entailed by (2) and (4), so I should have to reject either (2) or (4). Since I prefer (2) to (4), I should therefore have to reject (β). And that would seem to be the end of the matter. (In this reasoning, I of course presuppose that an "indisputable reason for believing in determinism" would not require me to accept without proof any proposition that I should prefer (β) to.)

I have defended (β) entirely on *a priori* grounds. But it would not surprise me too much to find that this proposition, which at present seems to me to be a truth of reason, had been refuted by the progress of science. Such refutations have happened many times. And it does not follow from the fact that they have happened that there is anything wrong with accepting on *a priori* grounds a principle that later turns out to be empirically refutable. One must simply realize that *a priori* convictions are as corrigible as any others.

I have earlier expressed some hesitancy about saying that I should reject (β) if science were to force me to accept determinism. I hesitate because this counter-factual supposition is very abstractly described. I wish to leave open at least the bare possibility that there is a way in which science might force me to accept determinism that would also force me to alter the ordering of preferences that I have expressed in the above list. I do not regard this as very likely; but who can be certain about what the future holds?

6.5 In this, the final section of this book, I shall outline its central argument.

The free-will thesis is the thesis that, very often, when we are faced with having to choose between incompatible courses of action, each of them is such that it is within our power to choose it. Or, more idiomatically, the free-will thesis is the thesis that we very often have a choice about what we are going to do.

Determinism is the thesis that, given the past and the laws of nature, there is only one possible future.

The free-will thesis and determinism are incompatible. That is, *incompatibilism* is true. This can be seen on the basis of several detailed arguments, all of which are elaborations of the following simple argument (the Consequence Argument):

> If determinism is true, then our acts are the consequences of the laws of nature and events in the remote past. But it is not up to us what went on before we were born, and neither is it up to us what the laws of nature are. Therefore, the consequences of these things (including our present acts) are not up to us.

One of these three detailed arguments—The Third Argument of Chapter III—is a particularly useful tool in a discussion of compatibilism because it isolates, as a separate premiss, the most doubtful thesis the incompatibilist must accept. That thesis is the validity of the following rule of inference:

(β) p and no one has, or ever had, any choice about whether p;

> If p then q, and no one has, or ever had, any choice about whether if p then q;
>
> *hence*, q and no one has, or ever had, any choice about whether q.

The proposition that this rule is valid, when carefully considered, disposes the mind to assent; it seems to be a truth of reason. But, for all that, it may be false. Still, it seems more likely to be true than certain of the incompatibilist's premisses. In particular, it seems more likely to be true than any conditional analysis of ability that is sufficiently complex to be able to "handle" the well-known counter-examples to simpler conditional analyses. This is the case simply because such analyses are too complex to be grasped as wholes and thus cannot even *seem* to be intuitively evident.

We should, therefore, be incompatibilists unless there is something objectionable about incompatibilism, something, moreover, that is *more* objectionable than the rejection of the apparently self-evidently valid inference rule (β). And indeed there is something objectionable about incompatibilism. The incompatibilist must either reject the free-will thesis or else accept the thesis that an agent often has a choice about whether a certain one of his inner states is followed by a certain overt act (the state being the cause of the act), even though neither the inner state nor anything else *determines* that act to occur.[22] I do find each of these alternatives objectionable, but the second seems to me to be far *less* objectionable than the rejection of (β). I therefore counsel accepting incompatibilism.

If incompatibilism is true, then either determinism or the free-will thesis is false. To deny the free-will thesis is to deny the existence of moral responsibility, which would be absurd. Moreover there seems to be no good reason to accept determinism (which, it should be recalled, is *not* the same thesis as the Principle of Universal Causation). Therefore, we should reject determinism.

This conclusion is, at least in principle, open to scientific refutation, since it is conceivable that science will one day present us with compelling reasons for believing in determinism. Then, and only then, I think, should we become compatibilists, for, in the case imagined, science has *ex hypothesi* shown that something I have argued for is false, and the weakest of my arguments are those that support incompatibilism.

Notes

PREFACE

1 In *Ethics and the History of Philosophy* (New York: 1952).
2 *Mind* (1934).
3 In Sidney Hook, ed., *Determinism and Freedom in the Age of Modern Science* (New York: 1958).
4 In Keith Lehrer, ed., *Freedom and Determinism* (New York: 1966).
5 Englewood Cliffs, NJ: 1966.
6 *The Journal of Philosophy* (1969).
7 Published as a pamphlet by Cambridge University Press, 1971.

CHAPTER I

1 Four very important problems about free will that we shall not consider are (i) the problem of free will and divine foreknowledge, (ii) the problem of free will and psychoanalysis, (iii) the problem of discovering whether Gödel's incompleteness results imply anything about human freedom, and (iv) the problem of discovering whether the conceptual impossibility of predicting one's own decisions implies anything about human freedom.

2 In my usage, *law of nature* and the physical modalities are inter-definable. I assume that, as etymology would suggest, the laws of nature and the laws of physics are the same, or, at least, that the former supervene upon the latter (that is, the laws of nature could not possibly have been different without the laws of physics also having been different).

3 *Psychological* determinism, the thesis that one's acts are determined by one's strongest motive, will not be discussed in this book. I can get no grip on the notion of a "strongest motive" and consequently have nothing to say about it.

4 The doctrine of immanent causation will be discussed in secs. 4.4 and 4.5.

5 To say that Tom has no cause is not to say that such things as Tom's coming to be and the fact of Tom's existence have no cause; nor is it to deny that Tom has an *aitia*.

6 *Causality and Determination* (Cambridge, 1971).

7 Jan Łukasiewicz "On Determinism", in Storrs McCall, ed., *Polish Logic* (Oxford: 1967). Perhaps an example would make Łukasiewicz's point clearer. Suppose t_1 is noon and t_2 is 1.00 p.m. Suppose the cause

of A occurred at 12.30, the cause of the cause of A at 12.15, the cause of the cause of the cause of A at 12.07.30, and so on, *ad infinitum*.

8 See sec. 4.4.

9 I doubt whether truth is necessary for lawhood. See sec. 1.5.

10 Perhaps there is more to a proposition's "supporting its counter-factuals" than this. If so, what more *is* there?

11 Or so most people now believe. Assume they're right for the sake of the example.

12 The remainder of this section derives mainly from Richard Taylor's classic paper "I Can", *The Philosophical Review* (1960).

13 In "Freedom to Act", in Ted Honderich, ed., *Essays on Freedom of Action* (London: 1973), Donald Davidson defends the view that the power to act is a "causal power". His thesis is consistent with mine. In Davidson's sense of 'causal power', the phrase 'if he wanted to speak French, he would' predicates a causal power of the person to whom it is applied. In my sense of 'causal capacity' it does not. For suppose a certain man would speak French if he wanted. It doesn't follow that there is any set of external circumstances such that if he were plunked down in those circumstances he would speak French (or do any other particular thing), for perhaps he doesn't want to speak French (or to do any other particular thing) and wouldn't want to under any circumstances. And, *a fortiori*, it doesn't follow that there is some set of circumstances in which he would speak French (or whatever) willy-nilly. I do not believe that the power to act *is* a "causal power" in Davidson's sense, but whether it is or not is a question that has nothing to do with the theses I have been advancing. See sec. 4.3 for a discussion of the power to act and conditionals whose antecedents involve states internal to the agent.

14 There seems to be no customary name for the conjunction of compatibilism with the thesis that we have free will.

15 R. E. Hobart, "Free Will as Involving Determination and Inconceivable Without It" (1934). P. H. Nowell-Smith, "Free Will and Moral Responsibility" (1948), J. J. C. Smart, "Free-Will, Praise and Blame" (1961).

16 See Richard Foley, "Compatibilism and Control Over the Past", *Analysis* (1979) and "Reply to Van Inwagen", *Analysis* (1980).

17 For more about "begging the question" and "where the burden of proof lies", see sec. 3.10.

CHAPTER II

1 C. D. Broad was a fatalist by the terms of this definition. The argument of his inaugural lecture, "Determinism, Indeterminism and Libertarianism" (in *Ethics and the History of Philosophy*, New York: 1952), might be summarized as follows: free will is incompatible with both determinism and indeterminism and is therefore impossible (though this bald summary does not do justice to Broad's beautifully finished lecture). In the present chapter we shall be concerned with fatalistic

arguments in a narrow sense (I resist the temptation to pun): those arguments that depend on the notions of time and truth. The question of the compatibility of free will with determinism and indeterminism will be considered in Chapters III and IV.

2 *The Collected Plays of W. Somerset Maugham*, (London: 1931), 298-9. The quotation is from "Sheppy", Act III.

3 There is a problem about defining *no matter what I do* (*he does*, etc.). Suppose you were to say "She would have died no matter what he had done", and a carping critic replied "That's not true! She wouldn't have died if he'd prevented her death, made an effective medicine out of the materials at hand, transported a doctor to her bedside by magic, or if he'd done any of a great variety of things." The obvious way of dealing with this critic is to stipulate that 'no matter what one does' means 'no matter *which of the things one can do* one does'. But if we accept this stipulation, then it will follow from fatalism that the man who delayed seeing a doctor about his cough till it was too late would have died of the disease the cough signalled *no matter what he had done* (since, according to fatalism, what he could have done and what he did coincide). And, in general, if we accepted this stipulation, it would be a consequence of fatalism that all events are strongly inevitable for everyone. That this is a consequence of fatalism is a thesis that one of the most prominent contemporary authorities on fatalism has been at pains to deny. (See Steven Cahn, *Fate, Logic, and Time*, New Haven and London: 1967, ch. 2, *passim*.) It would hardly do, therefore, to make this thesis true by definition. Perhaps the solution to this problem is to stipulate that *no matter what one does* means *no matter what choices or decisions one makes*.

4 To believe that God plays the role of a cosmic puppet-master would be to have a superstitious belief about God.

5 This is the infamous "idle argument" of antiquity, considered, according to Cicero, by Chrysippus.

6 For a detailed treatment of these issues, see Chapter V.

7 The one exception I know of is "Time, Truth, and Modalities" by "Diodorus Cronus" (Steven Cahn and Richard Taylor), *Analysis* (1965).

8 This is true in the same sense as that in which it is true that I use 'cardinal number' as a general term for the things people count with. But, of course, most numbers are too large for us to count with, and—in my view—most propositions are too complex for us to entertain. It would be more accurate, therefore, to say that I use *proposition* as a term for a certain class of objects, some of the simpler members of which are the things people *assent to*, etc. If anyone finds the "further" or "unentertainable" propositions mysterious, I ask him to lay aside his objections for the moment. Unentertainable propositions will play no role in the argument of the present chapter, though they will figure in our attempts to define determinism in Chapter III.

9 For the sake of convenience, I shall frequently use 'believe' and 'say' transitively when talking about the relations people bear to propositions, despite the fact that sentences of the form 'S says p' and 'S

believes *p*' are usually too odd-sounding for me to feel at all comfortable about them, except for the case in which '*p*' is replaced by certain 'wh'-nominalizations. For example, we certainly can't say 'John said Newton's First Law of Motion' and *my* ear doesn't much care for 'John believes Newton's First Law of Motion'—but 'John believes what Newton postulated about motion' is perfectly all right.

10 Thus, sentences containing indexical terms can, strictly speaking, be said to express propositions only in or relative to a situation or a "context of utterance", just as denoting phases containing indexicals can be said to denote objects only in or relative to a situation or context of utterance. We may therefore say that a sentence containing indexical terms expresses a given proposition in a given context of utterance, provided that the result of concatenating 'the proposition that' and that sentence denotes that proposition in that context of utterance.

11 We shall return to the topic of truth and falsity in sec. 2.7.

12 I use 'sound' and 'valid' in what have become their usual technical senses: a valid argument is an argument whose conclusion follows from its premisses; a sound argument is a valid argument with true premisses.

13 The remainder of this section owes a great deal to A. J. Ayer's essay "Fatalism", in *The Concept of a Person* (London: 1963).

14 I take it that when someone speaks these words, he uses the demonstrative pronoun to refer to the proposition expressed by the sentence the person he is speaking with has uttered, and not to the sentence uttered. To deny this would be like saying that in the following fragment of conversation,

> "How many have you invited to the wedding?"
> "Four hundred."
> "That's too many.",

the demonstrative pronoun refers not to the number four hundred but to the *words* 'four hundred'.

15 This paraphrase, I believe, captures Aristotle's view of truth-at-a-time. At any rate it is suggested by the language he uses in *De Interpretatione*, IX, particularly at 18b. A typical and especially suggestive passage is "... if a thing is white now, it was true before to say that it would be white, so that of anything that has taken place it was always true to say 'it is' or 'it will be'." (W. D. Ross (ed.), *The Works of Aristotle Translated into English*, vol. I (Oxford: 1928), tr. E. M. Edghill.) About twenty lines later, in discussing the alleged necessity of the events referred to in a correct prediction, he says, "... a man may predict an event ... and another predict the reverse; that which was truly predicted at the moment in the past will of necessity take place in the fullness of time. Further, it makes no difference whether people have or have not actually made the contradictory statements ...". Steven Cahn employs essentially this Aristotelian conception of truth-at-a-time. See his *Fate, Logic, and Time* (cited in note 3), 33 note 15.

16 This definition faces a great many purely technical difficulties. Suppose, for example, that no propositions were asserted in 10,000,000 BC

or earlier. Then, it would seem, it was true in 10,000,000 BC that no propositions had yet been asserted; or, at least, this would seem to be the right thing to say if the temporal qualification of the possession of truth makes sense. But, of course, if anyone had asserted this proposition in 10,000,000 BC he would have said something false.

17 This argument-form is essentially the principle that will be called 'Rule (β)' in the parts of this book that deal with free will and determinism. I have no wish to dispute the validity of this argument-form, for the validity of (β) comes very close to being the single premiss upon which the argument of this book is based. For a point about the relation of Rule (β) to fatalism see note 32, Chapter III.

18 *Metaphysics* (Englewood Cliffs, NJ: 1963), ch. 5.

19 Note that this point does not depend on our artificially extended sense of *in the absence of*. It therefore seems unlikely that Taylor's argument is defective owing to some incoherency in the notion of one's performing an act "in the absence of" conditions that, if they obtained, would obtain at times different from the time at which one performs the act.

20 Taylor has told me that he intended Principle (A) to apply only in the case of conditions causally but not logically necessary for one's acts. But what is the point of this restriction? Surely if it's plausible to suppose that I can't do a thing in the absence of a condition causally necessary for my doing it, then it's even more plausible to suppose that I can't do a thing in the absence of a condition logically necessary for my doing it. That is to say, if there were any good reason to reject the principle

> No agent is able to perform an act in the absence of a condition logically necessary for its accomplishment,

that reason would be an even better reason for rejecting the principle

> No agent is able to perform an act in the absence of a condition causally but not logically necessary for its accomplishment.

21 Richard Taylor, "I Can", *The Philosophical Review* (1960), 81.

22 This is as close as I can come to making sense of the syntactical *lusus naturae* (or *artis*) '(p) ($p \lor \sim p$)'. One might try 'Everything is such that either it or it is not the case that it'.

23 This argument-form certainly does not in any clear sense "presuppose" LEM.

CHAPTER III

1 "Freedom to Act" in Ted Honderich, ed., *Essays on Freedom of Action* (London: 1973), 139.

2 I know of only one fallacy that incompatibilists have been accused of that is not childish. In *Will, Freedom and Power* (Oxford: 1976),

155-6, Anthony Kenny charges that incompatibilists make use of the following rule of inference, which he contends is invalid:

> I cannot do so-and-so
> To do such-and-such is, in this case, to do so-and-so
> *hence*, I cannot do such-and-such.

(The incompatibilist, Kenny says, proceeds by substituting 'violate a law of nature' for 'do so-and-so' and expressions denoting unperformed acts for 'do such-and-such'.) Whether or not this inference form is valid, and I do not think Kenny presents a clear counter-example to it, I cannot see that any of the arguments of the present chapter depends on it, despite the fact that these arguments do depend on our inability to render false any proposition that is a law of nature.

3 In sec. 3.6 I shall explain in detail what I mean by *possible world* and related notions like that of truth "in" a world.

4 This point has nothing to do with the so-called "many-worlds" interpretation of quantum mechanics. What I call possible worlds are abstract objects: ways the universe might be. The "worlds" of the many-worlds interpretation of quantum mechanics, however, are concrete objects: universes.

5 Not that I *believe* that laws of nature are by definition true. See sec. 1.5. But I shall from now on assume that lawhood entails truth. This assumption could be dispensed with at the cost of minor complications.

6 This thesis would seem to entail that there are at least as many propositions as there are moments of time; and, presumably, there are as many moments of time as there are real numbers. To postulate an indenumerable infinity of propositions, most of which are not things that could possibly be thought of, owing to their unimaginable complexity, may seem to some people to be extravagant. But I do not see how to state the thesis of determinism without some "extravagant" assumption. Compare Richard Montague's criticism, in the opening paragraphs of "Deterministic Theories", of the characterization of determinism that he attributes to Laplace and Ernest Nagel. (*Formal Philosophy* (New Haven: 1974), 303 f.)

7 See Jan Narveson, "Compatibilism Defended", *Philosophical Studies* (1977).

8 The phrase 'possible in the broadly logical sense' is Alvin Plantinga's. See *The Nature of Necessity* (Oxford: 1974), 1 f.

9 There is one other way in which this definition may diverge from our intuitive notion of one's having the truth-value of a proposition within one's power. Consider the proposition that the safe is locked. Even if we were normally in the habit of talking of rendering propositions false, we should not normally say that an agent had it within his power to render this proposition false if he did not know, and had no way of discovering, the combination. But it may well be that a certain agent, who has no way of finding out the combination, is in the following situation: (i) he has it within his power to turn the dial left to 26, right

to 32, left to 5; (ii) it is not possible that he should do this and the past be as it was and the safe remain locked. Thus, by the strict terms of our definition, he can render false the proposition that the safe is locked. Therefore, it might be argued, what our definition really captures is something that is more like 's could, if he were lucky enough, render p false' than it is like 's can render p false'. But if this is so, it will not materially affect our argument. Our argument will, loosely speaking, proceed by deducing 'It is not the case that s can render p false', for arbitrary values of p, from determinism. If this thesis deduced from determinism is really best read 's could not, no matter how lucky he was, render p false', this fact would hardly undermine my claim to have demonstrated the incompatibility of free will and determinism. Moreover, the present definition has the useful consequence that 's can render p false' is a purely extensional context, a feature that might very well have to be sacrificed in order to produce a more intuitive result in cases like the case of 'He can render the proposition that the safe is locked false'.

10 Narveson, op. cit.

11 André Gallois, "Van Inwagen on Free Will and Determinism", *Philosophical Studies* (1977).

12 Many philosophers think that a "double temporal reference" is required to make ascriptions of ability fully explicit. That is, they think that the "real form" of ascriptions of ability is something like this: s could at t_1 have done A at t_2. I am not convinced by their arguments. I find 'Tom could have raised his hand at noon' ambiguous but clear—that is, I think it's clear what the two individually clear things this sentence might be used to say are—and 'Tom could at eleven o'clock have raised his hand at noon' sounds rather strange to me. I think the best way to understand sentences of this latter sort is like this: 's could at t_1 have done A at t_2' $=_{df}$'s could have (done A at t_2) and at t_1 it was not yet too late for s to do A at t_2'. That is, I prefer to take sentences of the form 's could have done A at t' as "basic" (whatever precisely that means) and to define sentences containing a "double temporal reference" in terms of these basic sentences, disambiguating brackets, and the notion of "not yet too late". I do not believe that my argument requires this rather special notion.

13 Cf. Narveson, op. cit. The possibility of this line of argument was first pointed out to me in conversation by Raymond Martin and Michael Gardner.

14 The speed of light is just under 3×10^8 metres per second. The difference is minuscule—about ninety times the muzzle velocity of a high-speed rifle bullet.

15 Oxford: 1974.

16 By 'possibility' I mean something like what philosophers have traditionally called 'logical possibility'. But I dislike this term intensely, since, in my view, many important possibilities and impossibilities do not owe their modal status to "logic", or not in any clear sense. It is, for example, as impossible as anything could be for the moon to be made

of cheese. This is just as much an impossibility as a round square; there is *no* sense in which the one is possible and the other impossible. But in what sense is the impossibility of the moon's being made of cheese "logical"? If anyone *does* think it's "possible" in any sense for the moon to be made of cheese, I recommend he read George Seddon's "Logical Possibility", *Mind* (1972). See also my "Ontological Arguments", *Noûs* (1977), and (for a discussion of the "green cheese" case) my review of R. G. Swinburne's *The Coherence of Theism*, in *The Philosophical Review* (1979).

17 I use 'object' simply as the most general count-noun. Thus, in my usage, everything is an object. I mean the word to have *no* implications beyond those that are, in the very strictest sense, consequences of this definition.

18 Assuming, that is, that our ordinary modal beliefs are correct, an assumption I shall feel free to help myself to when I am giving illustrative examples. But if Spinozism—a thesis strikingly at variance with our ordinary modal beliefs—were true, the possibility that Socrates teach Plato would include the second of these possibilities and would preclude, for example, the possibility that the Axis powers win the Second World War. Thus, if Spinozism were true, we should owe even more to Socrates' pedagogy than we had suspected!

19 Thus, those philosophers who go about saying loudly and defiantly, "There's only one possible world, the actual one!" are either Spinozists or fools.

20 This definition obviously entails that 'actual' does not mean 'existent'. All non-actual worlds *exist*, which is hardly surprising, since everything exists. (The golden mountain cannot be said to be a counter-example to this thesis, since there isn't any such thing as the golden mountain; no one can put forward the golden mountain as a counter-example to any thesis whatever, since there is no golden mountain to be put forward.) The thesis that non-actual worlds exist is simply a specification of the general truth that unrealized possibilities exist. (To deny this is to embrace Spinozism.) Some philosophers I have propounded this unremarkable proposition to have looked puzzled for a moment and then brightened and said, "Ah, I see—you mean they exist *as possibilities*." And yet if I had told these same philosophers that New York and London exist, they would *not* have looked momentarily puzzled and then have brightened and said, "Ah, I see—you mean they exist *as cities*." Perhaps this odd reaction has its roots in a confusion between possibilities and *possibilia*. If there were any such things as mere *possibilia*— which there aren't—they would be denoted by phrases like 'the golden mountain'. But a *possibile* is not the same as a possibility. Possibilities are denoted by phrases like 'the possibility that there be a golden mountain'. This phrase, of course, denotes something if and only if it's possible that there be a golden mountain.

21 My use of 'world' to denote comprehensive possibilities is not utterly at variance with ordinary English usage. In his article, "World", in *Studies in Words* (Cambridge: 1967), C. S. Lewis tells us that 'world'

has two main senses: 'the region that includes all regions' (the cosmos) and 'the state of affairs that includes all states of affairs'. And, surely, a (possible) state of affairs and a possibility are very similar things.

22 I prefer 'at' to 'in', since the former preposition is less likely to reinforce the widespread incoherent practice of thinking of possible worlds as things with insides (that is, cosmoi). But my usage is not consistent.

23 An equivalent definition: an object exists at a world if that world includes the possibility that that object exist. More generally, a proposition is true at a world if that world includes the possibility that that proposition be true. These definitions are equivalent because a counterfactual conditional having a protasis of the form 'If w were actual . . .' is equivalent to the corresponding strict conditional.

24 The first conjunct of the *definiens* is unimportant; it is there merely to restrict the application of 'Dx' to possible worlds, a function '$(\exists y)(Nxy)$' would have performed equally well. The second conjunct does the work.

25 I shall be forced to talk about the individuation of events in Chapter V.

26 The bars are, of course, as much a piece of imagery as the system of corridors. My use of them in this model is not meant to suggest that an agent is unable to bring about an event only in the case that some tangible and immovable barrier stands between him and the means necessary for bringing it about.

27 Perhaps there is only one "empty" world, only one world that contains no contingently existing objects. If so, this world is not relevant to our present concerns.

28 I doubt whether anyone has access, by the terms of this definition, to any set having a merely possible world as its single member.

29 I shall presently suggest a semantics for 'N', but only as a way of making the point that any very interesting semantics for this operator is going to be controversial.

30 In the remainder of this paragraph, I am going to be less careful about use and mention than is my habit.

31 Thomas McKay has proposed an interesting possible counterexample to (β). We should normally say that if someone throws a fair die in an honest game, then no one has any choice about the outcome of the throw. And most of us think that most gamblers have a choice about whether they practise their vice. But then the following instance of (β) could easily have true premises and a false conclusion:

> N Alfred throws a six
> N (Alfred throws a six $\supset$ Alfred plays dice)
> *hence*, N Alfred plays dice.

(The second premiss is true because the conditional embedded in it is a necessary truth.) *Respondeo*: Strictly speaking, Alfred does have a choice about whether he throws a six, at least provided he has a choice about whether he plays dice. He can avoid throwing a six by avoiding playing dice. What Alfred has no choice about is whether, *given that he plays dice*, he throws a six. That is—supposing that no one else has any choice about this either, and that Alfred does throw a six—N (Alfred plays dice ⊃ Alfred throws a six).

32 There is an argument about fatalism that parallels this argument about genetic determinism. What is essentially the argument for fatalism that we examined in sec. 2.5 can be stated in such a way as to make explicit use of (β). Let S be the (true) proposition that I shall shave tomorrow, and let *t* be some moment in the remote past. Availing himself of Rule (β), the fatalist argues:

> N S was true at *t*
> N (S was true at *t* ⊃ I shall shave tomorrow)
> *hence*, N I shall shave tomorrow.

In sec. 2.5, I argued that the first premiss of this argument was either meaningless, or, given a certain stipulation about what it might mean, doubtful. (Obviously no such move is open to us in relation to the arguments of the present chapter. The proposition that P_0 really *is* about the past and hence about what is outside our control. The proposition that S was true at *t* is made to look by a linguistic trick as if it were about the past. That is why the problem of fatalism is a problem to be dissolved by careful attention to the language of time and truth, while the problem of free will and determinism is deep and intractable and maddening.) This is a thesis about which the fatalist and I might have a serious philosophical discussion. But suppose that instead of saying this, I had simply denied that the above instance of (β) was valid. Then, I think, the fatalist would rightly have accused me of declining to make a serious contribution to the discussion, and so would any anti-fatalist who was really interested in getting to the bottom of the fatalist's puzzle.

33 In Chapter IV, the reader will remember, we shall examine two other arguments for compatibilism, the "Paradigm Case Argument" and the "*Mind* Argument". I shall not compare the premisses of these arguments with (β). The Paradigm Case Argument and two versions of the *Mind* Argument will be seen to suffer from defects more serious than an appeal to premisses less plausible than the validity of (β). The remaining version of the *Mind* Argument—there are three—will be seen to have the validity of (β) among its premisses.

34 I shall answer this charge in another way in sec. 5.8.

CHAPTER IV

1 "Divine Omnipotence and Human Freedom", in A. Flew and A. McIntyre, eds., *New Essays in Philosophical Theology* (London: 1955).

2 Ibid., 150.

3 W. P. Alston has suggested to me that this statement of (M) may be misinterpreted, so I shall say a few words more to try to make my

intentions plainer. The "table of instructions" consists entirely of conditionals, such as 'If you're in early middle age and a superior humiliates you by repremanding you in front of your subordinates, attempt to get revenge by spreading scurrilous rumours about his personal life, taking extreme care to see to it that these rumours can't be traced back to you'. The presence of the tiny device is causally sufficient for the subject's satisfying each of these conditionals; but it is time and chance that determine which of them the subject satisfies non-vacuously and which he satisfies only vacuously. Thus, (M) does not attribute omniscience to the Martians. They do not in general know what situations anyone is going to find himself in. But their "programs" for us are sufficiently comprehensive that every important contingency of human life is represented by the antecedent of one the conditionals that the program comprises.

4 Certain followers of Wittgenstein might say that if we made such a discovery we should no longer know *what* to say. But no one, I think, would feel tempted to say that we should simply continue to call people 'free'.

5 "An Empirical Disproof of Determinism?", in Keith Lehrer, ed., *Freedom and Determinism* (New York: 1966).

6 I have attempted in this brief discussion of Lehrer's reasoning to present an argument only for the conclusion that that reasoning is defective; I have not attempted a diagnosis. For a diagnosis, see my paper "Lehrer on Determinism, Free Will, and Evidence", *Philosophical Studies* (1972).

7 The most serious of these is that 'x can do y if he chooses' is no better a definition of 'x can do y' than 'x is beautiful if you look at it correctly' is of 'x is beautiful', or than 'x is poisonous if ingested' is of 'x is poisonous'. J. L. Austin has shown that 'he can if he chooses' cannot be regarded as the straightforward conditional it appears at first glance to be. ("Ifs and Cans", *Philosophical Papers* (Oxford: 1961).) I believe that the correct analysis of 'he can if he chooses' shows it to be a disguised conjunction: 'he can and if he doesn't this is only because he doesn't choose to and not because he can't'. Since this statement contains 'he can' as a conjunct, it is not going to be of much use to anyone who is interested in what 'he can' is compatible with.

8 See his review of Austin's *Philosophical Papers* in *Mind* (1964), and his "He Could Have Done Otherwise", *The Journal of Philosophy* (1967). I cannot resist quoting in its entirety a footnote to the latter:

> Presumably it was for reasons such as these that George Washington was said to be unable to tell a lie. The point was, not that he lacked the wit or skill or opportunity to do it, but that he was so good that he couldn't bring himself to deceive. Bayle quotes a seventeenth-century Walloon theologian, one de Wolzogue, who pointed out that, although God would have no difficulty in deceiving if he chose to deceive, nonetheless he cannot deceive since he cannot choose to deceive. De Wolzogue wrote: "God can deceive

if he will . . . but it is impossible for him to have such a will to deceive; it is also impossible for him to endeavor to employ his power for the execution of a deceit, whence I conclude that it is impossible for him to deceive." See Pierre Bayle, *A General Dictionary, Historical and Critical*, article "Rimini (Gregorio de)," note C. According to some Christians, an important point of difference between Mary and Jesus was that, while Mary could sin but never did, Jesus "has not merely not actually sinned, but also could not sin," the point being, again, that he could not undertake (choose, will, try, set out) to sin. Compare Ludwig Ott, *Fundamentals of Catholic Dogma* (Cork: Mercier Press, 1952), p. 169. Compare St. Thomas' treatment of the question, "Can God Do What Others Do?" in *On the Power of God*, Question II, Article 4.

9 "Cans Without Ifs", *Analysis* (1968-9).

10 As R. M. Chisholm showed in his review of Austin (cited in note 8), this definition could be improved by writing the *definiens* as follows:

There is something such that if x had chosen to do it, then x would have done y, and x COULD HAVE chosen to do it.

This definition would seem to avoid the difficulty illustrated by the Napoleon-Waterloo case mentioned earlier. But let us leave the definition as the text has it, since we shall be interested in other sorts of difficulties than those Chisholm's emendation is designed to obviate, and the emendation would cause our discussion of these other sorts of difficulties to be more complex than it need be.

11 Some philosophers have denied this, on grounds that are not clear to me. For a discussion of the question whether one's choosing to perform a certain act is itself an act, see Myles Brand's introduction to his collection, *The Nature of Human Action* (Glenview, Ill.: 1970), 14-16.

12 The desires that figure in the present example are "occurrent" and not "standing". This morning I wanted to visit the library to verify a reference and I also wanted to live to a ripe old age; but the latter desire, unlike the former, was never present to my consciousness, never before my mind. Thus the former desire (or "want", as too many philosophers insist on saying) was occurrent and the latter standing. I do not mean to imply that an unconscious person has no standing desires.

13 See his "'Can' in Theory and Practice: A Possible Worlds Approach", in M. Brand and D. Walton, eds. *Action Theory* (Dordrecht: 1976). Lehrer's analysis is not a conditional analysis, but it is sufficiently like one that various of its features may be "transferred" to typical conditional analyses with little modification. I should not want to give the impression that the analysis that follows in the text is equivalent to Lehrer's.

14 Can we define 'advantage' without using 'can' or some essentially equivalent term? (Does a 'can' grin residually up at us?) I am inclined to think that 'advantage' hides a 'can', but I will not press the point.

15 For an example of a compatibilist who, unless I have misunderstood him, has failed to grasp this simple point, see the papers by R. Foley

cited in note 16, Chapter I. I might mention in passing that there is a tendency among some compatibilists (including, I think, Foley) to treat their favourite conditional analyses as part of the thesis they call 'compatibilism'; that is, there is a tendency to treat this word not as a name for the thesis that free will and determinism are compatible, but rather as a name for something of this form: 'Because the following conditional analysis of *can* is correct . . ., free will is compatible with determinism'. This tendency should be resisted, if for no other reason, because it is possible to accept the compatibility of free will and determinism and to reject conditionalism. For an actual case of this, see Lehrer, "An Empirical Disproof of Determinism?", cited above.

16 For a conditional analysis of ability that does *not* have the consequence that any of the premisses of the First Formal Argument is false, see Carl Ginet, "The Conditional Analysis of Freedom", in P. van Inwagen, ed., *Time and Cause: Essays Presented to Richard Taylor* (Dordrecht: 1980). From now on, I shall generally use 'conditional analysis' to mean 'conditional analysis that supports compatibilism'.

17 The reader should be able to verify for himself that given the fairly precise notion of 'render false' that was introduced in sec. 3.4, the Analysis is incompatible with the truth of premiss (6).

18 We might expect from the preceding note that the correctness of the Analysis would entail the falsity of the premiss 'NL' of the Third Formal Argument—which is the premiss of that argument that seems intuitively to "correspond" to premiss (6) of the First Formal Argument —but this appears not to be the case. I do not think that this undermines my contention that the three arguments of Chapter III are essentially the same and stand or fall together. The three arguments represent three ways of "tightening up" the Consequence Argument and are in that sense essentially the same; but the three sets of technical devices used to tighten up the Consequence Argument differ markedly from one another and this had led to certain asymmetries among the premisses that superficially "correspond" to one another, with respect to their logical relations to the Analysis. I have chosen the Third Argument for detailed examination because I believe that the fact that the validity of (β) is the point at which the Analysis comes into conflict with that argument is of real philosophical interest, while the fact that the Analysis is in conflict with premiss (6) of the First Formal Argument—rather than with (5) or (4)—is pretty much an accidental result of the way in which I chose to define 'render false'.

19 Cf. P. A. Nowell-Smith, *Ethics* (Oxford: 1957), 282. The main sources of the arguments we shall be examining in the remainder of the chapter are Nowell-Smith's book, the *Mind* articles by Hobart, Nowell-Smith, and Smart cited in note 15 to Chapter I, and A. J. Ayer's "Freedom and Necessity" in his *Philosophical Essays* (London: 1954).

20 Except possibly 'unplanned' or 'unintended'. But this meaning will be of no help to the proponent of the first strand. The thief's repentance was certainly unplanned and he certainly had not intended to repent, but these facts have no tendency to show that his act was not free.

21 *I* might want to, in fact. See sec. 5.5.

22 Cf. Hobart, 7.

23 Of course the incompatibilist could make use of slippery-slope arguments, too. Consider, for example, the hypothesis (M) that we considered in our discussion of the Paradigm Case Argument in sec. 4.2. It would be easy enough to construct a sequence of stories according to the pattern provided by the second strand of the *Mind* Argument, in which the Martian device of that hypothesis is gradually turned into a natural part of the agent's brain.

24 W. P. Alston has pointed out to me that many of the medievals, most notably Aquinas, applied the notion of immanent causation to the human agent as well as to God.

25 See R. M. Chisholm, "Freedom and Action", in Keith Lehrer, ed., *Freedom and Determinism* (New York: 1966). Chisholm's later writings on free will, such as the first chapter of *Person and Object* (La Salle, Ill.: 1976), continue to make use of the concept of immanent causation, but this concept ceases to play a central role in Chisholm's exposition of his topic. See also R. Taylor, "Determinism and the Theory of Agency", in Sydney Hook, ed., *Determinism and Freedom in the Age of Modern Science* (New York: 1958), and ch. 9 of *Action and Purpose* (Englewood Cliffs, NJ: 1966).

26 "Actions, Reasons, and Causes", *The Journal of Philosophy* (1963).

27 *Causality and Determination* (Cambridge: 1971).

28 The second strand of the *Mind* Argument may be looked at as an attempt to show that apparent acts that are undetermined are really acts if and only if apparent acts that are caused by a freakish demon are really acts. It is interesting to note that the purely "Davidsonian" component of our second model entails that it is possible for a freakish demon to cause what are literally our acts: the demon need only produce in us the appropriate beliefs and desires. A similar point was made in sec. 4.2, in connection with the story of the Martian devices, though it was not really necessary in that context (discussion of the Paradigm Case Argument) for us to suppose that the Martian devices caused our acts: it would have sufficed to suppose that they caused what *seemed to be* or *felt like* our acts.

29 A similar point can be made about the first model, since, presumably, I can be the immanent cause only of events that are changes in natural parts of me.

30 Cf. R. M. Chisholm, "Comments and Replies", *Philosophia* (1978), 628-30.

31 An internal state of a certain type might cause an act of a certain type in a way very different from the way in which states of that type normally cause acts of that type. Suppose, for example, that mixtures of belief and desire cause our acts. Consider our thief, whose repentance was caused by the co-presence of a desire to carry out his mother's last wish and a belief that repentance would secure this end. When one is told a story like the story of our thief, one naturally takes the causation of act by inner state to be of a certain "natural" or "normal" sort—though

it would be very hard to spell out in any precise form what is meant by the words in scare quotes. But we can give examples of other sorts of causal linkage—'deviant', I shall call them—between inner state and overt act. Suppose, for example, that a certain thief desires to carry out his mother's last wish and believes that repentance will best secure this end; suppose that this mixture of desire and belief causes him to snarl at his own softness; suppose that his snarl is so violent that it precipitates a stroke, which in turn causes a temporary but frightening paralysis in the arm extended toward the poor-box; suppose the fear of God's wrath thus engendered causes the thief to repent. If causation is transitive, then a mixture of desire and belief has caused an act, but not in that natural or normal way that is what is intended by the adherents of a Davidsonian theory of the causes of action.

32 'Np', it will be remembered, stands for 'p and no one has, or ever had, any choice about whether p'.

33 By a "theory of choice" I mean a theory about what it is to *have* a choice, and not a theory about what it is to *make* a choice. A moment's reflection will show that these are not at all the same thing and that it is not obvious what the relation, if any, between them is. Consider the man who is locked in a room and who does not know it. He may certainly make a choice about staying, despite the fact that he has no choice about staying.

34 Alvin Plantinga has suggested to me that the thief may have had a choice about whether to repent owing to his having had a choice about whether, on the one hand, DB caused R, or, on the other, his desire for money and his belief that the poor-box contained money (DB*) jointly caused the event *his robbing the poor-box* (R*). We should note that the two desire-belief pairs, DB and DB*, both actually obtained; according to the theory Plantinga has proposed, what the thief had a choice about was which of these two potential causes became the actual cause of an effect appropriate to it. This may for all I know be the correct account of the "inner state" of a deliberating agent who has a choice about how he is going to act. But if this account is correct, then there are two events *its coming to pass that DB causes R* and *its coming to pass that DB* causes R** such that, though one of them must happen, it's causally undetermined which will happen; and it will have to be the case that the thief has a choice about which of them will happen. If this were so, I should find it very puzzling and I should be at a loss to give an account of it.

35 Strictly speaking, this puzzle arises only for someone who accepts both what I accept and also the second model of action. (The reader will remember that I have been pretending to accept the second model, as a literary convenience, though I in fact neither accept nor reject it.) But I am fairly sure that if I did accept (β) and the existence of free will, as I do, and also accepted some particular theory of action, then I should be forced to choose between the puzzling—though the puzzle might be a different one—and the inconceivable. The words to which this note is appended may be taken to represent what I *should* say if were able to see my way clear to accepting some particular theory of action.

36 I wish to thank W. P. Alston for his advice about sec. 4.4, which has led to changes in the structure of the argument of that section that I believe to be great improvements. Alvin Plantinga's comments on a draft of sec. 4.4 have saved me from making several blunders.

37 Suppose a philosopher believes in free will and in "immanent causation" in the sense of the present section. How will he reply to the argument that was presented in the text (p. 145) for the conclusion that an appeal to immanent causation merely "sweeps the incompatibility problem under the carpet"? I do not believe that this argument creates any *new* problems for him. I do not see why he should not simply reply as follows: "The thief was the immanent cause of R. Therefore he had a choice about whether DB was followed by R. Therefore he had a choice about whether R would occur. Therefore he had a choice about whether *his being the immanent cause of R* would occur—simply because he had a choice about whether R would occur." The philosopher I have imagined appeals to the principle, 'If x and y have actually occurred and if x caused y, and if a certain agent had a choice about whether y would occur, then that agent had a choice about whether x would cause y'. This principle seems quite reasonable.

CHAPTER V

1 *Système de la nature X*, xxi (tr. H. D. Robinson).

2 This is in a way unfair. They believed they were giving arguments. But their arguments were merely emphatic elaborations of the thesis that free will is an illusion.

3 "Deliberation and Foreknowledge", *American Philosophical Quarterly* (1964).

4 I use the term 'incompatible' very loosely. In the present loose sense, two contemplated acts may be incompatible simply because the agent has already decided not to perform both.

5 Or so it seems to me. W. P. Alston has told me that he doubts whether the effects of a total abstention from deliberation would be as radical as that. They would certainly be pretty drastic, though.

6 *Logic Matters* (Oxford: 1972), 279.

7 P. T. Geach, *Reason and Argument* (Oxford: 1976), 9.

8 "The Principle of Alternate Possibilities", *The Journal of Philosophy* (1969).

9 These sections are a somewhat simplified version of my paper "Ability and Responsibility", *The Philosophical Review* (1978). Readers interested in the fine points of the argument may wish to consult that paper.

10 This schema and the instance of it that follows involve the agent's intentionally refraining from performing a given act. Of course not every case in which we might want to consider holding an agent responsible for failing to perform some act is a case in which the agent intentionally

refrains from performing that act: he may never even have considered performing that act. This distinction between two ways of failing to perform a given act is of no importance for our present purposes. The points made in the text would be equally valid if we had chosen to examine a case in which the agent failed even to think of performing the act whose non-performance we are considering holding him responsible for.

11 Perhaps it is debatable whether this phrase designates a particular.

12 But I doubt whether they can be anticipated. The objects of anticipation and other "future-directed" attitudes would seem to be universals.

13 Perhaps the last of these phrases could also be used to name an event-universal. We seem to be using it this way if we say, "What Bill saw happening in the garden happens all too frequently," but, I think, we use it to name a particular when we say, "What Bill saw happening in the garden last night will live in infamy", or "could have been prevented with a little foresight". The phrases "the fall of the Alamo" and "the death of Caesar", however, seem to be suited only for denoting particulars: even if the Alamo had fallen twice, even if Caesar, like Lazarus, had died twice, we could not say, "The fall of the Alamo has happened twice" or "The death of Caesar has happened twice." This is not due, or not due solely, to the presence of the definite article in these phrases, for we can say, "The thing Bill fears most has happened twice."

14 From Davidson's contribution to a symposium on events and event-descriptions in Joseph Margolis, ed., *Fact and Existence* (Oxford: 1969), 84.

15 "The Individuation of Events" in Nicholas Rescher, ed., *Essays in Honor of Carl G. Hempel* (Dordrecht: 1969), 225.

16 Might *logically*, that is. A determinist could admit this point and consistently maintain that it was *physically* impossible for that event to have had different effects.

17 Or so it seems to me. Other philosophers—Cartesians, for example —will have a different view of the matter.

18 Cf. Saul Kripke, "Naming and Necessity", in Donald Davidson and Gilbert Harman, eds., *Semantics of Natural Language* (Dordrecht: 1972), 312-14.

19 A theory of event-particulars that is inconsistent with the view presented in the text is held by R. M. Martin and Jaegwon Kim. See Martin's contribution to the symposium referred to in note 14, and, for Kim's latest published views on events, "Causation, Nomic Subsumption, and the Concept of Event", *The Journal of Philosophy* (1973). If we abstract from the particular twists that each of these authors gives to his own account of events, we may say that, on the "Kim-Martin" theory, the class of events is the class of substance-property-time triples. For example, Caesar's death is the triple ⟨Caesar, being dead, 15 March 44 BC⟩. (Strictly speaking, the term '15 March 44 BC' in the preceding sentence should be replaced with a term designating the precise instant at which Caesar died.) A Kim-Martin event *happens* just in the case that its first term acquires its second term at its third term. However useful

Kim-Martin events may be in certain contexts of discussion, I do not think it is correct to think of them as particulars. They are, rather, highly specified universals, just as the property *being the tallest man* is a highly specified—in fact, "definite"—universal (cf. note 24). This property, though only one man can have it, is none the less such that it *could have* been possessed by someone other than the man who in fact has it. Similarly, any Kim-Martin event that happens *could have* been caused by quite different antecedent events from those that in fact caused it. To suppose that event-particulars have this feature is to violate my intuitions, at any rate, about particulars. An additional problem: every Kim-Martin event is such that there is one particular moment (its third term) such that the event must happen just at that moment if it happens at all. But surely Caesar's death might have happened at least a few moments earlier or later than it in fact did, just as a given man might have been born, or even conceived, at least a few moments earlier or later than he in fact was.

20 Nothing in PPP1 corresponds to the parenthetical qualification 'that state of affairs obtains and' in this principle. So far as I can see, to say of a given event-particular that it "happens" is equivalent to saying that it exists. And, of course, there exist no events that do not exist. Thus there exist no events that do not happen. But states of affairs may exist without obtaining, just as propositions may exist without being true or properties without being instantiated. Cf. note 20, Chapter III.

21 Or, at least, this *may* be true. We shall later see that if Caesar would have been murdered by someone else if the conspirators hadn't murdered him, then this state of affairs does not, strictly speaking, obtain *because* the conspirators murdered him.

22 For a discussion of the propriety of applying the term 'universal' to "states of affairs" in the present sense, see note 24.

23 By Carl Ginet and Nicholas Sturgeon.

24 Perhaps some philosophers would be disinclined to call the property of being the heaviest statue there ever was or will be a *universal*, on the ground that a universal must be "sharable", must be capable of being exemplified by more than one object. And, for similar reasons, it might be held that what I have called 'states of affairs' are not true universals, since each of them either obtains or fails to obtain without further qualification, whereas a state of affairs that was truly a universal should be capable, say, of obtaining in 1943 but not in 1956, or of obtaining in both Britain and the United States but not in France. Well, let us say that our "states of affairs" and properties like being the heaviest statue are, if not "true" universals, at least *cross-world universals*. A property or other abstract object is a cross-world universal if there are worlds w_1 and w_2 such that x falls under it in w_1 and y falls under it in w_2 and $x \neq y$. (I use the words 'fall under' with deliberate vagueness; what "falls under" a property is whatever has it; what "falls under" a state of affairs is whatever arrangement of particulars realizes it.) If this usage is an extension of traditional philosophical usage, it is a very natural one; I call, for example, C(Gunnar kills Ridley) a 'universal' because it is not "tied to" any given arrangement of particulars.

25 I do not mean to give the impression that one never brings about any state of affairs. For example, granting the correctness of the Warren Commission Report, Lee Harvey Oswald brought about C(Kennedy dies on 22 November 1963). But it is not true that Oswald brought about C(Kennedy dies). That state of affairs was brought about by God or by Adam and Eve or by no one at all. Moreover, it *is* true that Oswald brought about the event-particular, Kennedy's death.

26 Strictly speaking, the antecedent of this conditional *entails* only the "minimal free-will thesis" (see sec. 3.9). But I suppose no one would seriously maintain that the minimal free-will thesis was true and the free-will thesis false.

27 The function of 'even partly' will be explained in note 28.

28 If the words 'even partly' were omitted from the sentence-form that 'N*p*' abbreviates, then (B) might be open to counter-example. Suppose, for example, that Smith kills the elder of the Jones twins and that the younger is killed by a bolt from the blue. It is at least arguable that in that case neither Smith nor anyone else is responsible for the fact that both the Jones twins are dead. But then the following argument has true premises and a false conclusion if the words 'even partly' are omitted from the reading of 'N*p*':

N Both the Jones twins are dead;

N (Both the Jones twins are dead ⊃ the elder of the Jones twins is dead);

hence, N the elder of the Jones twins is dead.

But it seems evident that, in the case imagined, Smith is at least *partly* responsible for the fact that both the Jones twins are dead. A perhaps more troublesome case arises if we substitute 'Tom throws a six' for '*p*' and 'Tom plays dice' for '*q*' in (B). I should be inclined to say that, if Tom is indeed responsible for playing dice, then he is *partly* responsible for the fact that he throws a six, since he could have avoided throwing a six by avoiding playing dice. Anyone who finds this response artificial and contrived may wish to replace the reading of 'N*p*' in the text with '*p* and no human being or group of human beings is responsible for the fact that *p* or for any of the logical consequences of the fact that *p*'. If we think of a logical consequence of a fact as a "part" of that fact, then this reading may be regarded as a refinement of the reading given in the text. And it is clear that in this sense Tom can be responsible for a "part" of the fact that he throws a six, to wit, for the fact that he plays dice.

CHAPTER VI

1 See sec. 1.3.

2 Although, as we shall see, this supervention is merely statistical if quantum mechanics is right.

3 Or, at any rate, this is as likely to be true as the corresponding thesis about classical states is in the case of classical mechanics. Cf. Richard Montague, "Deterministic Theories", in Richmond H. Thomason, ed., *Formal Philosophy: Selected Papers of Richard Montague* (New Haven: 1974), 332-6.

4 Cf. N. R. Hanson, "Quantum Mechanics, Philosophical Implications of", in Paul Edwards, ed., *The Encyclopedia of Philosophy* (New York and London: 1967), vol. 7, p. 45.

5 That is, in a theory according to which observable variables like position and momentum are determined. We have already seen that quantum mechanics itself is in a sense a deterministic theory, though it does not in general yield deterministic predictions of the values of observable variables.

6 See Max Jammer, *The Philosophy of Quantum Mechanics* (New York: 1974).

7 J. Andrade e Silva and G. Lochak, *Quanta*, tr. from the French by Patrick Moore (New York: 1969), 162.

8 By Jauch and Piron, for example. For a reasonably accessible presentation of their argument, see ch. 5, 6, and 7 of Josef M. Jauch, *Foundations of Quantum Mechanics* (Reading, Mass.: 1968).

9 Cf. C. D. Broad, *The Mind and its Place in Nature* (London: 1925), 113.

10 This is not to say that there are no plausible *a priori* arguments for the conclusion that every event has a cause. Perhaps there are.

11 Leibniz, of course, believed that this world's being the best of all possible worlds was a sufficient reason for its being actual, despite the fact that *this world is the best world* does not entail *this world is actual* (for if that entailment did hold, then the other worlds would not be possible; that is, they would not be possibly actual).

This would seem to be a flatly incoherent position. If Leibniz is right, then the possibility that the best of all possible worlds *not* be actual exists, though this possibility is, in his view, unrealized. But what is the *sufficient reason* for this possibility's being unrealized?

12 Someone might worry about whether this arguably impredicative definition leads to paradoxes of self-reference. It does not. The following model shows this. Identify a proposition with the set of worlds in which it is true, as we did in sec. 3.3. The conjunction of two propositions will then be their intersection and a conjunct of a proposition will be any proposition of which it is a subset. Thus, every proposition is a conjunct of itself. On this model, 'P' denotes the set whose only member is the actual world (provided there are at least two possible worlds: if there is only one world, all propositions are necessary and 'P' fails to denote), a set that can be singled out without paradox. Cf. this identification of P in our model with the identifications made in the parenthetical remark that follows in the text.

13 That criterion of identity is not really necessary for the argument. If we rejected it, we should have to replace our second principle with the principle that no contingent state of affairs can have a state of affairs

to which it is logically equivalent as its sufficient reason. And this seems plausible enough.

14 It follows from this result that PSR does indeed entail determinism, for the simple reason that determinism is a thesis that, conceived very abstractly, asserts only that certain true propositions are entailed by certain other propositions; but if truth and necessary truth coincide, then any set of true propositions is entailed by anything whatever.

15 Cf. the discussion of Baron Holbach in sec. 5.2.

16 For another example, see the discussion of the relation between physical possibility and the power to act in sec. 1.4.

17 I use the word *illusion* in Freud's sense (*Die Zukunft einer Illusion*, ch. 6): the alchemists' belief that lead could be turned to gold and Columbus's belief that a fifteenth-century ship could reach land by sailing west from Europe were illusions, despite the fact that they were *true*. For an example of a fine mind in the grip of scientism, read Carnap's intellectual autobiography in P. A. Schilpp, ed., *The Philosophy of Rudolf Carnap* (La Salle, Ill.: 1963).

18 I hope that the fact that I have discussed quantum mechanics at some length has not given the opposite impression. My purpose in discussing quantum mechanics was simply to make it clear that, if it was ever reasonable to believe that science supported determinism (the general thesis, that is, not the thesis that human beings are "for all practical purposes" determined), it no longer is. Thus one reason our philosophical forebears may have had for believing in determinism is not a reason we have.

19 This, of course, is a tendentious term. I would describe myself as holding a "scientific world-view" if the term had not become associated with a certain metaphysic (one having no real connection with the achievements of science) that I reject.

20 One sometimes finds another fear mixed with the fear of being caught out: the fear of being swept into the dust bin. This is the fear that the progress of science—or perhaps changing social attitudes attributable to the progress of science—will leave one's views not so much refuted as irremediably old-fashioned.

21 See Bertrand Beaumont, "Hegel and the Seven Planets", *Mind* (1954).

22 This dilemma, strictly speaking, faces only the incompatibilist who accepts our second model of action. But some such dilemma will face any incompatibilist who holds any very explicit theory of action.

Index

actuality 232n
agent causation *see* immanent causation
Alston, William P. vi, 234n, 238n, 240n
Andrade e Silva, J. *quoted* 196, 244n
Anscombe, G. E. M. vi, 4, 139
Aristotle 31, *quoted* 33, *quoted* 34, *quoted* 228n
astrology 198f
Austin, J. L. 235n
Ayer, Sir Alfred 228n, 237n
Ayers, M. R. v

Beaumont, Bertrand 245n
Brand, Myles 236n
Broad, C. D. vi, 226n, 244n
Broglie, Louis Victor de 196

Cahn, Steven 227n, 228n
'can' 8-13
Carnap, Rudolf 245n
causation 65, 138-41, *see also* immanent causation; Principle of Universal Causation, The
chance 128f, 144
Chisholm, Roderick M. vi, 115, 136, 152, 163, *quoted* 235n, 236n, 238n
Chrysippus 227n
Cicero 31, 227n
compatibilism 13, 74-8, 101, 102-5, 106-52, 222f, *see also* Compatibility Problem, The; incompatibilism
Compatibility Problem, The 2, 16, 17, 18, 19, 190
compulsion 17
Conditional Analysis Argument, The 16, 19, 106, 108, 114-26, 150
Consequence Argument, The v, 16, 56, 222, 237n
'contra-causal freedom' 14f

Darrow, Clarence 153
Davidson, Donald *quoted* 55, 137f, 140f, *quoted* 167, 168, 169, 226n, 241n
deliberation 19, 30, 154-61, 204f, 209, 240n
determinism 2-8, 20-22, 58-65, 85f, 94, 95, 100f, 111f, 183-8, 188f, 190-204, 205-21 *passim*, 222f, 245n, *see also* 'hard determinism'; indeterminism; psychological determinism; 'soft determinism'
Diodorus Cronus 31
divine foreknowledge 225n

Edwards, Paul 244n
Einstein, Albert 195
Epictetus 31
events, individuation of 167-70, 241n, 242n
existence 232n

Farrer, Austin v
fatalism 1, 23-54, 234n
Flew, Antony 106-12, *quoted* 107, 234n
Foley, Richard 226n, 236n
Frankfurt, Harry vi, 19, 162-82
Franklin, R. L. v
free will 8-13, 19-22, 86-91, 153-89, 204-21, 222f, *see also* free-will thesis, the; 'of his own free will'
free-will thesis, the 14, 65-8, 87, 91, 243n
Frege, Gottlob 79
Freud, Sigmund 153, 245n
future contingencies *see* fatalism

Gallois, André 231n
Gardner, Michael 231n
Geach, Peter 81, 158, *quoted* 159, 240n

Ginet, Carl vi, 237n, 242n
Gödel incompleteness results 225n

Hanson, N. R. 244n
'hard determinism' 13f
Harman, Gilbert 241n
Hegel, G. W. F. 218, 245n
Hobart, R. E. vi, 134, 226n, 237n, 238n
Hobbes, Thomas 154, 155, 190
Holbach, Paul-Henri Thiry, Baron d' 153-60 *passim*, *quoted* 153, 245n
holism 215f, 217
Honderich, Ted 226n, 229n
Hook, Sidney 225n, 238n
Hume, David 190

immanent causation 4, 135-7, 145, 151f, 225n, 238n, 240n
incompatibilism 13, 15ff, 55-105, 111f, 126-52 *passim*, 222f, *see also* compatibilism
indeterminism 3, 126ff, 148, 191-7, 205-21 *passim*, 222f
inevitability 23-9
introspection, knowing of one's free will by 204f

Jammer, Max 244n
Jauch, Josef M. 244n

Kant, Immanuel 218
Kenny, Anthony v, 229n
Kim, Jaegwon 241n
Kripke, Saul 241n

Laplace, Pierre Simon, Marquis de 143, 193f, 201, 230n
Law of the Excluded Middle, The 50-4
laws of nature 3, 5-8, 9, 14f, 60-5, 85, 92, 111f, 185, 202, 225n, 230n
Lehrer, Keith vi, 113-14, 115, 119f, 225n, 235n, 236n, 238n
Leibniz, G. W. 244n
Lewis, C. S. 232n
'libertarianism' 13f
Lochak, G. *quoted* 196, 244n
Lucas, J. R. v
Łucasiewicz, Jan 5, 225n

Margolis, Joseph 241n
Martin, Raymond 231n
Martin, Richard M. 241n

Maugham, W. S. *quoted* 24, 27, 227n
McCall, Storrs 225n
McIntyre, Alasdair 234n
McKay, Thomas 233n
Melden, A. I. v
Mill, John Stuart 190
Mind Argument, The 16f, 106, 126-52, 234n, 238n
miracle, the concept of a 14f
Montague, Richard 230n, 244n
Moore, Patrick 244n
moral responsibility 19f, 29f, 104f, 161-89, 206ff, 243n

Nagel, Ernest 230n
Narveson, Jan 230n, 231n
Naylor, Margery vi
necessary truth 96, 184
Neumann, J. von 196
Nowell-Smith, P. H. 226n, 237n

O'Connor, D. J. v
'of his own free will' 17

Paley, William 218
Paradigm Case Argument, The 16, 106-12, 150, 204, 234n, 238n
physical possibility and impossibility 3, 9, 85, 225n, 245n
Piron, C. 244n
Plantinga, Alvin vi, 79, 203, 230n, 239n, 240n
possibilia 232n
possibility and impossibility 231n, *see also* physical possibility and impossibility
possible worlds 59, 78-82, 84, 85, 96f, 186, 230n, 232n, 233n
predicting one's own decisions 225n
Principle of Alternate Possibilities, The 162-82
Principle of Sufficient Reason, The 21, 202-4, 244n, 245n
Principle of Universal Causation, The 3, 191, 223
propositions 31-4, 53, 58f, 227n, 228n
psychoanalysis 225n
psychological determinism 225n
psychological laws 63f

quantum mechanics 52, 60, 191-7, 215, 216, 217, 230n, 243n, 244n, 245n

Rescher, Nicholas 241n
responsibility: see moral responsibility
Robinson, H. D. 240n
Ross, Sir David 228n

scepticism 210–13
Schilpp, P. A. 245n
"scientific world-view" 217, 245n
scientism 215–18, 245n
Seddon, George 232n
Smart, J. J. C. 226n, 237n
socio-biology 99–101
'soft determinism' 13f
Spinoza, Baruch 204
state of the world at an instant 59f, 84
states of affairs, individuation of 171,
    241n, 242n
"strongest motive" 225n
Sturgeon, Nicholas 242n

Taylor, Richard vi, 42, 43–50, quoted
    48, quoted 49, 136, 154, 226n,
    227n, 229n, 238n
Thomas Aquinas, St. 238n
Thomason, Richmond H. 244n
Traditional Problem, The 2, 20-2,
    190–223
truth and falsity 31–4, 53
    at a time 34–43, 228n
Twain, Mark 63, 153

universal causation: see Principle of
    Universal Causation, The
universals 171, 175–80, 241n, 242n

van Inwagen, Peter 232n, 235n, 237n,
    240n

Walton, Douglas 236n
Wittgenstein, Ludwig 235n